Spatial Perspectives
on Problems and Policies

Social Areas in Cities

Volume II
Spatial Perspectives on Problems and Policies

Edited by

D. T. HERBERT

Senior Lecturer in Geography,
University College of Swansea

and

R. J. JOHNSTON

Professor of Geography,
University of Sheffield

JOHN WILEY & SONS
London · New York · Sydney · Toronto

Library of Congress catalog card number 75-30943
ISBN 0 471 37305 2

Photosetting by Thomson Press (India) Limited, New Delhi.
Printed at Unwin Brothers Limited, The Gresham Press, Old Woking, Surrey.

To

Our Parents and Families

Preface

Urban studies have become extremely popular in the last two decades and a number of important books have been produced on topics such as those dealt with here. Indeed, the social geography of the city is almost an overpopulated field and some brief justification for yet another book might be valuable. Our view is that no book to date has provided an overall synopsis at a high level. Introductory texts give brief mention to many, if not all, of the topics covered here, but most take a fairly narrow viewpoint, based often on only one of the social sciences whose methods and findings are relevant to work on social areas—sociology, economics, psychology and political economy. Hence, we have attempted to cover the whole field of urban studies as they refer to social areas and decided that the best way to face this daunting task was to commission a series of chapters by experts on particular aspects of the field, who would be able to approach their particular topic within a wider view of the whole.

Publication of a book in two separate volumes imposes particular strains upon the second volume as its predecessor, from which its discussions are intended to form a logical extension of ideas, may be unread and will certainly by physically removed. It is important to stress, therefore, that the overall book, *Social Areas in Cities*, was conceived as a whole and is published in two volumes for practical reasons. The two volumes, although forming distinctive compartments, are closely related and one function of this preface must be to outline the contents of the first volume and to demonstrate the relationships which it bears with this present volume.

Volume I was concerned with the ways in which urban research has provided detailed examinations of residential patterns, of the institutional and societal frameworks within which they have emerged, and of the processes which have produced them. More than any other task, that of residential differentiation came to dominate research by urban geographers in particular in the 1960's and social area analyses and factorial ecologies featured very prominently in the published literature. The emphasis upon this field of research reflected important trends within the wider study of human geography. As a research methodology, residential differentiation studies became increasingly reliant upon statistical inputs and provided an arena for the development and application of quantitative approaches. Factor analyses and cluster analyses in particular, perhaps the most widely used statistical procedures in human geography, are strongly associated with this field of study. Residential differen-

vii

tiation studies have reached high levels of attainments on several fronts and the relevant chapters in Volume 1 reflect this fact. A range of technical analytic procedures, suitable for the objectives of distinguishing and characterizing urban residential patterns is now well understood; the 'art' of regionalization has attained a high level of systematic scientific method. To the extent that quality and availability of data inputs allow, the 'dimensions' of residential differentiation have been identified and labelled for many parts of the world. Similarly, the possible spatial generalizations or models of urban form have been tested and classified. Any city for which suitable statistical information exists can now be readily subjected to a residential differentiation analysis and the results which are obtained can be seen in a general comparative context. At this scale of analysis, urban residential patterns act as a mirror-image of the relevant society; social stratifications are reflected in the geographical space of the city.

Although this acknowledgement of the link between societal structure and city space was always apparent and became very explicit in social area analysis, *sensu stricto*, and in use of the concept of social space in relation to factorial ecology, it was rather later in time that the focus of attention was moved from pattern identification to the task of examining the processes which underlay patterns. An interest in process tended to be subservient to the aims of generalizing upon form and distribution. The Concentric Zonal Model (Burgess, 1925) is one of the best known of the intra-urban models of growth and structure but as Rees (1970, p. 307) has suggested of Burgess, 'He missed the point of his own model of the city. The movement of people from one residence to another *as the city grows* is the very mechanism by which the zones and natural areas . . . are created'. Burgess was writing over half a century ago but it is still true to say that geographers working upon patterns much more recently have been slow to recognize and study the related processes. Even when studies were made of movements within the city, their value was reduced because they were conceived and reported in aggregate terms. So, Hoyt (1939) studied the movement of high grade residential *areas*; Morrill (1965) described the process of *ghetto* expansion in American cities. This concern with area expansion, with the assimilation of groups and with modified forms of the invasion and succession process, although valuable within its own terms of reference, understated the complexity of residential mobility processes within the city. The shift to a behavioural stance is often ascribed to a paper by Wolpert (1965)—though Rossi (1955) was an important precursor in the social science literature—and the importance of recognizing the individual household as the decision-making unit was accepted by geographers and led to new forms of research into residential change. The chapter by Adams and Gilder in Volume I provided a detailed study of residential change as an individual decision-making process. If this school of research into the nature of decision making, into the spatial terms of reference of mobility, and into the problems of measuring activity spaces, awareness spaces, and search spaces, had a misconception, then it was an overdue belief in the existence of choice and in the rationality of the individual as a decision-making unit (Herbert, 1973).

It has become increasingly clear that for large sections of society it is the constraints rather than the choices facing the individual household which are the most real and effective factors. Constraint operates at all stages of the residential mobility process, its effects are differential and the most disadvantaged sections of society are those with the least choice (Rex, 1968). The general notion of a rational selection process in residential mobility which could be defined and modelled in a sequential way (Brown and Moore, 1970), has been criticized. Gray (1975, p. 234) argued, 'By assuming and providing support for the belief that people are free to prefer and choose from a range of options and that individuals and families control their own life chances, urban geographers have, by default, accepted, aided, and supported the existing structure of society and hindered a true understanding of reality.' Such critical viewpoints of the earlier research into residential mobility are tenable in the sense that, as has already been stated, too little attention has been paid to the role of constraints. Constraints have however been insufficiently detailed rather than ignored. The major constraint of cost has often been taken for granted and only handled in an implicit way; models of the decision-making process have assumed elements such as a free market and the availability of housing. Again, an emphasis upon constraint can go too far. However great the constraints, there can be very few situations of no choice whatsoever. This situation will vary from one society to another but there is evidence in Britain, for example, that choice does operate within the local authority housing sector through the mechanisms of the housing waiting lists and the possibility of transfers within the public sector (Herbert, 1972).

The processes underlying urban residential patterns are not merely those relating to the mobility characteristics of individual households. There are other decision makers who operate through the mechanisms of the housing market whose roles are equally important. The land owners, the developers, the professional agencies of finance and housing sales, and the planners are all key elements in the supply of houses; they rarely operate in unfettered space but rather in a mosaic of inherited fabrics, imbued with diverse economic and social values, and controlled by a range of factors from social prejudice to planning regulations. Each actor in the supply side of the housing market has power, how much power will vary over time and from one societal context to another.

Variations in societal context are also of importance in that they are representative of different systems of values, ethics, and political economies which pervade the whole scenario within which decision making at all levels takes place. Any research which is concerned with society's problems faces questions of value judgements and interpretations. The extent to which the established order is seen as a force for good or for evil will in part be a reflection of the system of values of the individual researcher; there is a 'crisis of identity' involved. In common with other disciplines geographical research must be aware that attitudes about the nature of society may become incorporated into a pattern of thought, a system of values, which may or may not be made explicit. Harvey (1973) argued, from a specified set of values, that the existing social order and its accompanying inequities was being supported by much urban research which has been 'counter revolutionary' in its effects. Similarly, it has been argued that much research is misdirected and (Gray, 1975, p. 232) argued that 'The structural analysis of capitalism and its various spatial manifestations is the core problem facing geographers studying urban processes and sociospatial forms'. The structural analysis of capitalism is a tall order for the social sciences as a whole let alone for urban geographers but the questions raised by this 'school of thought' have undoubtedly enriched the content and quality of debate in social geography and have helped to point research effort in new directions.

The real objective of Volume I has been to provide a detailed summary of the actual achievements of urban research concerned with social areas and to identify those conceptual frameworks which provide both a wholistic view and a platform from which further analyses can be presented. It is a research record of very considerable advance over a relatively limited period of time. It has been, perhaps understandably in the time-specific context within which it emerged, a research tradition with priorities of measurement and model building but one which has retained an awareness of constraints and the problems of the real world. Those constraints are discussed in Volume I but not from a set of values which places societal 'revolution' as a desirable goal. Certainly by the 1970's there was growing evidence of a more central concern with urban problems and the shift in emphasis from analysis of pattern to study of process was in keeping with this trend. Study of residential mobility processes leads to analysis of the supply side of the housing market, to the 'gatekeepers' of the system, such as policy makers in central and local government, and the managers of financial institutions, such as banks and building societies. Analyses of spatial processes and form have taken increased account of the societal contexts within which they have occurred, the city is a segment of society and its extraction for study as a unit is recognized as a step of convenience.

Whilst the contributors to Volume I provided detailed statements of research into urban residential patterns and the forces and conditions which produced them, the starting points for Volume II have been the spatial outcomes, the detailed and diverse urban environments of which the city is now composed. Research which contributors now seek to examine is more explicitly concerned with the role of environment as a stimulus for social behaviour, with the closer identification of problems which occur within the sociospatial framework of the city and with the kinds of policies which have been proposed to ameliorate these problems. This concern reflects the increasing awareness of social problems and a diminishing interest in quantitative procedures as ends in themselves. The writers of the first four chapters in Volume II, who are professional geographers, have arrived at this research frontier from prior concerns with spatial processes and form in the context of residential areas. Links clearly exist between process and form on the one hand and urban environment as stimulus on the other, which are carried forward in the chapters of this present volume. Whilst some of the links are direct, housing allocation procedures by local authorities, for example, a decision-making process with spatial manifestations, can 'create' problem estates, others, inevitably, are a good deal less so. Identified patterns of social areas, whilst valuable as sampling frameworks and as guidelines to further and more detailed analyses, have not in themselves proved particularly useful as diagnostic parameters of social problems (Baldwin, 1975). The detailed structural mosaics of residential areas, which geographers have become so adept at characterizing, become little more than incidental sources of background information as more sensitive indicators of particular types of social conditions prove necessary (Herbert, 1975).

The remaining three contributors to Volume II are social scientists, who although interested in the spatial aspects of cities, have their emphases within their respective disciplines. There is cohesion to the volume in that although every chapter has a specific theme, each contributor examines an aspect of behaviour or a set of attitudes in relation to qualities of the urban environment, to territories, to groups in areas, and to locational characteristics; for most of the contributors the real problems of urban areas and the policies related to them are never very far from sight. Whereas on some of the themes, such as that of local community, we might hope to approach a definitive statement, most of the chapters are concerned with fields of study which, in spatial terms at least, remain at relatively early stages of development. As one of our contributors concludes 'we have a long way to go'.

As editors, we were responsible for the structure of the volume, for the selection of authors, and for the final production; each author is of course responsible for his or her own view. In assisting us with our tasks, we are grateful to the contributors for agreeing to participate, for their acceptance of our idiosyncrasies and for their good-natured reaction to our badgering. To our publishers, who launched us on the project and guided us through it, we are grateful for their help: and the final product would never have emerged without the work of a number of secretaries and technical staff, notably at the Universities of Canterbury and Sheffield for Ron Johnston and at the University College of Swansea for Dave Herbert, but also at all of the institutions at which our contributors are or were based.

REFERENCES

Baldwin, J. (1975). 'Social area analysis and studies of delinquency'. *Social Science Research*, **3**, 151–168.
Burgess, E. W. (1925). 'The growth of a city'. In R. E. Park, E. W. Burgess and R. D. McKenzie, *The City*, University of Chicago Press, Chicago. pp. 47–62.
Brown, L. A. and Moore, E. G. (1970). 'The intra-urban mobility process: a perspective'. *Geografiska Annaler B*, **52**, 1–13.
Gray, F. (1975). 'Non-explanation in urban geography'. *Area*, **7**, 228–235.
Harvey, D. (1973). *Social Justice in the City*, Edward Arnold, London.
Herbert, D. T. (1972). *Public Sector Housing, Residential Mobility and Preference*, unpublished discussion paper, Department of Geography, University College of Swansea.

Herbert, D. T. (1973). 'The residential mobility process: some empirical observations'. *Area*, **5**, 44–48.

Herbert, D. T. (1975). 'Urban deprivation: definition, measurement and spatial qualities'. *Geographical Journal*, **141**, 362–372.

Hoyt, H. (1939). *The Structure and Growth of Residential Neighbourhoods in American Cities*, Federal Housing Administration, Washington, D.C.

Morrill, R. L. (1965). 'The negro ghetto: problems and alternatives'. *Geographical Review*, **55**, 339–361.

Rees, P. H. (1970). 'Concepts of social space: toward an urban social geography'. In B. J. L. Berry and F. E. Horton (Eds.) *Geographic Perspectives on Urban Systems*, Prentice Hall, New York. pp. 306–394.

Rossi, P. A. (1955). *Why Families Move*, Free Press, New York.

Wolpert, J. A. (1965). 'Behavioural aspects of the decision to migrate'. *Papers of the Regional Science Association*, **15**, 159–169.

D. T. HERBERT
R. J. JOHNSTON

Summary of Contents of Volume I

Spatial Processes and Form

List of Contributors

DR D. T. HERBERT — *University College of Swansea*

PROFESSOR R. J. JOHNSTON — *University of Sheffield*

PROFESSOR COLIN R. BELL — *University of New South Wales*

ELIZABETH GITTUS, M.A. — *University of Newcastle-upon-Tyne*

PROFESSOR T. R. LEE — *University of Surrey*

HOWARD NEWBY, B.A. — *University of Essex*

DR C. J. THOMAS — *University College of Swansea*

Contents

An Introduction

D. T. Herbert and R. J. Johnston

A demonstration of the facts of spatial segregation and the reality of urban social areas and the provision of a series of insights into the processes which have produced them has been a major contribution of social geography. The main body of the research literature is concerned with these questions and it might be argued that with their discussion and investigation a threshold of spatial study has been reached. As already suggested, however, there are other qualities to residential area besides the established facts of their spatial identity and arrangement and beyond their coincidence with particular social groups. How can social processes be fitted into the urban mosaic? Does residential area affect as well as reflect social behaviour? To what extent does territory have meaning as a local social system? Do the spatial images which urban people possess coincide with the social topographies which geographers and planners recognize? Increasingly, researchers who study the city have shown an un-willingness to restrict themselves to pattern description or to the analysis of aggregate statistics. The more interesting questions now may be more directly answered by looking—perhaps, initially, at an individual level—at the key processes of social interaction, at the spatial effects of social inequalities and at the conditions which produce them. In studying the numerous strands of social processes, attitudes and behaviour, the main academic task is to specify the spatial qualities which are involved and to assess their relevance. Such an emphasis promises to fill a recurrent vacuum in social science research, parti-cularly where it is concerned with the planning process. Stewart (1972), in a discussion of possible reasons for the failure of social scientists to cope with urban problems, suggested that, with the exception of geographers, they had historically shown little concern for the spatial implications of their various approaches. It is important to increase this concern and to demonstrate the role of spatial qualities. Geographers have consistently argued this theme in their own research, and, as Jones (1975, p. 8) has com-mented, 'It is almost a truism that space is not merely a medium in which society moves and acts but a variable we can no longer ignore'.

If geographers have a perspective to contribute, they also have a good deal to receive and acknowledge from social science research. Many concepts and theories which form key elements of their perspective are derived from

1

other disciplines, of which social ecology, sociology and social psychology are recent examples. This is acknowledged in Harvey's (1970) plea for research at the interface of disciplines and, particularly, for a general theory of the city which relates social processes to spatial form and combines elements of the sociological and geographical imaginations. That this should be a two-way beneficial process of the exchange of ideas is obvious; perspectives should be complementary rather than contradictory and the acquisition of knowledge should be cumulative rather than duplicative. As Harvey (1970) has suggested, a successful strategy must appreciate that spatial form and social process are different ways of thinking about the same thing.

Some qualities of spatial form are easily identified. A map on which schools are located is a point distribution; a social area map is a regionalization of the city into its component territorial parts; and a territory when examined in detail has elements of structure which include its plan or design, the form and quality of its buildings and the density with which it is occupied. Other spatial qualities, those concerned with the relationship between form and social process, are more complex, but it is with their characters and roles that this second volume is concerned. Already in some of the chapters of volume one some of these complexities have been met. Residential area has been regarded as an indicator of societal structure; the orderly social geography of the city is the product of like individuals making like decisions on where to live within the framework of constraints which society imposes. Beshers (1962) argued that if social structure existed as an aggregate, its effects must be revealed in residential areas which in themselves act as symbols of social position. This preoccupation with the aggregate scale (and it must be acknowledged that most research on patterns within cities has been based upon aggregate statistics usually derived from censuses) raises the familiar problems of ecological fallacy. Clearly, this is a problem, but research based upon aggregate data ackonwledges its existence and offers findings which apply at that scale. It can be argued that within a measurable probabilistic framework useful generalizations can be made and that the aggregate is the scale at which most planning decisions have to be formulated. Jones (1956), in an early discussion of cause and effect in human geography, suggested ways in which behaviour on the aggregate scale can be regarded as a statistical expression of the total individual behaviour of a given population. 'Although individuals may act in a certain way for an almost infinite variety of reasons, many of which may seem "irrational", on the scale of society as a whole these acts seem to conform to a limited number of patterns which can be "explained" "scientifically"' (Jones, 1975 p. 6). While the hazards of ecological correlation must be avoided, what Berry (1971) has called the individualistic fallacy, or a refusal to treat the collectivity as such, is also averted.

It is the identification of patterns in behavioural data which suggests that spatial implications exist. There are numerous examples to suggest that the geographical expression of many forms of behaviour is ordered and closely related to variations in the urban structures upon which they are imposed.

Forms of social interactions, such as links with kin and friends, have repetitive spatial expressions when controls are introduced for measures such as social class and age; everyday activities, such as work trips and shopping trips, seem to conform to a few simple rules of spatial behaviour; and many types of deviance and deprivation are heavily concentrated in particular parts of a city. There is a spatial order which demands explanation. In the discussion so far, this spatial order has been viewed as a mirror image in geographical space of societal order, with social stratification reflected through the housing market. This line of explanation contributes to an understanding of the spatial order in behavioural terms, but is not sufficient. In order to understand the other sources of explanation, the relevant spatial factors must be identified.

The concept of distance-decay is the most strongly established spatial factor in studies of behaviour. Central place theory (with its definite position in the development of human geography) rests upon the assumption that, given alternative opportunities of equal attraction at different locations, consumers will choose the nearest place. Many other models of spatial behaviour have used the basic notion that increasing distance will diminish interaction. Harvey suggested that along with threshold, range of good and measurement of spatial patterns, distance-decay was one of the four empirical themes which dominated the quantitative revolution in human geography. While recent research has shown that distance-decay needs to be qualified for more detailed individual study, it retains a central position in the formulation of laws of spatial behaviour. Most studies using the distance-decay function are facets of an economic theory of location; distance itself is a surrogate for time and cost, from which are derived spatial variations in information and opportunities (Johnston, 1973). When more 'social' phenomena are studied, distance-decay is more evidently a blunt instrument and other factors need to be considered.

URBAN ENVIRONMENTS

The whole idea of examining relationships between environment and behaviour conjures a 'ghosts in the cupboard' response from many geographers. A more traditional geographical view of environment—as natural order or physical setting—has little usefulness, however, in the study of the modern city. As a setting, the built urban environment is the relevant parameter. This environment is composed of a morphological framework, the pattern of streets and buildings, with a degree of variety which is related to the age of the city and the number of 'morphological phases' through which it has passed. Each section of the built urban environment has distinctive features: some suffer disadvantages of age and outmodedness; others gain prestige as heritages of the past; all will be invested with values, both economic and social, and present a diversified stage for behavioural patterns to be enacted upon.

The extent to which the built urban environment is an influence upon social behaviour is still debated, but most would heavily qualify the independence of its effects. A number of detailed research projects, which are frequently quoted in support of environmental design influences, have in fact been conducted in exceptional circumstances. 'Festinger and his colleagues studied married ex-servicemen who were all postgraduate engineering students. Kuper studied rehoused working class people. Whyte dealt with such a homogeneous group that he labelled its members "organization men"' (Brown, 1973, p, 28). Some of the conclusions from the study by Festinger (Festinger, Schachter and Back, 1950) are often taken as extreme positions of architectural determinism. 'The architect who builds a house or who designs a site plan, who decides where the roads will go and will not go, and who decides which direction the houses face and how close together they will be, also is, to a large extent, deciding the pattern of social life among the people who live in those houses' (Pahl, 1970, p. 105). The notion that the built urban environment could have such influence acquired particular significance when it infiltrated planning practice and certain physical design principles became tools of social planning. Of these the neighbourhood unit was the best known and has been used in attempts to foster desirable levels of locality identification and localized social relationships.

More recent sociological research has been strongly critical of attempts to show a design influence upon behaviour. Gans (1972), who was particularly concerned with planning practice, argued that there was now considerable evidence that physical environment does not play as significant a role in people's lives as the planners believe. Buildings were of secondary importance in comparison with economic, cultural and social relationships; while bad designs could hinder activities and good design could aid them, design *per se* does not significantly shape human behaviour. Kuper (1953) showed that design might provide bases for increased antagonism rather than increased friendship; Mitchell and coauthors (1954) suggested, from their study of housing estates in Liverpool and Sheffield, that it was not possible to assert that the spatial position of houses contributed to the formation of friendships. More recently, however, N. Taylor (1973) and Newman (1972), among others, have indicated the role of design as alternatively a constraint to, or an opportunity for, various types of behaviour.

There is clearly a middle ground between views of extreme architectural determinism and those of its critics who would want to discount any influences whatsoever. The built urban environment is the context of social interaction and is obviously involved; 'good' design is always desirable, but in the last resort the built urban environment is one variable along with others which are influential. Michelson (1970) suggested a series of circumstances which might promote an element of spatial determinism in human friendship patterns. These included common characteristics of inhabitants, particular life-cycle stages and need for mutual aid. 'In short, spatial proximity often based on the position and outlook of doors may determine interaction patterns, but this normally only occurs under conditions of real or perceived homogeneity in the population and where there is need for mutual aid' (Michelson, 1970, p. 190). Anne Buttimer (1971) suggested a need to find a balance between involvement in neighbourhood and privacy in family life and Stewart (1972) stated that, while local physical arrangements were not irrelevant to ways in which individuals or groups behave, they were not the main determinants.

Besides the role of built urban environment in the promotion of contact and social interaction, some researchers have concentrated upon the deleterious effects of bad urban facilities. Narrow and restricted streets and overcrowding are all well studied facets of the bad urban environment. During the decades of social reform in the late nineteenth and early twentieth centuries, it seemed clear to researchers that the atrocious living conditions of the inner parts of the Western industrial city were directly responsible for the many undesirable qualities of the life-style of their inhabitants. To some extent they were right. Standards of health, for example, improved considerably when changes in living conditions were made possible. Over a range of behavioural traits, however, it is clear that improvements in the built urban environments have had little effect; in British rehousing projects, for example, social groups with a high incidence of delinquency and crime have simply transferred those characteristics from one form of environment to another. Michelson (1970), in a review of pathology and the urban environment, concluded that assertions of the adverse effects of bad environments were inconclusive. Only limited effects had been documented, the physical referent was ambiguous, the salience of intervening factors had not been adequately assessed and dependent pathologies had not been precisely defined. Only where housing conditions were desperately inadequate did they lead directly to physical and social pathologies.

A clear message from research on several fronts is that, if we wish to examine the environmental context of behaviour, a definition of environment as an urban built form is inadequate. The total environment within which an individual lives is much more than a framework of streets, buildings and spaces; it is populated, it is active and it is a contextual framework of attitudes, values and many forms of behaviour. Objective qualities of number, densities, social class, age and the like form one dimension of the social environment; activities, beliefs and traditions form another. Recognition of the social environment or the social milieu as one context for the study of individual behaviour opens up many new and promising avenues for research. The emphasis shifts from the need to study the influence of design to the need to understand to influences of those who live in close proximity. Residential area provides at least one reference group; others may be provided by work, school or interest location, but residence is likely to be the most important of these. How important the residential social environment is will vary with qualities such as age, education and personality; two concepts which seek to examine its relevance are neighbourhood effect and the idea of urban neighbourhood itself.

As a concept, neighbourhood effect recurs in several chapters of this second volume, yet its development in a systematic way is of recent origin. Neighbourhood effect suggests that within a locality or territory, a set of values may exist which have achieved some level of concensus over time and are transmitted to individuals within that locality or territory. Some studies (Robson, 1969) have suggested that such values may be generally accepted and typify an area; others see them as being particular to sub-groups within the area. The concept of delinquent sub-culture (Cohen, 1955; Mays, 1968), for example, is normally used to describe a set of deviant values held by youths within certain districts of a city; the individual youth for whom these youths form a peer group or a reference group is particularly at risk. Robson (1975) has recently exemplified the general idea of a neighbourhood effect. An area of manual workers, he suggested, provides a very different environment both physically and socially, from that of white-collar households. Two households with otherwise identical characteristics would be different objects if one lived in one type of area and the second in the other. Attempts to demonstrate and to measure the neighbourhood effect are proceeding on several fronts and will be exemplified in the chapters which follow. Measurements based upon aggregate statistics allow inferential statements of individual and neighbourhood effects; results of controlled household surveys provide more direct kinds of evidence. Methodologies are also available whereby the bases of individual behaviour can be examined at a more detailed scale, and social network analysis and reference group theory provide conceptual tools which may prove valuable in this respect. As yet, however, few empirical studies of any precision with a spatial referent (see, however, Walker, 1975) have been forthcoming, and there may be considerable practical problems in their application.

URBAN NEIGHBOURHOOD

All writers who introduce the term 'community' rightly stress its complexity. In their review of the meaning of the term, Bell and Newby (1971) noted that ninety-four definitions had been identified, but for them the three common strands in the majority of definitions were social interaction, common ties, and territory. For the city, the urban neighbourhoods are its locality-based communities. As Stewart (1972) has noted, the idea of a single urban community is untenable, for cities almost always contain many sub-communities with identifiable, stable patterns of relationships, both locally and non-locally based. It has been argued (Blowers, 1973) that urban neighbourhood is best viewed in typological terms; the five types of neighbourhood suggested were awareness, physical, homogeneous, functional and community. To prove that urban neighbourhoods exist as known, physically distinctive segments of the city occupied by broadly uniform groups of people has been the function of the first volume of this text. It is a more difficult task to show the extent to which our social areas are also coincident with local activity systems and possess a sense of place—a feeling of 'community'. Many sociologists have become increasingly critical of the concept of community neighbourhoods, observing correctly, as Dennis (1968, p. 80) does, that the importance of social system local communities has diminished considerably over time, but also displaying a reluctance to acknowledge any residual significance. Pahl suggested that 'Any attempt to tie particular patterns of social relationships to specific geographical milieux is a singularly fruitless exercise' (Pahl, 1968, p. 293).

To be as dismissive as this of the role of locality in the overall pattern of social systems is to adopt an untenable position. It can be accepted that it is possible for individuals to become antagonistic to neighbours, for individuals to have all their social contacts outside their residential localities and to be aspatial in their interaction patterns, and for individuals to be isolated or to have no awareness of 'neighbourhood'; but the great majority of people are not like this. Whatever their predilections, levels of mobility and interests, parts of their social lives are enacted upon a local stage. Some life-cycle stages tend to be more locality-based than others; the very old and the very young have little mobility and mothers with young children are similarly constrained. The mobile middle class may be more able to operate in non-place communities, but local ties still form important segments of their activities. Each individual has a system of activity network which changes through time and has hierarchical qualities both in terms of intensity and of spatial dimensions. Within the broader urban sub-community there are hierarchies of locality and from recent studies Pahl (1970, pp. 119–120) suggests that small groups of eight to twelve houses form foci of positive relationships. Several researchers have suggested that territory has a latent importance when particular issues arise, such as a planning decision which affect the area as a whole (Bell, 1968) or situations of conflict (Boal, 1969) which crystallize a sense of place in threatened communities. It is argued, therefore, that although the traditional form of the close-knit urban community has been modified over time it has not disappeared and that locality is a variable to be considered in the analysis of social interaction. Stacey (1969) defined a social system as a set of interrelated social institutions covering all aspects of social life and the associated belief systems of each. A local social system occurs when such a set of interrelationships exist within a geographically defined locality. This poses the most complete and demanding definition of local community, as Dennis does in his discussion of the neighbourhood community idea (Dennis, 1968), but no one wants to argue that this type of form is common now. Locality, territory, spatial proximity and the local social environment offer one context from which to study behaviour; it is partial and complements other perspectives. In this role it cannot be disregarded.

In this discussion of those spatial qualities which are of recurrent importance to the context of this second volume of the book, we have examined the broad categories of distance relationships, environmental contexts and the concept of urban territory. Two further qualities which require some examination are the idea of spatial images and the spatial implications of social inequalities in the city.

An influence of social psychology upon human geography is of very recent origin and, although there were earlier papers, those by Lowenthal (1961) and Kirk (1963) were perhaps the first to reach a wide audience. A central role of this influence was to suggest a new environmental context, which Kirk termed the behavioural environment. The assemblage of facts which comprises total reality will enter the behavioural environment of man, but 'only in so far as they are perceived by human beings with motives, preferences, modes of thinking, and traditions drawn from their social, cultural context' (Kirk, 1963, p. 367). Researchers, therefore, in assessing the spatial qualities which are possessed by a section of the city, should consider how those qualities are perceived by its inhabitants. The total reality which a district possesses may be less important than the partial awareness of it which is held by the individual.

To the methodologies developed to define sub-areas or neighbourhoods should be added attempts to measure the mental maps of their occupants; to the classifications of sub-areas should be added the preference ratings of the population. The implications of acceptance of this new type of environment context have far-reaching effects upon the study of spatial qualities.

'RELEVANCE'

Demonstration of the facts of social inequalities in cities and comprehension of the processes which produce them has been implicit in much social geographical research. The research methodologies which have been developed to study overall patterns of residential differentiation are easily adapted to probe more selectively and locate areas of social deprivation within cities. Researchers concerned with particular forms of deprivation or deviance, such as mental illness (Giggs, 1973), have shown that these are highly concentrated in particular parts of the city. Whilst there are areas of multiple deprivation (Boal, Doherty and Pringle, 1974), some forms of deprivation may have specific types of spatial distribution (Herbert, 1975). This alliance of concentrations of disadvantage with particular districts has led to the adoption of area-based policies (United Kingdom Department of Education and Science, 1967). For many geographers, however, an implicit concern with social problems and a set of transferable methodologies are not enough. Harvey (1972, p. 6) suggested that although the 'quantitative revolution' has run its course, 'There is a clear disparity between the sophisticated theoretical and methodological framework which we are using and our ability to say anything really meaningful about events as they unfold around us'. Harvey has also argued that more empirical studies of conditions of urban life in the inner city are not needed; in his terms they are 'counter revolutionary' in the sense that they allow 'bleeding heart liberals' to pretend they are contributing to a solution when they are not. These views have promoted a considerable debate and have found considerable support (Gray, 1975). There has also been an increasing awareness of the need to respond to social problems. Strategies for response differ. Harvey (1972) has strongly argued the lessons to be learned from a study of Marx and his works; Morrill (1970, p. 8) did not so favour revolutionary change: 'The key is to retain the institution of private property whilst instituting social control over its exchange and circumscribing its power over people'; while Berry (1972) was less willing to condemn the effects of individual initiative, private decision-making and competitive determination of success.

Academic researchers have become increasingly aware of social problems and have increasingly directed their enterprise more directly towards them. While, as Robson (1975) suggests, such studies do not directly ameliorate polarities in city life, they do reveal more strikingly their less attractive facets and have directed attention towards the processes and mechanisms which produce them. These activities may be dubbed 'counter revolutionary', but it is likely that the 'revolution syndrome' is not the correct one. Different kinds of social justice, new patterns of spatial equality and a reduction of societal divisions will not emerge overnight in Western cities. For many, the record of the mixed economy is by no means bad, for changes have occurred and have been in the right direction; evolution, though perhaps at a discouragingly slow pace, in some areas, is the more correct model. The more persistently and clearly the facts are demonstrated, the more clearly they are investigated and then the more effects they are likely to have. Informing a public with an increasing social conscience and reaching, and being involved in, the decision-making processes which affect cities, are objectives of no small significance. Thus, the philosophy, to which this book is addressed, is that immediate social problems require urgent remedial action, and some at least of this action can be spatial in its nature, whether by positive discrimination to certain areas or by social engineering through alteration of an area's population structure and general behavioural milieu. Such policies, it is realized, will not get at the root causes of many social problems which lie in the social structure which spatial structures reflect—you don't improve your looks by doctoring the mirror. But they may forestall an unfortunate revolution, caused by despair and frustration, while the twin processes of education and research produce a population aware of, and ready to produce, the radical changes needed to produce the better, more equal society.

CONTRIBUTIONS TO VOLUME II

The study of those forms of consumer behaviour which are a response to the need for urban services has been the cornerstone of modern human geography. Christaller's theory of central places has been variously regarded as providing the first comprehensive model of spatial behaviour and the main—if not the only—indigenous theory in human geography. This relatively long tradition of behavioural analysis has produced a considerable research literature which has evolved from a simple test of the initial axioms of central place theory to attempts at restatement of some of its more fundamental concepts. A small number of basic factors have always featured prominently in studies of consumer behaviour, and it is here that the friction of distance and the more general ideas of distance-decay have received closest attention. The nearest centre hypothesis, suggesting that other things being equal a consumer will use the nearest centre at which a particular good or service is available, remains a prop in the central place model. Colin Thomas, with the particular brief of examining the utility of extant theories within the city, explores the inheritance from the older models of central places and identifies the main avenues into which current research activity is being channelled. He demonstrates the debt which is owed to the early models, both in explanation of spatial patterns of distribution centres and their development, and in allowing rational generalizations on the form of consumer behaviour. He also shows how medical services are amenable to research strategies normally applied to retailing. Despite the continued revelance of aspects of more traditional central place theory, dissatisfaction with its details arise on several fronts. These include its over-reliance upon the concept of 'economic man' and its comparatively weak predictive power in attempts to explain modern consumer behaviour.

Although contextual factors are important in the study of consumer behaviour (Colin Thomas argues, for example, that socioeconomic status differences need to be examined more closely and that there is a relationship between residential differentiation and service provision), the main feature of their relevance is the way in which individual consumers react to 'trade-offs' in selecting a service centre. Relevant parameters include the age, wealth, sex and family circumstances of the consumer, on the one hand, and the distance, quality and attractiveness of the centre, on the other. These parameters need to be articulated to give the bases for new ground rules of *collective* behaviour, but there is little hint in the literature that the environmental contexts in which the individual is placed have any particular independent relevance. We are assessing the relative qualities of points in space—locations of consumer and service—not the relational qualities of areas. In this sense, the chapter differs from others in this section of the book in that it identifies no neighbourhood effect or concept of relational space but rests upon more traditional parameters as a basis for explaining behaviour. Any similarity between the consumer behaviour of occupants of a particular area is a function of the similarity of individual qualities of the occupants and the identical distance to services, rather than a product of some communicated consensus.

If these more traditional parameters hold sway in studies of consumer behaviour, it is in the analysis of voting behaviour that the extra dimension of neighbourhood effect has been explored most systematically. Indications of the importance of contextual variables have often been provided; Segal and Meyer (1969), for example, suggested that the climate of opinion in communities where people lived is a significant contributor to an explanation of voting behaviour. Ron Johnston's chapter focuses squarely upon the question of neighbourhood effect and asserts that location is not a passive variable but may warp behaviour in distinctive ways. A relatively small, but nevertheless impressive, literature on voting behaviour provides evidence of neighbourhood effects. The causes of such effects are not yet fully defined, but there is a body of evidence to demonstrate the salience of the residential mosaic as an influence on social activity. Geographical literature on voting behaviour is symptomatic of new emphasis in urban social geography in many ways. Distance as a variable in the traditional sense has little relevance, as polling stations are placed very close to users—see, however, A. Taylor's (1973) study of the effect of perceived distance in a local election—but distance as a variable in interaction with social qualities and processes requires close attention. The extent to which the candidate is known by the voters, the effectiveness of the local campaign and the intensity of relational space within the electoral district are all considerations which involve both social processes and spatial qualities.

Social deviance is a form of behaviour which has attracted an enormous amount of attention across a wide range of social science disciplines. Its attractions as a field of study include its distinctiveness—minority deviant groups stand out as anachronisms in societal structure and the 'unusual' always exerts a certain magnetism—and the immediacy of the practical problems which it poses. Social deviance is not, of course, one phenomenon; the term covers a diversity of behavioural forms for which numerous typologies exist. David Herbert's chapter does not attempt to cover the whole of this range, but selects a cross-section which is, in some ways, representative of the whole. Some deviance is involuntary, particularly medical deviance which includes mental illness, and other forms of deviance are voluntary, in that individuals consciously decide to infringe rules which have been prescribed for a society; the division in this dichotomy is by no means always clear. Social deviance frequently reveals a clear spatial expression, in that when its incidence is mapped there are heavy concentrations in particular, limited, parts of the city. Attempts to explain these concentrations can involve both the idea of a mirror image effect—the spatial concentration reflects a societal distribution and the intervening fact of an orderly social geography—and a neighbourhood effect, which suggests that a contaminating influence can be exerted within residential areas. areas. While the 'drift hypothesis'—that afflicted persons accumulate in particular urban districts *after* they become deviant—is an example of an alternative way of explaining the spatial distribution of deviance, the questions of societal distribution and the individual 'becoming' deviant have attracted a plethora of theoretical approaches.

Close examination of neighbourhood effect has been little evident in deviance studies, where the ecological tradition has more basic ingredients of social mapping and the ecological correlation of aggregate data. Possibilities of extending analysis occur with this kind of data, with methodologies, which adopt more specific hypothesis-testing frameworks, and with more detailed investigations arrived at examining area differences and the influences of variables which constitute the physical and social environments. Johnston (1975) has proposed analytical methods for the isolation and measurements of 'ecological effects' in the study of delinquent behaviour. As with other fields of behavioural study, ongoing research into social deviance faces severe data problems. Official published statistics are often not available at a sufficient level of detail nor in terms of classifications which are most suitable for academic research. Problems of reliability, comprehensiveness and bias exist, but in situations where no other sources are available and individual surveys are both time-consuming and expensive, they remain sources which have to be used.

In studying social deviance, researchers are dealing with real problems faced by society and must retain a consciousness of a responsibility to contribute towards solutions. This is not to argue that all research activity in this type of field should be dominated by the question of relevance; research can be instigated and carried through for purely academic reasons and the Cardiff study of delinquency reported in the chapter had, as its initial impetus, a desire to extend the methodology of residential differentiation by developing an area-sampling framework and investigating the contextual bases for a particular form of deviant behaviour. The approach and findings, however (in common with much social geographical research), were relevant to the practical problem and 'spin offs' were possible. There are studies of deviance which are specifically stimulated by the societal problem—much recent research (by American geographers) has been the result of concern with rising crime rates—and which are problem-orientated. An equally important role, however, is to contribute to the fund of information which is available to policy-makers; the composition of this fund will be diverse and will rest properly upon the contributions of many disciplines and their distinctive perspectives. Where more direct involvement in decision-making processes on policies occur, academics are likely to rely less upon their professional skills, as practised in research, than upon their individual abilities of judgement and compromise.

Questions of relevance and the role of research in the promotion of area-based policies are particularly pertinent to urban education. Here, as David Herbert's chapter indicates, the geographical research tradition is thin, but a diverse literature has thrown up observations relating to spatial qualities. These observations are often incidental in projects which have their emphasis elsewhere, but despite this many policies in the social services—and in the field of education in particular—have become area-based. The observed concentration of problem children in specific urban territories and the uneven distribution of low educational attainment over the city's schools and residential areas have been used as bases for designing selective policies of positive discriminations. In both the United States and Britain, educational policy-makers have boxed around with policies which have strong spatial implications; some of these—including bussing in the United States and designation of 'stress' schools in Britain—have achieved levels of notoriety. There have been reactions against area-based policies and it is recognized that in themselves they are insufficient, but all of this activity has occurred within the context of a major welfare service with minimal involvement by professional geographers. Recently, as studies reported in this chapter show, geographers have taken up the specific spatial questions affecting educational planning. Catchment areas and school locations are two of the problems which have now attracted the attention of spatial analysts. If a cautionary note can be sounded from a review of initial American exercises of this kind, it is of the need to communicate professional advice in an unambiguous way. The questions faced by educational planners are straightforward. What is the best location for a new school? What systems of catchment areas will secure the 'best' allocation with stated criteria? How can inequalities of resource distribution and management be minimized? If the answers are not simple, they must be comprehensible.

Whereas the first four chapters in this volume are by professional geographers who emphasize spatial qualities and the research frontiers of their own discipline, the last three are by social scientists from other disciplines whose approaches are inevitably—and desirably—dissimilar. All of these four authors, however, have previously written of urban matters in ways which acknowledge and use spatial variables and a common bond between each chapter is their concern with the meaning of urban neighbourhood and the sense of place. Several of the key spatial qualities recurrent in this book use urban neighbourhood as a concept and as a reality; the task now is to explore its meaning in both these contexts. Terence Lee, who has many claims to be an innovator in research into cognitive mapping within the city, considers the interface of social psychology and social geography in his discussion of city structures in the mind. His discussion of imagery in psychology provides a concise statement of many of the derived concepts which geographers have begun to use extensively in their research. The recent survey of cognitive mapping in geographical studies (Gould and White, 1974) provides ample evidence of the impact of these concepts. From this basis of the initial ideas and their lineage, Terence Lee is able to trace their translation into urban research at a variety of levels. The city-wide imagery of Lynch (1960), the distinctive work on neighbourhood perception and the attempts to adapt this type of approach to the needs of planning practice are examined in some detail. It has been the arrival of this new dimension, perhaps more than any other, which has pulled up social geographers with a jolt. Notions of non-economic man, behavioural environments and the blatantly obvious fact that individuals make spatially relevant decisions from the bases of imperfect knowledge, have had profound effects upon research. In the context of urban neighbourhood, the idea that the term the territory, and the values attached to it, are variously defined by occupants is now readily accepted; the problems are to measure and to generalize.

Colin Bell and Howard Newby seek to comprehend the meaning of urban neighbourhood within a broader framework of reference than that adopted by Terence Lee. Their concern is partly historical, in that they examine the antecedents of a local sense of identity and the forces which promoted it; partly methodological, in that they examine the role of classical social thinkers in labelling the dichotomies and differences within the range of socially interactive situations; and partly real and contemporary, in that they seek to examine the role of locality in the emerging pattern of urban politics. In methodological terms, questions of definition are critical and much of the confusion in the literature of the social sciences may have arisen from the proliferation of definitions attached to terms such as community. Bell and Newby draw a distinction between community, as the objective group to which individuals belong, and communion, which exists only through real and affective bonds. Although discussions in the abstract are crucial, the development of good analytical techniques to deal with empirical situations are of equal importance, and here social network analysis and the idea of housing classes (Rex, 1968) are identified as capable of application. It is in this empirical context of assessing the reality of urban neighbourhood that links with the research tradition of urban social geography are clearest; the position in the housing market and stage in the life-cycle, which are regarded as the best—albeit crude—predictors of the spatial location of individual families in urban structure, figure prominently in the literature of residential differentiation. Urban neighbourhood, or more generally local social system, has a clear and comprehensible place in the historical roots of society. Its independent role has become blurred and variegated with the complexities of a liberalizing and technologically changing way of life, and its main role in the near future may be as a basis for emerging political movements and as a means of maintaining identity and 'grass roots' affiliations.

The more practical consideration of the role of neighbourhood as a base for community power and political action recurs in the chapter by Elizabeth Gittus on deprived areas and social planning. Her emphasis upon those aspects of sociological theory and research, which are relevant to this particular spatial manifestation of poverty, reinvokes ideas of social networks, reference groups and the local bases of community action. We are reminded that the social sciences have a long tradition of research which has sought to portray the polarities in urban living standards and has maintained a close involvement with 'action research' and direct involvement with campaigns for social reform and with pleas for area-based policies. Research into poverty has had to face the question of definition and the difficulties of attaching measures to a relative and often personalized concept. It has had to face the fact that, within any designated deprived area, diversity will exist. There is diversity in the sense that not all individual members of the area will be deprived in the same ways, or to the same degree, or at all. There is diversity in the sense that the strength of social bonds between individuals and area will vary and that this variation does not necessarily relate to levels of measurable deprivation. Immigrant populations pose particular problems because the general conditions of deprivation, which they may share with sections of the white population, are exacerbated by their membership of minority groups against which discrimination exists. For academics who are stirred by the needs of the underprivileged, it is often minority groups such as these upon whom attention is focused. Their problems are self-evident, and their deprivation can often be both multiple and generational and shows little evidence of disappearing over time. As Elizabeth Gittus points out, one form of deprivation which can be mitigated is the lack of information and of access to available resources and welfare.

A strong theme in the chapter by Elizabeth Gittus is that, in the past, separation of approaches to urban problems has been much less distinct than it has more recently become with increasing specialization. There are both merits and disadvantages in this separation, but the important thing is to acknowledge that each approach has its 'relevance value'. We are probably best able to pursue our professional skills within our own terms of reference, to the solution of both academic and practical problems, but the point arrives when the gap between spatial and social thinking has to be bridged and resources have to be pooled in order to make the fullest sense of a complex urban question and in order to provide the fullest basis of information from which decisions affecting lives in cities have to be made.

The chapters in this volume can only claim to have approached the study of environments and behaviour within the city along a limited front. The limits imposed were principally those of an emphasis upon spatial qualities and an acceptance of a particular level of generalization. As a product of society, the city has a complexity and multi-stranded composition which reflects society as a whole; at any one point in time, it both contains a heritage of past structures and values and the contemporary forces for change. Researching this phenomenon is a hazardous business; while single 'strands' are analytically desirable, isolating them imposes an artificiality upon the research strategy. Use of the 'social area' as a strand has some advantages of synthesis. If the city is a mosaic, its 'social areas' are its component parts. The weaknesses and strengths of 'social area' lie in its level of generality. On the one hand, the understanding of individual behaviour is blurred; on the other, it presents a practical unit for which meaningful generalizations can be made and—eventually—practical policies can be formed. The city poses a multitude of problems and requires a multiplicity of approaches; this volume enunciates the potential contribution of one of these approaches.

REFERENCES

Bell, C. (1968). *Middle Class Families*, Routledge and Kegan Paul, London.
Bell, C., and Newby, H. (1971). *Community Studies*, George Allen and Unwin, London.
Berry, B. J. L. (1971). 'The logic and limitations of comparative factorial ecology'. *Economic Geography*, **47**, 209–219.
Berry, B. J. L. (1972). 'Revolutionary and counter revolutionary theory in geography—a ghetto commentary'. *Antipode*, **4**, 31–33.
Beshers, J. M. (1962). *Urban Social Structure*, The Free Press, New York.
Blowers, A. (1973). 'The neighbourhood: exploration of a concept'. In *The City as a Social System*, Urban Development Unit 7, The Open University. pp. 49–90.
Boal, F. W. (1969). 'Territoriality on the Shankill—Falls Divide, Belfast'. *Irish Geography*, **6**, 30–50.
Boal, F. W., Doherty, P., and Pringle, D. W. (1974). *The Spatial Distribution of Some Social Problems in the Belfast Urban Area*, The Northern Ireland Community Relation Commission, Belfast.
Brown, Hedy (1973). 'Man and his environment: a psychological introduction'. In *The City as a Social System*, Urban Development Unit 6, The Open University. pp. 13–44.
Buttimer, Anne (1971). 'Sociology and planning'. *Town Planning Review*, **42**, 145–180.
Cohen, A. (1955). *Delinquent Boys: The Culture of the Gang*, The Free Press, New York.
Dennis, N. (1968). 'The popularity of the neighbourhood community idea'. In R. E. Pahl (Ed.), *Readings in Urban Sociology*, Pergamon, Oxford.
Festinger, L., Schachter, S., and Back, K. (1950). *Social Pressures in Informal Groups*, Stanford University Press, California.
Gans, H. J. (1972). *People and Plans*, Penguin, Harmondsworth, Middlesex.
Giggs, J. A. (1973). 'The distribution of schizophrenics in Nottingham'. *Transactions, Institute of British Geographers*, **59**, 55–76.

16

Gould, P., and White, R. (1974). *Mental Maps*, Penguin, Harmondsworth, Middlesex.

Gray, F. (1975). 'Non-explanation in urban geography, *Area*, **7**, 228–235.

Harvey, D. (1970). 'Social processes and spatial form'. *Papers of the Regional Science Association*, **25**, 47–69.

Harvey, D. (1972). 'Revolutionary and counter revolutionary theory in geography and the problem of ghetto formation'. *Antipode*, **4**, 1–13.

Herbert, D. T. (1975). 'Urban deprivation: definition, measurement and spatial qualities'. *Geographical Journal*, **141**, 362–372.

Johnston, R. J. (1973). *Spatial Structures*, Methuen, London.

Johnston, R. J. (1975). 'Areal studies, ecological studies, and behaviour'. *Transactions, Institute of British Geographers* (in press).

Jones, E. (1956). 'Cause and effect in human geography'. *Annals, Association of American Geographies*, **46**, 369–377.

Jones, E. (1975). *Readings in Social Geography*, Oxford University Press, Oxford.

Kirk, W. (1963). 'Problems of geography'. *Geography*, **48**, 357–371.

Kuper, L. (1953). *Living in Towns*, The Cresset Press, London.

Lowenthal, D. (1961). 'Geography, experience, and imagination: towards a geographical epistemology'. *Annals. Association of American Geographers*, **51**, 241–260.

Lynch, K. (1960). *The Image of the City*, Harvard University Press, Cambridge, Massachusetts.

Mays, J. B. (1968). 'Crime and the urban pattern'. *Sociological Review*, **16**, 241–255.

Michelson, W. (1970). *Man and His Urban Environment*, Addison-Wesley, Toronto.

Mitchell, G. D., Lupton, T., Hodges, M. W., and Smith, C. S. (1954). *Neighbourhood and Community*, Liverpool University Press, Liverpool.

Morrill, R. L. (1970). 'Geography and the transformation of society'. *Antipode*, **2**, 4–10.

Newman, O. (1972). *Defensible Space*, Macmillan, New York.

Pahl, R. E. (Ed.) (1968). *Readings in Urban Sociology*, Pergamon, Oxford.

Pahl, R. E. (Ed.) (1970). *Patterns of Urban Life*, Longman, London.

Rex, J. (1968). 'The sociology of a zone in transition'. In R. E. Pahl (Ed.), *Readings in Urban Sociology*, Pergamon, Oxford.

Robson, B. T. (1969). *Urban Analysis*, Cambridge University Press, Cambridge.

Robson, B. T. (1975). *Urban Social Areas*, Oxford University Press, Oxford.

Segal, D. R., and Meyer, M. W. (1969). 'The social context of political partnership'. In M. Dogan and S. Rokkan (Eds.), *Quantitative Ecological Analysis in the Social Sciences*, The M.I.T. Press, Cambridge, Massachusetts. pp. 217–232.

Stacey, M. (1969). 'The myth of community studies'. *British Journal of Sociology*, **20**, 134–146.

Stewart, M. (Ed.) (1972). *The City: Problems of Planning*, Penguin, Harmondsworth, Middlesex.

Taylor, A. (1973). 'Journey time, perceived distance, and electoral turnout—Victoria Ward, Swansea'. *Area*, **5**, 59–62.

Taylor, N. (1973). *The Village in the City*, Temple Smith, London.

United Kingdom Department of Education and Science (1967). *Children and Their Primary Schools*, H.M.S.O., London.

Walker, R. L. (1975). 'Urban sub-areas as sampling frameworks: a further development'. *Town Planning Review*, **46**, 201–212.

Chapter 1

Sociospatial Differentiation and the Use of Services

C. J. Thomas

The areal expansion and the increasing functional complexity of urban life in Western cities in the twentieth century has resulted in a prodigious growth in the quantity and variety of services required by urban consumers. The range of services varies significantly in character and with respect to the agencies which provide them, so that their locational patterns and associated behavioural usage are also variable. Nevertheless, three centrally distinct but marginally overlapping categories can be suggested.

Numerically, the most important are the services normally provided in shopping centres. These comprise retail outlets; personal services such as hairdressers, dry-cleaners and photographers; professional services such as banks, estate agents and solicitors; and a range of catering and entertainment facilities. Their unity derives from the fact that their locational patterns have resulted from the competitive decisions taken by a large number of small suppliers relative to perceived consumer demand, although, in recent years, the influence of large supply organizations and the extension of physical planning controls have tended to complicate the situation.

A second category of medical services comprising general practitioners and hospitals can be suggested. These services are closely connected functionally and are significantly different from the first group. The locational decisions of general practitioners are not market-orientated to the same degree, but are restricted, usually by professional or by governmental licensing controls. In the case of hospitals, the individual units tend to be larger relative to the scale of the system as a whole and, therefore, less responsive to changes in the nature and location of demand, while in some countries their location policies have been subject to a greater degree of public control than shopping facilities.

The third category comprises public utilities such as local government administrative offices, public libraries and the police and fire services. Their location policies are already subject to near-complete public control and have little dependence upon a competitive market mechanism.

The intention of this chapter is to indicate the relationship between socio-spatial residential differentiation in the city and the development of patterns of

17

service facilities with their associated patterns of consumer behaviour. Initially, an analysis will be made of the manner in which service centres emerge in cities, indicating cross-cultural variations which have been observed. This will be followed by a more detailed investigation of the manner in which residential differentiation leads to systematic spatial variations in systems of service centres. Attention will then be focused on studies of consumer behaviour to indicate, from the alternative demand viewpoint, the degree to which a knowledge of sociospatial differentiation can contribute to an understanding of the use of services. An attempt will also be made to indicate the degree to which a comprehensive theory of intra-urban consumer behaviour has been developed and its relationship to the mosaic of social areas.

Most attention will be concentrated on the development and use of shopping centres. Services available in shopping centres are numerically the most important, while significant proportions of medical services and public utilities are either located in or are closely associated with shopping facilities. Also, the greatest number and the most frequent journeys to service facilities are generated by shopping centres. Thus, the majority of the analytical methods and substantiative findings associated with the investigation of the provision and use of services in cities are derived from studies of shopping facilities.

In contrast, the other services have been neglected until relatively recently. However, since 1966, following the intermittent publication of the findings of the Chicago Regional Hospital Study by R. L. Morrill and associates at the University of Chicago, considerable geographical interest has been developed in the medical service sector and an extensive body of literature is now available (Morrill and Earickson, 1968a, 1968b, 1969; Morrill and Kelley, 1970), although this activity has not been matched for public utilities, where investigation is still at an exploratory stage (e.g. Symons, 1971). The additional insight which these studies have contributed to the analysis of the development and use of service facilities will be incorporated into the discussion where applicable. However, it must be stressed that due to the differences in the nature of and controls over the specific categories of services, both the locational decisions— which determine their spatial patterns—and the associated consumer decisions —which relate to their use—are not totally comparable. Considerable variation occurs with respect to the degree of public control over the location of the different services, while, in general, consumers have a much greater range of choice and a more frequent need for shopping facilities than for either medical services or public utilities. Thus, considerable caution has to be exercised in extrapolating findings beyond the confines of a particular service type.

PATTERNS OF SERVICE FACILITIES AND SOCIOSPATIAL DIFFERENTIATION

The development of shopping centres and central place theory

In the early stages of city growth, consumer demands for goods and services are usually satisfied by business establishments concentrated in the central area. With urban expansion, a point is very soon reached when significant numbers of people are located too far away from the emerging central business district (C.B.D.) to be conveniently supplied with the most frequently required goods and services. The usual response of the business community to this situation is for new suppliers of the most ubiquitously required, lowest-order functions to establish their premises in locations central to the increasingly dispersed population. If dispersion of demand continues unabated, it becomes feasible for increasingly more specialized functions to decentralize. Ideally, these additional functions will gravitate to the most nodal of the original non-central locations and thereby create a series of second-order service centres. These centres will not achieve the degree of specialization of the C.B.D. because they will be less accessible to the city-wide population necessary to support the highest-order functions. The remainder of the original non-central service locations will continue to provide the lowest-order functions in positions interstitial to the higher-order centres. These would form a third order of centres.

This process would ideally create a nested hierarchical spatial pattern of service centres in cities, conceptually similar to the central place structure derived by Christaller (1966) for rural settlement patterns. In fact, while this process could be postulated from empirical observation, it has been provided with an academic foundation in central place theory by Berry and Garrison (1958), and the close relationship between the hierarchy of service centres in the settlement pattern and the hierarchy of service centres in cities was further elaborated by Berry (in Garrison and coauthors, 1959). Human behaviour is assumed to conform to the economic man concept. Both suppliers and consumers of services are credited with perfect information and the ability to make economically rational decisions. The theory assumes that an optimal location decision is made by the suppliers of services and that every consumer undertakes an economically rational journey-to-consume (Pred, 1967). The suppliers' decision is assumed to be determined by the 'threshold' concept, which states that a service will not be provided in a location unless a local market capable of supporting it at a profit exists. The market population will normally be located beyond the maximum sphere of influence ('range') of any other centre supplying the service. The journey-to-consume is assumed to be determined by the 'range' concept. The consumer will normally travel to the nearest centre within whose 'range' he happens to live, in order that the time-cost budget of the journey is minimized.

In real-world situations, consumers will normally require a considerable number of goods and services in varying amounts and with varying frequency. Consequently, varying numbers of the different types of establishment will be required to provide them and, in general, the consumer will be prepared to travel greater distances for the less-frequently required goods. The interaction of the behavioural norms with the specific requirements will logically result in a nested hierarchical system of service centres (Christaller, 1966). This will normally comprise many low-order centres and fewer larger centres providing all the lower-order goods but, in addition, providing goods and services which are less frequently required. The market areas for each hierarchical level will not overlap.

The concepts developed in central place theory have been used subsequently as an explanation for both the patterns of shopping centres in cities and the manner in which they change in relation to changing societal circumstances. At any one point in time the distribution of facilities is assumed to be adjusted to the nature of consumer demand, which in turn is determined by the density and distribution of the urban population, the types of goods and services required and the transport facilities available. In addition, changes in the organizational structure of retailing can also create disequilibrium, which ultimately expresses itself in changes in the pattern of service centres and associated consumer behaviour.

The application of these concepts to the study of intra-urban service centres has been most widely developed in the North American literature. Berry and others (1963) indicated that Chicago maintained a central commercial dominance until 1910, but, by 1935, 75 per cent. of business establishments were located outside the C.B.D. Commercial land use extended in ribbons along most grid and arterial routeways and at the busiest intersections outlying business centres developed which could be differentiated into neighbourhood, community and regional hierarchical orders, depending upon their degree of centrality to the surrounding population. The essentially linear pattern was related to the dependence of the population on public transport routes in the densely populated inner suburbs.

By 1950, widespread changes in the nature of urban society created pressures which accentuated the process of service centre decentralization and generated major changes in the spatial pattern of commercial activity. The growth in car ownership and the associated improvement of urban highways considerably improved intra-city mobility. Associated increases in the desire for spacious living resulted in urban residential densities decreasing from the typical 80 000 per square mile of the inner suburbs to 2000–10 000 per square mile of the post-war suburb. In addition, increases in affluence accentuated demand for specialized goods at the expense of the convenience outlets and, at the same time, economies of scale in retailing indicated the advantages of larger retail organizations and larger individual outlets (Simmons, 1964).

The greater dispersion of the population, the enhanced consumer choice afforded by increased mobility, changing buying patterns and changes in the nature of retailing all tended to create pressures favourable to the development of planned car-orientated shopping facilities in the outer suburbs, most of which have been developed in nodal locations on rapid transit routes.

The newly developed centres have tended to increase in size from neighbourhood to regional status as personal mobility has increased. The American Urban Land Institute has suggested the following hierarchical orders (Kivell, 1972):

1. Neighbourhood centres: consisting of 2 750–9 290m² of retailing space

providing mostly day-to-day requirements and serving a catchment area of 5 000–50 000 people.

2. Community centres: providing a greater depth of merchandising and based upon a junior department store. Typically, these offer 9 290–27 500 m² of selling space and cater for 50 000–150 000 people.

3. Regional centres: offering a full depth and variety of convenience, comparison and specialist goods, and including at least one department store. In size they range from 27 500–92 900 m², they provide up to 8 000 car parking spaces and they service a population of 150 000–500 000.

In contrast, spatial fragmentation has also been accentuated because improved mobility has allowed locational specialization of retail conformations. Specialization has occurred by product, particularly for infrequently purchased goods such as automobiles and furniture, and also by social class, manifest in the development of high status fashion centres or by concentrations of low status discounters, generally in accordance with the income characteristics of the districts in which they are located. In addition, a great variety of highway-orientated functions such as service stations, restaurants, drive-ins and motels have accentuated the linear pattern of commercial land use.

At the same time, the commercial structure of the inner city has been subject to 'commercial blight' (Berry and others, 1963). The suburbanization of the middle and high status population and their replacement by low income white and, particularly, negro groups has occurred. As a result of the loss of spending power, the hierarchical status of the inner suburban retail ribbons has declined substantially. Retailers of the higher-order goods and the least efficient of the excess convenience goods traders have gone out of business. Vacancy rates of a third to a half have developed before stabilization has occurred at a lower level, often accompanied by a physical reorganization of the remaining premises at nodal points on the former ribbons. A general air of dilapidation usually remains and the functional significance of the centres has diminished to neighbourhood or even to corner shop status. From a subsequent detailed study of the Hyde Park–Kenwood district of Chicago, it was apparent that this process was significantly accelerated by the demolition of the poorest residential property in urban renewal schemes (Berry, Parsons and Platt, 1968).

The overall process of change, in the absence of comprehensive planning controls, was stated by Berry and others (1963) to result in 'spatial anarchy', and this was considered by Cohen and Lewis (1967, p. 36) to be a highly detrimental development: '... the fragmentization of shopping facilities by clustering them along heavily traveled roads rather than their development into new "downtowns" may represent one of the great "missed" land use opportunities of our time'.

Nevertheless, a commercial structure consisting of three systems of aggregations was recognized (Figure 1.1), which in functional terms were not considered to be mutually exclusive categories. This was underlined by Boal and Johnson (1965) in their study of commercial ribbons in Calgary. Both an older ribbon

22

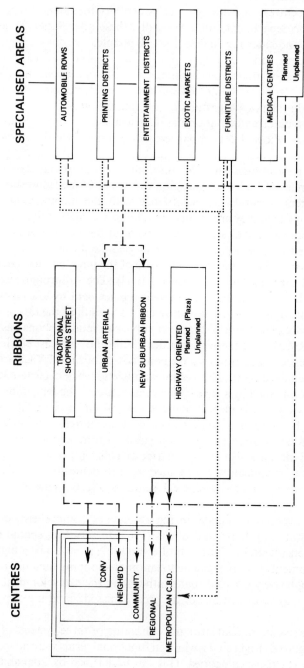

FIGURE 1.1 The metropolitan commercial structure. (Reproduced by permission of B. J. L. Berry and University of Chicago Department of Geography, Research Papers, 1963, Table 2, p. 20)

TABLE 1.1 Commercial ribbons: Calgary

| | Establishment group (percentages) | | | Special Functional |
| | | Ribbon | | |
	Hierarchic	Highway-oriented	Urban arterial	
17th Avenue South (inner suburban ribbon)	62.7	12.8	21.3	3.2
Macleod Trial (new arterial ribbon)	21.2	49.2	12.7	16.9

Reproduced with the permission of the Canadian Association of Geographers from F. W. Boal and D. B. Johnson, 1965.

near to the C.B.D. and a new suburban ribbon along a main arterial road incorporated establishments which could be included in any of the functional categories, despite their apparent morphological unity (Table 1.1).

However, while central place theory has provided a conceptual framework which contributes to an understanding of the development and change of patterns of shopping facilities in cities, in detail it is considered to lack explanatory and predictive precision. Pred (1967) suggested that dependence upon the economic man concept was the most significant weakness. Suppliers and consumers of services were considered more likely to be 'boundedly rational satisficers', concepts derived from the work of H. A. Simon (1957). They are unlikely, due to individual and environmental constraints, to have perfect information relating to spatial economic opportunities. Also, rather than attempting to economically optimize their behaviour, they are likely for social reasons to be satisfied with less. However, these alternative concepts have yet to be incorporated into a modified central place theory.

More specifically from the supplier viewpoint, Webber (1972) considered Pred's proposals to be intuitively correct but incapable of further refinement. Instead, he suggested that the introduction of the concept of 'uncertainty' into the decision-making process is potentially more fruitful because it might be incorporated into a modified economic location theory. Uncertainty, he suggests, results in a greater centralization of economic activity than central place theory predicts. Uncertainty concerning the location decisions of rivals tends towards an overestimation of the advantages of agglommeration in centralized, least-risk locations (Hotelling, 1929). Similarly, uncertainty concerning the 'states of nature', such as the future rate of economic growth, tends to accentuate the advantages of a major market location where instability is likely to be least evident, while the manner in which innovation and learning diffuse through economic systems from the most central to the least central locations tends to promote the influence of geographical inertia in the development patterns of economic activity.

With respect to the development of intra-urban patterns of shopping facilities, empirical evidence to support these contentions was suggested for Melbourne by Johnston (1968). It appeared that the advantages of inertia associated with the nodal attributes of the early suburban shopping centres located at railway stations significantly precluded a localized decentralization process in later years.

However, Webber's thesis was largely developed at the regional and national scale and still awaits rigorous testing in the urban situation. Nevertheless, the ideas expressed appear worthy of further investigation.

Cross-cultural comparisons

The commercial structure described for Chicago has been widely accepted as a model for the North American situation (e.g. Simmons, 1966), but its application in the wider context of Western industrial society has to be viewed with caution. Elsewhere, living standards have not advanced to the same degree, so that the associated levels of suburbanization and personal mobility have not been reached. Consequently, the commercial structures are usually more akin to the North American situation in 1950. This has been illustrated for Britain (Davies, 1974) and for New Zealand (Clark, 1967). A four-level hierarchy was demonstrated for both Coventry and Christchurch, broadly commensurate with the convenience, neighbourhood, community and C.B.D. categories of Chicago. The absence of a regional level between the community and the metropolitan C.B.D. can be related to the vastly different scale of the cities studied. The ribbon commercial form was noted in the inner suburbs of both Coventry and Christchurch, but they functioned in a hierarchical manner analogous to the North American traditional shopping street rather than demonstrating the considerable functional variety of the recently developed ribbons. A typical pattern of shopping centres in British cities is illustrated for Coventry in Figure 1.2.

However, in recent years the forces which transformed the North American situation have become increasingly apparent elsewhere. Johnston and Rimmer (1969) have indicated for metropolitan Melbourne a similar process of adjustment to that demonstrated in the United States. Since the late 1950s a number of unplanned and planned centres at all hierarchical levels have been developed in the Melbourne suburbs, and by 1965 there existed six large planned centres, one of which, Chadstone, was of regional significance (Johnston and Rimmer, 1967). In addition, the initiation of the process of commercial blight was demonstrated for the inner suburban areas in which recent Southern European immigrants were concentrated.

Similar developments have occurred throughout Western Europe since the mid-1960s. This has resulted in the widespread development of car-orientated suburban superstores or hypermarkets (at least 25 000 sq.ft. of selling space), particularly in Germany, as well as planned centres of community and regional significance (Dawson, 1974; National Economic Development office, 1971). More specifically, by 1972, 212 hypermarkets and four regional centres had been completed in France (Smith, 1973). Similar trends have been noted in

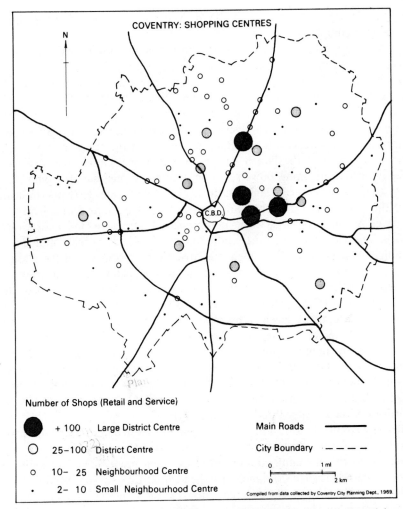

Number of Shops (Retail and Service)

⬤ + 100 Large District Centre

◯ 25–100 District Centre

o 10– 25 Neighbourhood Centre

· 2– 10 Small Neighbourhood Centre

Main Roads ——————

City Boundary – – – –

0 ⊢————⊣ 1 ml
0 ⊢————⊣ 2 km

Compiled from data collected by Coventry City Planning Dept., 1969

FIGURE 1.2   Coventry: shopping centres. (Compiled from data collected by
Coventry City Planning Department, 1969)

Britain, although the centres have been mainly of neighbourhood or community
significance (Kivell, 1972).

In part, the international differences noted can be related to detailed variations
in affluence, personal mobility, the nature of the suburbanization process, the
incidence of historical settlement nodes in the suburbs and the rate of retail
innovation. However, of more fundamental significance in explaining both
current variations and the degree to which the North American experience
will be replicated elsewhere is the influence of urban planning controls. In
North America, despite the fact that many individual centres are planned,
comprehensive controls over the changing commercial structure have been
lacking. The relative location of unplanned and planned developments has

only been marginally influenced by land using zoning, and this has resulted in the present complex structure.

In Australia, evidence suggests that, apart from the provision of neighbourhood and community facilities in areas of new housing, little planning control has been exerted. Instead, the development of new centres has been related to the assessment of demand by essentially private initiative (Dawson, 1974; Johnston and Rimmer, 1969), and a similar situation exists in France and Germany (Smith, 1973). However, European evidence increasingly suggests that future adjustments will be influenced by more stringent planning controls than was typical of the North American experience. Despite an absence of effective urban planning powers, a comprehensive regional shopping centre was proposed for Paris in 1968 (Smith, 1973), while Waide (1971) has indicated that the future pattern of shopping centres in metropolitan Copenhagen will be developed in accordance with a comprehensive structure plan incorporating two major regional centres, thirty community centres and a range of more locally significant facilities. In Britain, in the absence of a comprehensive planning strategy to accommodate the new developments, planning authorities have tended to use their powers to protect either existing retailing interests or their investment in, and potential tax revenue to be derived from, successful town centre redevelopment schemes by restricting large new suburban or out-of-town centres. Nevertheless, the wider issues and potential alternatives are recognized by many professional planners (e.g. Buchanan and Partners, 1968), and the Greater London Council has incorporated a comprehensive regional shopping centre structure in the Greater London Development Plan, including the construction of the first regional centre at Brent Cross in North London (Greater London Council, 1969).

In these circumstances, it might be suggested that in countries in which well-developed planning frameworks exist the adjustment of the commercial structure to the changing circumstances is much more likely to modify the existing hierarchies in accordance with the idealized system suggested by Vance (1962) for San Francisco and reiterated by Simmons (1964) for Toronto, rather than allow the complications which have emerged in the United States. In both these schemes the C.B.D. was seen as the seller of mass goods to the captive market of the inner suburbs and the seller of the highest-order speciality goods for the whole city region, while a complimentary series of regional centres were suggested as the sellers of mass goods to individual suburbs. In addition, a range of small neighbourhood and corner store functions were considered suitable to supplement the structure for frequently required or emergency purchases.

The influence of sociospatial differentiation

Whatever the general hierarchical structure of shopping centres, it is usually subject to detailed variation in different parts of the city. This reflects diversity in the nature of consumer demand, which is influenced by a number of interrelated factors. Of prime significance in this respect is the residential density of the urban population. This has tended to decllne both over time and with distance from the city centre (Rees, 1970). In areas of high residential densities the lowest-order functions (those with the lowest thresholds and restricted ranges) are able to establish in isolated locations, resulting in a profusion of low-order facilities. In areas of low residential density such functions are, by themselves, unable to attract trade from a sufficiently wide area to be economically viable. Instead, they have to cluster with other functions to create sufficient combined attraction to extend their range to encompass the necessary threshold population. As a result, in low density areas the lowest-order centres will tend to be larger and more widely spread then in high density areas (Johnston, 1966).

Superimposed upon the effects of the density surface is the complicating influence of residential differentiation by socioeconomic status, which generally tends towards a sectoral pattern (Hoyt, 1939). The expenditure available to the high status groups creates demands for a greater choice of more specialized goods and services than their lower status counterparts. This, in combination with their higher levels of personal mobility, tends to result in less frequent shopping trips, but to higher-order centres, though these do not necessarily involve a larger and more difficult journey to the C.B.D. (Evidence to support these behavioural contentions will be presented in a later section.) This tends to result in the elimination of isolated stores and small centres and the development of a relatively larger number of middle- and high-order centres in high status areas and the converse in low status areas (Johnston, 1966).

Additional empirical support for the relationship between socioeconomic status and detailed structural variations in the hierarchy is evident from the literature. Johnston and Rimmer (1967) indicated for Melbourne that the majority of the large planned suburban shopping centres developed by 1965 were located in those suburbs which were characterized by the highest personal incomes and levels of car ownership, while locational specialization by social class has already been referred to for Chicago (Berry and others, 1963). A similar consideration is suggested by Schiller (1971) to explain the recent relocation tendencies of specialist services such as imported car agencies, high status fashion boutiques and expensive antique shops in the higher status parts of the Outer Metropolitan Area of London.

At a more detailed scale of investigation, Davies (1968) demonstrates the close adjustment of the social class and income characteristics of residential areas in Leeds and their associated shopping facilities. Two residential areas equidistant from the C.B.D. were defined, one with a medium separate income unit of £1 276 and the other £733. In general, their shopping facilities were similar, each with one main shopping centre, five local shopping parades and five and six isolated stores respectively. The number of establishments and functions clearly indicated the expected pattern of a larger, more specialized centre in the high income area, although the greater relative importance of low-order facilities in the low income area was not immediately apparent. However,

28

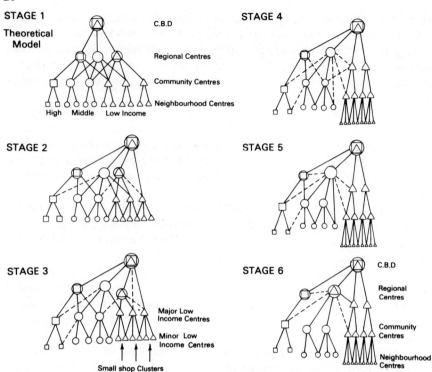

FIGURE 1.3   A developmental model of hierarchical sub-systems of shopping centres. (Reproduced by permission of the Institute of British Geographers, from R. L. Davies, 'structural models of retail distribution: analogies with settlement and urban land use theory, *Transactions of the Institute of British Geographers*, vol. **57** (1972), Figure 6, p. 70)

when the major and minor subsidiary functions were included in the analysis, a greater number and variety of functions were indicated in the lower income area, in accordance with the expected pattern.

Based upon the evidence of studies such as these, Davies (1972) proceeded to suggest a hypothetical model, outlining the development of hierarchical sub-systems of shopping centres within a four-level hierarchy which might be expected to be associated with spatial variations in the socioeconomic status of consumers (Figure 1.3).

Additional hierarchical variations are considered to be related to the principal mode of transport available to the initial residents of different parts of cities (Johnston, 1966). Prior to the development of mass public transport, residential densities were necessarily high and few locations had particularly advantageous nodal attributes, the combined influence of which tended to create a scattered distribution of shopping facilities. Following the development of public transport, the stopping points on the routes achieved greater accessibility and nucleated shopping centres often resulted in these locations. However, in inner-city situations, frequent stopping points encouraged the expansion of centres along the lines of the routes. This often created a ribbon pattern in which frequent duplication of shop types occurred, although the concentration of the higher-order functions at the original nodal points was usually maintained.

Alternatively, in situations where railways influenced residential development, a different pattern resulted. Stops were usually less frequent and often coincided with the locations of pre-existing settlements. The consumer demand resulting from suburban growth near these locations, combined with their accessibility, resulted in the development of relatively large shopping centres (Johnston, 1968). In detail, the hierarchy was directly related to the distance between stations. Stations equidistant from one another developed centres of similar hierarchical order, and the further apart the stations were, the higher was their order. Intervening stations developed at a later date were usually associated with smaller centres than might be expected from their locational characteristics, a fact explained by the difficulty of overcoming the advantages of the earlier centres.

Suburbs developed in association with high levels of car ownership demonstrate additional variations. The enhanced personal mobility of consumers reduces dependence upon restricted local facilities so that they are able to exert greater discrimination in their choice of shopping opportunities. This tends to encourage the development of middle- and high-order centres at particularly accessible points on the highway network, although in a system unconstrained by land use planning this can also result in the dispersal of some functions along the highway network.

Lastly, the location of a residential area relative to the C.B.D. can also influence the nature of the shopping hierarchy which it develops. In general, the closer an area is to the competitive influence of the C.B.D., the less likely it is to develop middle- and higher-order centres.

The combined influence of these factors creates variable patterns of consumer demand to which the distribution of centres adjusts. Stated in its most general form, this demand surface can be considered to comprise two cases:

1. The inner city: tending to house the lowest status groups at the highest densities in the oldest dwellings. The high densities of the poorer, less mobile elements of the community are able to support a greater-than-average number of low-order centres and isolated corner shops, but proximity to the C.B.D. obviates any tendency for new high-order centres to develop. Consequently, such areas will tend to be well represented with the lower-order and older elements of the hierarchy.

2. The outer suburbs: tending to house the highest status groups at the lowest residential densities. The low densities militate against the widespread development of lower-order and isolated facilities, but promote a stronger tendency to clustering in nodal locations. The high levels of personal mobility and retail expenditure located at a distance from the competitive influence of the C.B.D. accentuates the clustering tendency and promotes the development of new high-order facilities in a relatively small number of nodal

points on the transport network. Consequently, such areas will be well provided with the higher-order and newer elements of the hierarchy.

Such variations were demonstrated for Chicago, where the central lower income zones supported only a two-level hierarchy comprising a neighbourhood level and smaller shops, while, in the outer higher income zone, neighbourhood, community, shopping goods and regional level centres were recognized (Berry and others, 1963). Corroborating evidence was provided by Johnston's (1966) study of the spatial distribution of the central place hierarchy of Melbourne. The higher density inner-city areas supported many isolated low-order stores, while the outer lower density suburbs demonstrated a significantly greater clustering tendency, with the lowest level centres significantly larger than the lowest level of the high density area.

Clearly, more complicated variations could be envisaged if middle status areas were introduced into the scheme or if high status inner-city areas and low status outer suburban areas were considered. In these circumstances, systematic hierarchical variations might be expected to accord with the effects of the factors already discussed, the percise patterns depending upon the relative significance of each in individual cases.

Thus, it might be concluded that variations in the hierarchy of service centres will tend to reflect the nature of residential differentiation in the city.

The medical services system

The majority of the geographical literature relating to the provision of systems of medical services in cities has been developed in the United States. The services have been provided on a fee-for-service basis, so that the market considerations of profit maximization and the ability of the consumer to pay have strongly influenced the structure of the resulting system. For this reason, the process of development and the resulting structure of the health care delivery system closely parallels patterns of shopping facilities (Earickson, 1970).

The locational behaviour of physicians is indicative of these considerations. The medical profession is bound by codes of conduct which prevent advertising. Thus, the best location for a practitioner is a shopping centre visited by his potential patients. As a result, Earickson indicates that 83 per cent. of physicians in Chicago are located in commercial centres and that, furthermore, there is a distinct tendency for the higher the degree of specialization of the physician, the higher the hierarchical status of the centre in which he is established. Similarly, changes in the location of physicians over time closely follow the changing pattern of demand of their middle and high status patients. This initiates a process closely analogous to commercial blight in the sphere of retailing. De Vise (1971) illustrates the drastic decline in the numbers of physicians in selected inner suburbs in Chicago, 1950–70, associated with their transition from middle-class white to low status negro communities (Table 1.2), and the concomitant imbalance in the distribution of physicians in favour of middle and high status suburbs.

TABLE 1.2 Change in number of physicians in selected
Chicago communities, 1950–1970

Chicago communities	Number of physicians	
	1950	1970
East Garfield Park	65	2
West Garfield Park	161	12
North Lawndale	83	16
Kenwood–Oakland	41	9
Woodlawn	125	37

Reproduced by permission of *Antipode* from P. de Vise,
1971.

The locational determinants of hospital services are considerably more complex. Hospitals vary with respect to the type of care and the degree of specialization offered. Generally, the larger the hospital, the more specialized the service, although the relationship is complicated by the possibility of providing specialist services such as pediatric, obstetric and geriatric care in relatively small single-purpose units. There may also be variation in hospital type according to religious affiliation and to the degree to which they will accept Negro and charity patients. Patients also vary with respect to the level of specialist care their ailment requires, to their preference for hospitals with particular religious affiliations and to their ability to pay for care. These considerations approximate to the shopping situation and it is assumed that the interrelationship between the supply and demand criteria result in the development of a hierarchy of hospitals which is conceptually similar to the hierarchy of shopping centres. In fact, it is apparent in Chicago that there exists a close relationship between the accessibility of a hospital and its hierarchical status, a relationship which Earickson (1970) attributes to the same agglommerative and centrality considerations which create a similar effect in the shopping centre hierarchy.

However, the analogy between the two systems cannot be taken too far. Hospitals are not necessarily located in shopping centres, principally because their services are less frequently required and, therefore, not subject to the same rigorous accessibility constraints. Also, some types of hospital, such as sanitoria and infectious disease units, have particular environmental requirements. Nevertheless, they are generally located close by, probably due to their partial dependence upon the same public transport facilities and highway network. In addition, hospital location tends to be less responsive to changes in the location of consumer demand than either shopping facilities or physicians. General hospitals are extremely expensive and relatively large indivisible units, so that there is a time lag of approximately five years between a newly developed residential area reaching a threshold population and the start of construction even of a community hospital (Earickson, 1970), while locational inertia is even more marked in the cases of the highly specialized hospitals in city centres. The effects of the resulting imbalances in the location of supply and demand are overcome in the short term by patients undertaking relatively long journeys, a situation which has adverse effects upon the less mobile elements of the community, who are likely to be those in greatest need.

The provision of medical services in the United States has an additional point of contact with the system of shopping facilities. Its free enterprise basis has resulted in a lack of comprehensive planning-controls over its spatial structure. Organizational diversity is endemnic. Four major organizational categories occur, most of which themselves have divided responsibilities between federal, state and county administrative levels. Currently, the most important is the non-profit organizations comprising hospitals controlling 70 per cent. of general hospital beds, medical societies and health planning coordination councils. Private practitioners constitute a second group, while commercial enterprises such as health insurance interests, nursing homes and drug companies are also of considerable importance. Finally, government agencies in recent years have become increasingly important. The relative significance of these bodies can be roughly indicated by existing methods of payment for health care: 50 per cent. direct private payment, 25 per cent. health insurance, 23 per cent. government assistance and 2 per cent. philanthropic (Ardell, 1970). The complexity of control has resulted in a considerable operational inefficiency and has accentuated the lack of responsiveness of the system to existing and changing patient requirements.

As a result of the existing deficiencies in the system, academic studies have concentrated upon two closely related themes. The first considers policies designed to produce social equality of access to medical services by reducing existing income and racial barriers (de Vise, 1971). The Federal Medicare and Medicaid programmes initiated in 1966 to assist the aged and poor respectively represent an exploratory step in this direction. The second considers the need to promote a comprehensive health services planning system which can be effectively coordinated with urban planning agencies to create spatial equality of access to health facilities (Ardell, 1970; Frieden and Peters, 1970). A first step in this direction was taken in 1966 with the provision of government funds to encourage the development of comprehensive 'Areawide' health planning.

Clearly, the shopping and medical service systems in American cities have significant features in common. It seems likely, therefore, that the investigation of one system is capable of providing insight into the operation of the other, as long as their detailed differences are appreciated.

This situation is not typical of all Western societies. The manner in which medical services are financed and the extent to which they are subject to government control vary considerably. In this respect, the British National Health Service represents an opposite extreme to that in the United States. Medical services are financed and controlled by the government and are available without charge. The Ministry of Health introduced a tripartite organizational structure in 1948 to replace the variety of private and voluntary general hospitals and private medical practitioners. Hospital authorities were created to administer general hospital and specialist medical services, executive councils to coordinate the services of general practitioners and related services, and local health authorities to administer public health services such as domiciliary care and preventive medicine. These organizations have functioned largely as autonomous entities, and this has created considerable problems of coordination. Nevertheless, a much less complex organizational structure has resulted than is the case in the United States, and a strongly developed hierarchical ordering of services is apparent.

England was divided into fourteen regions with populations of approximately three million for health planning and administration. These areas were controlled by regional hospital boards and each contained a regional hospital, usually associated with a university medical centre, offering the most specialized services. For operational purposes, the regions were subdivided into districts of 100 000–200 000 population, controlled by management committees responsible for approximately 1 000 hospital beds. Initially, these were housed in a variety of small single-purpose hospitals and clinics, which reflected the historical development of the hospital system. However, the growing demand for increasingly specialized services and the constant shortage of manpower and capital asserted the organizational and economic advantages of agglomeration. This culminated in the Hospital Plan of 1962, which proposed the general district hospital to integrate all existing hospital services into single units of 1 500–2 000 beds to serve populations of 200 000–300 000 (Ministry of Health, 1962).

Below this level the situation was more confused. In most cases, primary medical care was provided by general practitioners, each serving approximately 2 500–3000 persons, although significant imbalances have been apparent in the peripheral regions of the country and in the less-attractive parts of the major cities. In addition, the Ministry of Health encouraged general practitioners to create larger group practices to serve 10 000–15 000 people (Shannon and Dever, 1974). These were to be operated from health centres, providing a wider range of more specialized diagnostic and therapeutic out-patient facilities than the smaller practices, in order to allow the hospitals to concentrate on more serious ailments. It was also possible for the local health authorities to cooperate in the development of, or to initiate, health centres of this type. This policy was designed to integrate general practice with the provision of public health services, but, in practice, due to financial limitations and the cautious attitude of general practitioners to the possibility of local authority control, developments in this direction were slow (Ryan, 1968). In fact, Buttimer (1971) indicated that by 1969 only 131 such centres were in use, 79 under construction and few had developed out-patient clinics or specialized diagnostic services.

Over the years, the problems of coordination associated with the tripartite structure increasingly created pressures for change. As a result, administrative reorganization came into effect in 1974 (Office of Health Economics, 1974). The new system was designed to promote greater efficiency in the health care delivery system by introducing a unitary system of control and by defining more clearly the hierarchical allocation of responsibilities. Control and planning were to be the principal functions of the upper levels of the hierarchy, while the provision of care was to be organized locally in accordance with the needs of the population. In effect, there was to be a maximum delegation downwards, matched by accountability upwards; in addition, a sound management structure was to be created at all levels (Department of Health and Social Security, 1971).

The Department of Health and Social Security is responsible for overall resource allocation. In England, the coordination of planning proposals at the regional level is effected via fourteen regional health authorities, and full operational and considerable planning responsibility has been devolved to the ninety area health authorities. The latter are the key units in the new structure and they employ the majority of the National Health Service staff. Spatially, they coincide with the recently reorganized metropolitan district and county units of local government. This was designed to promote coordination of the medical services with the social welfare, school health and environmental health services of the local authorities. Below this level, a system of district management teams is responsible for the provision of hospital, general practitioner and community health services for populations of approximately 250 000. Where possible, these units were based upon the service areas of the general district hospitals.

The problems of coordination associated with the health care delivery system of the United States appear to have been largely resolved in Britain by this structure. Also, access to medical services in Britain is available on a more socially equitable basis. Nevertheless, the system is not without potential problems. Government controlled services tend to concentrate on the development of an efficiently functioning supply system, with standards of efficiency gauged essentially from the managerial viewpoint. Buttimer (1971, p. 32) stated the case of the following terms: 'Primary attention is implicitly given to the economics and/or engineering of the supply system rather than the appropriateness of service to demand'. The varying needs of the consumer were assumed, until 1974, to be represented by lay members of the various administrative committees, but in practice their roles tended to be divided ambiguously between the representation of public opinion and managerial responsibility. Thus, supply and demand did not necessarily combine to provide a mutually satisfactory system. The decisions to develop general district hospitals and to amalgamate general practitioners into health centres were suggested respectively by Buttimer (1971) and Sumner (1971) to reflect largely the managerial perspective—the need to provide more specialized medical services and to improve administrative efficiency. However, both decisions reduced the accessibility of medical services to the consumer, with scant attention given to the social implications of these actions. These studies did not categorically state that radically different decisions would have been reached if the consumer viewpoint had been introduced more formally into the decision-making process. Clearly, the medical and managerial decisions still had to be accommodated. Rather, it was suggested that if a socially optimal spatial allocation of medical services is to be developed, considerations relating to both the supply system and to consumer demand have to be incorporated into the decision-making process in a mutually interdependent manner.

To overcome this problem, the control of service provision has been devolved to the most local level, so that the needs of the population might be accurately judged. In addition, community health councils have been created to represent public opinion, although, as currently constituted, these are virtually powerless (Office of Health Economics, 1974). In theory, such a solution could be successful, but in the absence of strong consumer organizations it is likely that the managerial viewpoint will continue to dominate decisions concerning the provision of services.

The health care delivery systems of the United States and Britain represent extremely different situations. Other countries demonstrate aspects of each in varying degrees of significance. In fact, in Europe alone, Babson (1972) has suggested a fourfold categorization of hospital organizational types, depending upon the nature and degree of central control (Table 1.3). Furthermore, he suggests that invariably a cross-cultural evolutionary process is operating which is tending towards the comprehensive government control

TABLE 1 3 European hospital system types

Basic organizational pattern	Principal characteristics	Countries illustrative of pattern
Scandinavian	Considerable local autonomy	Denmark Finland Iceland Norway Sweden
Eastern European	Centralized ownership and control	U.S.S.R. Poland East Germany Czechoslovakia Hungary
Central European	Provincial governments responsible for hospital services	Germany Austria Switzerland
Latin–Benelux	Diverse ownership with complex Administrative controls	France Belgium Italy Netherlands

Reproduced by permission of Pitman Medical Publishing Co. Ltd. from J. H. Babson, 1972, Figure 1.1, p. 4.

of health care delivery systems. Similarly, Shannon and Dever's (1974) comparative spatial evaluation of health care delivery systems in the U.S.S.R., Sweden, England and the United States stresses the advantages of a regionally centralized administrative organization combined with a decentralized system of service provision.

Nevertheless, it might be suggested that the future investigation of the development and operation of medical service systems in cities is likely to maintain an underlying unity with studies of services in general. Despite organizational variations, there still exists a need to match the supply system with consumer demand. In fact, exploratory geographical investigations of the location of primary medical care (Sumner, 1971) and hospital facilities (Buttimer, 1971) in Britain both stress the importance of the need to concentrate on the relationship between supply and demand in the system.

SERVICE CENTRES, SOCIOSPATIAL DIFFERENTIATION AND CONSUMER BEHAVIOUR

In the previous section, systems of service centres in cities were assumed to be adjusted to the social characteristics of the differing residential areas. The implication, which is made explicit in central place theory, is that for a particular type and grade of services a consumer will tend to use the nearest centre offering such services. Thus, from a knowledge of social area differentiation and the spatial structure of the service system under review, the vast majority of behavioural interaction might be predicted with ease.

However, the strength of these relationships was assumed rather than demonstrated. By focusing attention directly upon studies of consumer behaviour, the remainder of this chapter intends to explore further the relationship between the residential location of consumers and their behaviour, and the closely associated effects of social differentiation. It is also intended to indicate the degree to which a comprehensive theory of intra-urban consumer behaviour has been developed and its relationship to an appreciation of sociospatial differentiation in the city.

As the literature relevant to this subject is extensive and a considerable variety of approaches exist, a basic division is made between the normative and the behavioural approaches.

The normative models

Normative behavioural assumptions are the basis of central place theory and spatial interaction theory, both of which postulate assumptions or norms which are considered to determine the development of an optimal aggregate pattern of spatial behaviour.

Although the basic postulates of *central place theory* have been known for some time, most empirical tests of the theory have been confined to determining whether a reasonable approximation of the structural facets of the system

TABLE 1.4 Consumer patronage of nearest centre

Totals	Sample size	Number purchasing	Percentage using nearest centre	Percentage using nearest centre within 200-yard 'indifference zone'	Percentage not purchasing
Grocery	495	488	57.4	63.1	1.4
Vegetables	495	336	62.8	66.4	32.1
Meat	495	459	46.8	52.1	7.3

Compiled from household interviews, and maps of household and business centre location. Reproduced by permission of the Association American Geographers from W. A. V. Clark, 1968.

exists in the real world. If this proved to be the case, it was assumed that supplier and consumer behaviour conformed to the theoretical norms. However, it is possible that inference based upon a knowledge of structure results in a serious mis-statement of behavioural realities. This view has been taken by a number of workers who have tested directly the behavioural assumptions of the theory. Specifically, the hypotheses which have been subject to empirical analyses are:
1. The explicit assumption that a consumer will visit the nearest centre supplying a good or service.
2. The implicit assumption that there is not a significant difference in the distance travelled for the same goods or services for different sized centres.

A study by Clark (1968) of a random sample of Christchurch shoppers indicated that only 50–60 per cent. of convenience shopping trips could be predicted by the nearest centre hypothesis (Table 1.4), while similar findings were reported by Ambrose (1967–68) for the Sussex coast urban area. Also, it was apparent that in the five-level hierarchy in Christchurch, consumers did travel further to the C.B.D. and to other high-order centres than to lower hierarchical levels for a wide range of goods and services, so refuting hypothesis 2 (see Table 1.4). More recently, Day (1973) has also tested the movement minimization hypothesis in a London New Town. Nearly all the interviewees lived closer to a neighbourhood centre than to the town centre, yet only 37 per cent. of the food purchases were local and only 36 per cent. of clothing purchases were made in the town centre, the remainder going to higher-order centres further afield.

Similar findings have been reported for the use of medical services in the United States (Morrill, Earickson and Rees, 1970). In the inner city of Chicago only 55 per cent. of patients visited the nearest physician and this fell to 35 per cent. in the outer suburbs. The situation was similar for hospital visits. Only 55 per cent. of inner-city patients travelled to the nearest hospital and 30 per cent. of suburban patients. The hospital case reflects the nature of the two-stage trip via a physician referral and the fact that only 45 per cent. of inner-city and 25 per cent of suburban physicians are affiliated to the nearest hospital. However, also of fundamental significance in explaining these patterns was the influence of consumer preference for particular physicians or hospitals, possibly related to religious adherence or to the constraints imposed upon access to the services by financial or racial barriers.

However, Christaller (1966) did recognize two situations in which the behavioural assumptions might deviate from the norm. These are highlighted by Pred (1967) for the shopping situation, and they rest on the assumption that a shopper will sometimes attempt to maximize total travel effort, often by combining shopping with some other activity (multipurpose trip), rather than merely minimizing the travel cost for the individual good. Thus, a consumer may obtain both low- and high-order goods from a high-order centre which is more distant than the closest low-order centre, or may travel to a distant centre if sales price savings exceed additional transport costs. If these cases had been comprehensively incorporated into central place theory rather than recognized as minor deviations from the norm, it is possible that the behavioural shortcomings indicated in the literature might be substantially accounted for.

However, other features detract from the utility of the behavioural assumptions of central place theory as a comprehensive explanation of intra-urban shopping behaviour. The concept of the 'boundedly rational satisficer' was assumed to apply as much to the consumer as to the supplier of services (Pred, 1967). Thus, consumer behaviour is likely to be socially sub-optimal rather than economically optimizing. In addition, particularly at the intra-urban scale, the range of possible alternative shopping opportunities is constantly increasing. This is a direct result of improvements in personal mobility and of increasing consumer awareness related to developments in education and advertising, and is demonstrated in the development of overlapping hinterlands of shopping centres at all hierarchical levels (Berry and others, 1963).

Therefore, it might be concluded that the nearest centre assumption of central place theory provides only a partial explanation for behaviour in the intra-urban context. The residents of particular areas in cities generally display variable patterns of behaviour. Nevertheless, the assumptions of the theory provide a useful introduction to the study of consumer behaviour, and their critical appreciation has stimulated additional research which is currently attempting to develop a more comprehensive understanding.

Spatial interaction theory attempts to provide a more comprehensive explanation of consumer behaviour than central place theory. The assumption that behaviour is explained by the simple rule that consumers will use the nearest offering of a service is discarded. Instead, behaviour is assumed to be determined by a more complex trade-off of the advantages of size (or more generally attraction) of the centres against the disadvantages of distance (or more generally disincentive) of the consumers to the centres. This was derived from the 'law of retail gravitation' (Reilly, 1931) and is intuitively based upon empirical observations of shopping behaviour in the inter-urban context.

At the intra-urban scale, the wider range of shopping opportunities within relatively short distances renders the two-centre interaction situation of the original formulation inappropriate. In these circumstances, Huff (1963) considered it more likely that more than one centre will be used by a particular residential area with varying degrees of probability, in direct proportion to the relative attraction of the centre, in inverse proportion to some function of distance between the centre and the residential area, and in inverse proportion to the competition of all other centres in the system. These assumptions were independently incorporated into a probabilistic reformulation of the gravity model by Lakshmanan and Hansen (1965), designed to estimate the shopping expenditure flows between any residential area (i) and shopping centre (j) in a system:

$$S_{ij} = C_i \frac{\dfrac{A_j}{D_{ij}^{b}}}{\displaystyle\sum_{j=1}^{n} \frac{A_j}{D_{ij}^{b}}}$$

where S_{ij} = the shopping expenditure of residents in area i spent in centre j
$\quad\quad A_j$ = the size (or index of shopping attraction) of centre j
$\quad\quad D_{ij}$ = the distance from area i to centre j
$\quad\quad b$ = an exponent empirically calibrated to express the distance–disincentive function operating in the system under investigation
$\quad\quad C_i$ = the total shopping expenditure of residents in area i.

By calibrating the model using known origin–destination data for metropolitan Baltimore, it was found to provide an approximate description of existing behaviour. The model was then rerun incorporating possible future residential areas and service centre structures. Estimates of the probable turnover of each centre and associated trip characteristics were produced as output and this was used to evaluate the planning potential and problems which might be associated with alternative strategies.

A partial adaptation of the gravity formulation has subsequently been applied to the modelling of patient trips to medical services. An aggregate study of the origins of patients in a variety of Chicago hospitals suggested that their behaviour conformed to the assumptions of the gravity model. The larger, more specialized hospitals drew their patients from the widest areas, while the decline in the frequency of patients attracted per unit area with distance from the larger hospitals was systematically lower than for the small hospitals (Morrill and Earickson, 1968b). These findings were used as the basis for a compound gravity-simulation model which was considered suitable for the evaluation and planning of medical service systems. (Morrill and Earickson, 1969; Morrill and Kelley, 1970). The model was structured in two parts to accommodate the patient-to-physician and patient-to-hospital situations and each part could be disaggregated by the level of care required, the religious preferences of the patients and the financial and racial constraints to which patients were subject. The gravity-interaction notion was used to define the probabilities of patients using particular physicians or hospitals in accordance with empirically derived information relating to known consumer preferences. The potential patients were then allocated from residential areas to the services by a Monte Carlo simulation routine, in order to incorporate a random behavioural element in the model.

The model was run in at least three stages. Initially all patients were allocated to the services that the empirically derived assumptions indicated that they would most like to use, irrespective of known capacities of individual service clusters. A second stage reallocated patients from overdemanded to under-demanded locations by an iterative procedure until a balance was reached A third alternative stage relocated underdemanded services to overdemanded locations. Additional variations were also possible. The religious, financial and racial constraints could be relaxed or new services or residential areas could be added to test their effect upon the operation of the system. The comparison of the outputs of the different allocations provided information useful for the evaluation and planning of the system.

The gravity model has been criticized because, like central place theory, it proposes a theory of aggregate consumer behaviour without a sound basis in behavioural investigation (Jensen-Butler, 1972). The normal assumptions may be important determinants of behaviour but they are intuitively derived rather than theoretically developed (Huff, 1961) and may, therefore, be associated with behavioural interaction in a non-explanatory manner. Consequently, additional detailed investigation of the behavioural dynamics of trips is necessary before the model can be considered to provide a comprehensive explanation of behaviour—a cautionary note which has also been expressed with respect to analyses of the use of medical services (Morrill and Earickson, 1969).

In fact, a number of additional approaches incorporating different behavioural assumptions have already been suggested for the spatial interaction process (Wilson, 1974). These have been derived from the intervening-opportunities model of Stouffer (1940) and the entropy-maximizing framework of Wilson (1970). A comparative appraisal of these alternatives is not possible here because they, like the gravity model, await rigorous behavioural validation at the intra-urban scale. Suffice it to say that alternatives to the gravity formulation are worthy of investigation in the development of an explanatory model of consumer behaviour.

Thus, a variety of spatial interaction formulations are being developed to model consumer behaviour. Already versions exist which approximately describe the complex patterns of behaviour between residential areas and service facilities, and suggest that they relate systematically to a trade-off of the attractions of centres against the disincentives associated with travelling to them. It is also clear that the use of the models for explanatory and predictive purposes awaits a more rigorous validation at the intra-urban scale, and there are also outstanding problems associated with the availability of adequate data inputs (Jensen-Butler, 1972; Mottershaw, 1968).

The behavioural approaches

The limitations associated with the aggregate behavioural assumptions of

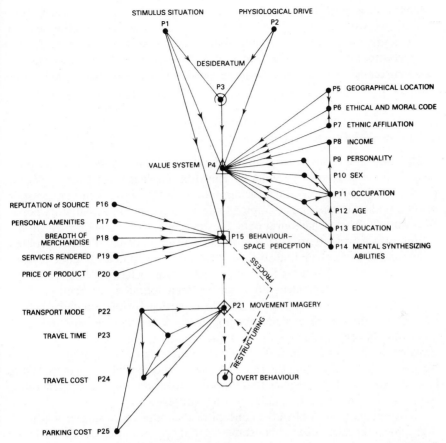

FIGURE 1.4 Huff's conceptualization of the consumer decision-making process. (Reproduced by permission of the Regional Science Association, from D. L. Huff, 1960, Figure 6)

the normative models strongly indicated the need for further research into both the nature of and motivations behind consumer behaviour. This has stimulated research which concentrates upon contributing to the development of a theory of consumer behaviour from information derived from the individual scale of investigation.

The interrelationships between the resulting research foci can be illustrated with reference to Huff's (1960) conceptualization of the consumer decision-making process (Figure 1.4). Huff suggested that behaviour was the result of the interaction of three compound factors, complicated by each having a partly objective and partly perceptual facet. The first comprised the effects of geographical location and social differentiation; the second the nature of the available service facilities, and the third, the influence of personal mobility considerations.

The theoretical behavioural approach attempts to develop an alternative theory of consumer behaviour which subsumes the factors suggested by Huff and is, therefore, closely analogous to the normative models. The empirical behavioural approach concentrates more specifically upon the clarification of the effects of factors such as residential location and social stratification. The cognitive approach has similar foci of attention, but concentrates upon the perceptual dimension of consumer decision-making. The latter two approaches currently aim at the *refinement* of existing theory, but do not exclude the ultimate development of an alternative model. Each approach will be considered in turn.

The theoretical behavioural approach

The most ambitious attempt to develop an alternative theory of consumer behaviour derives from the work of Rushton, Golledge and Clark (1967) in rural Iowa. They demonstrated the limitations of the nearest centre hypothesis of central place theory and attempted to develop alternative explanatory postulates directly from behavioural data. The concepts were subsequently applied to the intra-urban situation by Clark and Rushton (1970). A major problem is acknowledged in the initial study and fully developed in a subsequent paper (Rushton, 1969a); this is the fact that structure and behaviour in a system are in a state of interdependent adjustment. Behavioural generalizations from survey data are, therefore, descriptions of the particular situation under review, rather than theoretical explanatory postulates which can be expected to be applicable beyond the scope of a unique situation. Rushton (1969a, p. 391) explains the situation in the following terms: 'In the study of spatial behaviour we are interested in finding the rules for spatial choice which, when applied to any unique distribution of spatial opportunities are capable of generating spatial behaviour patterns similar to those observed.'

To overcome this problem the concept of the indifference surface was used. A graphical representation of consumer spatial opportunities was devised with the Y-axis representing increasing centre size and the X-axis increasing distance from the consumer to a centre. Particular centre size groupings and distance zones were designated in accordance with the character of the area under investigation, so that a specific number of possible spatial opportunities were defined (e.g. Figure 1.5 illustrates thirty locational types).

From a shopping behaviour survey, a data matrix was obtained which indicated for each shopper the actual type of location visited for a good and the alternatives, given his unique residential position. From this data, a centre attractiveness index or revealed space preference was computed for each cell in the graph, which indicated the relative attractiveness of each locational type in accordance with the choices expressed by the total sample population. This was obtained from the expression:

$$I_{ij} = \frac{A_{ij}}{P_{ij}}$$

where i = the arbitrarily defined centre size groups (in this example, 6)

(a) Locational Types

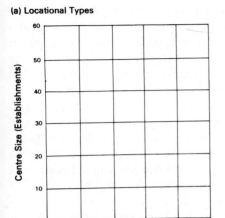

Centre Size (Establishments)

Distance of household to Centre (miles)

(b) Centre Attractiveness Indifference Curves for the purchase of a specific product.

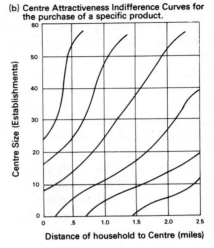

Centre Size (Establishments)

Distance of household to Centre (miles)

FIGURE 1.5   The construction of indifference curves

j = the arbitrarily defined distance zones from households to the centres (in this example, 5)

A_{ij} = the number of sample households who chose to patronize a town in the ith centre size group and the jth distance zone

P_{ij} = the number of sample households whose residential location would allow them to interact with a town in the ith centre size group and the jth distance zone

Isopleths were drawn in accordance with the values of I_{ij} in each cell and they constituted centre attractiveness indifference curves for the particular good studied (Figure 1.5). They describe the preferences of the sample population for all the spatial opportunities available to them and express the expectation that consumers will be indifferent between all spatial opportunities on any curve but will prefer any alternative on a higher curve to one on a lower.

The procedure by which any particular centre is assigned to its corresponding locational type abstracts spatial choice and spatial structure from their unique context. In this way a rank ordering of all spatial opportunities is derived from the aggregate spatial preferences of the respondents, rather than descriptions of behaviour in particular spatial contexts.

What then has been the success of this method in the derivation of theoretical postulates to explain consumer behaviour? The indifference curves derived from the index of attraction express graphically the hypothesis that sample households should patronize, whichever centre had the highest attractiveness index relative to their specific location. This was tested by comparing the extent to which the indifference curves derived from observed behaviour were capable of independently generating the same spatial choices, given only the location of the sample households. In the intra-urban context of Christchurch, its predictive capability was consistently below 50 per cent. for a range of convenience goods and services (Clark and Rushton, 1970). Clearly, the index of attraction did not represent a significant improvement upon the nearest centre hypothesis. This is perhaps not surprising considering that the indifference curves represent a description of the average response of the sample population. Unless a substantial majority of the population responded in precisely the same way to similar shopping opportunities, it is unlikely that the indifference surface would generate more than an approximate prediction of behaviour. In fact, spatial interaction theory and empirical investigations (see next section) indicate that such a degree of behavioural determinism does not occur in practice. Consequently, it might be suggested that if this methodology is to develop comprehensive behavioural postulates it will at least have to be disaggregated with respect to the social characteristics of the population which are known to be associated with behavioural variations, and, even then, some kind of probabilistic formulation might be more suitable.

In addition, as with spatial interaction theory, this approach has not yet solved the problem of explanation. The indifference curves describe the average preference of the sample households for the specified shopping opportunities in terms of an assumed trade-off of the advantages of increasing centre size against the disadvantages associated with greater distance. However, the manner in which these two variables influence the decision-making process is not apparent at present. This was recognized by Rushton (1969a, p. 395): '... preferences for towns with values for these two attributes do not necessarily represent preferences for the quantities of the attributes themselves, but rather preferences for intermediate entities which themselves are functions of the observed attributes.'

A sounder appreciation of the nature and operation of the 'intermediate entities' will have to be developed before this approach will be able to derive comprehensive postulates of consumer behaviour rather than descriptive behavioural norms, albeit independent of unique spatial structures.

Subsequent developments have concentrated upon improving the method of deriving indifference curve preference structures rather than resolving the methodological problems. Instead of using the attractiveness index derived for a simple comparison of actual and potential interactions to express the relative attractiveness of spatial opportunities, a more rigorous method has been adopted. The relative frequencies with which one locational type was chosen over another when both are present has been computed from similar behavioural data. From this information can be derived a proximity matrix, indicating the perceived similarity between any two of the spatial alternatives. Such a matrix is used as input to a non-metric multidimensional scaling procedure to recover a scale which indicates the relative preferences for the locational types (Jensen-Butler and Petersen, 1973; Rushton, 1969b) from which can be derived the indifference surface of spatial choice. This method has been shown by Rushton (1971), using hypothetical data, to be a sounder method of recovering a preference structure than the attractiveness index, but it awaits practical application in the intra-urban context.

Clearly, this approach is still in a formative stage, but it promises to produce interesting results if the outstanding methodological problems can be resolved.

The empirical behavioural approach

Studies undertaken under this heading provide considerable information relevant to the evaluation and improvement of the existing theories of consumer behaviour. The strength of the relationship between the residential location of consumers and their behaviour has been investigated, as well as the significance of social area differentiation to an understanding of consumer behaviour. Three types of study can be recognized. The first is concerned with the functioning of service centres and uses information obtained by interviewing shoppers within centres; the second focuses on the aggregate responses of consumers to existing facilities; and the third upon the detailed investigation of specific factors influencing behaviour—the latter two approaches obtaining information from sample households drawn from residential areas.

From the first category, the conclusions most relevant to this discussion concern the trade areas of centres. There is a general tendency for shopping centres of all hierarchical levels to draw the greatest proportion of their customers from neighbouring areas, although the higher the hierarchical status of the centre the wider will this area be. There is also a significant tendency for trade areas to overlap both within and between hierarchical levels (e.g. Berry and others, 1963; Brush and Gauthier, 1968). These findings suggest behaviour consistent with the intra-urban version of the gravity model and a similar situation has already been indicated for the use of medical facilities (Morrill and Earickson, 1969).

Recent studies of planned suburban shopping centres have indicated the manner in which these behavioural generalizations are adjusting to changes in the hierarchy of services. Johnston and Rimmer (1969) demonstrated that two new regional centres in the Melbourne suburbs had significantly wider spheres of influence than the older unplanned centres of similar status. In the cases of both planned centres, approximately 70 per cent. of their customers were drawn from a distinct suburban sector within four miles, compared with a figure of three miles for most of the older unplanned centres. It was also apparent that the planned centres were developing at the expense of older intermediate level centres within their spheres of influence, while also beginning to function as C.B.D. substitutes. Consequently, it was suggested that new consumer behavioural tendencies were emerging. For convenience goods, local neighbourhood and corner shop facilities were widely used, the planned regional centres provided a high-order intermediate level which met most normal requirements, while the C.B.D. continued to maintain considerable importance for the highest-order speciality goods. These contentions were supported by an analysis of the centres usually visited by shoppers interviewed at the two planned centres (e.g. Table 1.5).

Similar findings emerge from Dawson and Murray's (1973) study of a planned regional centre in Perth. The same extensive sectoral trade area developed

Table 1.5 Preferences of Chadstone shoppers, Melbourne (percentage of customers)

Goods	Local centres	Chadstone	C.B.D.
Food	80.7	18.3	1.0
Clothing and drapery	17.6	58.2	24.2
Furniture and floor coverings	17.4	34.3	48.3
Electrical appliances	24.5	39.0	36.5
Household hardware	26.3	52.8	20.9

Reproduced by permission of the Department of Human Geography, Australian National University, Canberra, from R. J. Johnston and P. J. Rimmer, 1969, Table 4.5, p. 69.

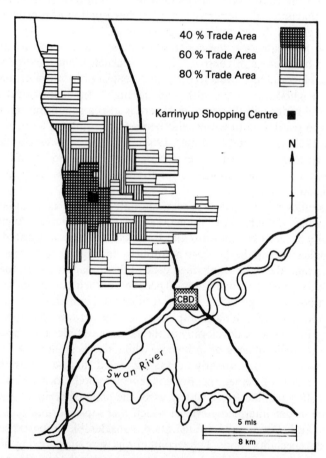

Figure 1.6 Trade area of Karrinyup shopping centre: Perth. (Reproduced by permission of J. A. Dawson and I. D. Murray, 1973, Figure 3)

(Figure 1.6), essentially at the expense of smaller intermediate level centres (community and neighbourhood), conclusions which were also reached in the Hague (Gantvoort, 1971) and for centres of sub-regional status in Britain (Thorpe and Kivell, 1971; Thorpe and coauthors, 1972).

However, this type of study can only provide an indication of patterns of consumer behaviour. The research method introduces an element of bias into the investigation, since analysis is limited to the shoppers using the small number of centres investigated. Consumers living in the trade areas of the centres under review who do not use these centres are lost to the analysis and the extent of this loss cannot be estimated. Thus, the evidence of these studies has to be supplemented by investigations of the behaviour of consumers systematically sampled from particular residential areas, if a comprehensive appreciation of patterns of consumer behaviour is to be obtained.

A study of the shopping behaviour of a random sample of consumers living in the Sussex coast urban area is an early example of the second approach (Ambrose, 1967–68). This was more concerned with the factors influencing the frequency rather than the spatial attributes of shopping trips. The frequency of shopping for a range of goods was shown to decline with distance from a centre, but to increase with household size, although evidence was also presented to refute the nearest centre hypothesis of central place theory.

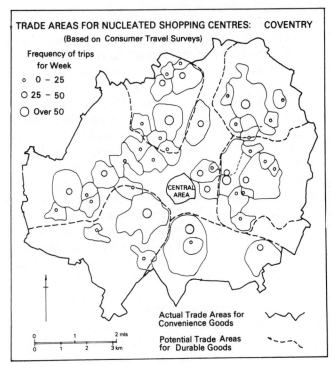

FIGURE 1.7   Trade areas for nucleated shopping centres: Coventry (Reproduced by permission of R. L. Davies, 1973, Figure 12)

A much more comprehensive examination of shopping behaviour was conducted by Davies (1973). A shopping diary for a single week, recording the origin and destination of trips, mode of travel, major purpose, items purchased and shops visited was obtained from a random 1 per cent. sample of the residents of Coventry. This provided considerable descriptive information concerning the nature of shopping behaviour. Journeys for convenience and durable goods for each day of the week suggested recognizable patterns. The central area appeared to serve the entire city for durable goods, while also attracting a significant proportion of convenience goods trips. Most of the convenience goods trips were concentrated on the various lower-order centres, and there was some evidence to suggest a limited number of durable goods trips to the district level. On the basis of this evidence, a tentative trade area map was produced, indicating approximately the hinterlands of the neighbourhood (convenience goods) and district (durable goods) centres. The hinterland of the central area was assumed to cover the whole city (Figure 1.7). This information indicated the continued importance of a strong residential location effect upon behaviour, particularly for convenience goods, and a considerable orderliness in the journey to shop. This led Davies (1973, p. 42) to support the applicability of the modified behavioural postulates of central place theory, rather than those suggested by spatial interaction theory: 'Consumers shop either within their immediate surroundings or alternatively go to the nearest largest centre to them.' This situation is likely to be widely replicated in the British context (Day, 1973), particularly where planning authorities have encouraged the hierarchical arrangement of neighbourhood and community centres and have discouraged the newer forms of decentralized facilities typical of North America.

Exploratory evidence to indicate that variations in the socioeconomic characteristics of the shoppers resulted in considerable deviations from the aggregate behavioural responses was also presented by Davies. Frequency of shopping was highest for the lowest social classes, youngest age groups and largest households, while the lower status groups were most likely to start their shopping trips from home. The highest status groups shopped more frequently by car and tended to travel further to higher-order centres than their lower status counterparts, while the least mobile were the youngest and oldest families. To highlight behavioural extremes associated with social class, an additional analysis was undertaken of the highest income groups and the immigrant community. The less mobile immigrants were found to have a much higher dependence upon lower-order centres for all goods, while for clothing and furniture 49 per cent. and 35 per cent. respectively of the higher income groups travelled beyond Coventry to higher-order facilities. This suggested that for a comprehensive understanding of intra-urban shopping behaviour considerable attention should be paid to the spatial variations in the socioeconomic characteristics of the residential areas.

In North America, there is also evidence to suggest that despite widespread decentralization of service facilities a degree of orderliness in shopping behaviour remains. Brush and Gauthier (1968), working in the peripheral areas of metropolitan Philadelphia, attempted to discern basic spatial patterns of behaviour. Despite a strong tendency towards overlapping hinterlands, the service centres where found not to have lost their local identity. Centres with 100–300 establishments maintained recognizable hinterlands up to three miles in diameter, while centres of 20–100 establishments had discernible local trade areas. More detailed evidence is provided by Holly and Wheeler (1972) for the metropolitan area of Lansing, Michigan (1970 population 375 000). Origin–destination data for shopping trips aggregated by census tracts are obtained for 1965 and factor-analysed to describe the basic interaction patterns. Correlation coefficients were computed for the destinations in the matrix, so that the dimensions derived from the factor loadings indicated groups of destinations which were basically similar in terms of the patterns of trips drawn from origins. The factor scores consequently indicated the groups of origin zones which were associated with the particular destination dimensions. Eight rotated factor dimensions were found to 'explain' just under 50 per cent. of the variance and no single dimension accounted for more than 10 per cent. This relatively low level of explanation indicated a considerable degree of variation in shopping behaviour in the city. Nevertheless, each of the eight dimensions of shopping interaction could be related to a specific sector of the city which was identifiable in terms of their particular socioeconomic character-istics (Figure 1.8), while no single factor identified exclusively with the C.B.D.

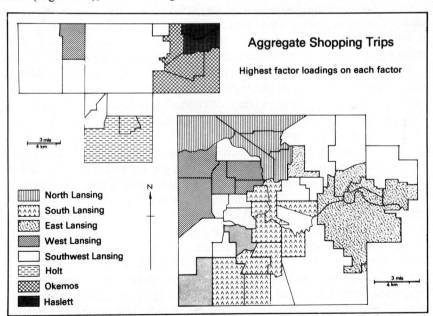

FIGURE 1.8   Lansing, Michigan: dimensions of shopping interaction (Reproduced by permission of Urban Studies, University of Glasgow, from, B. P. Holly and J. O. Wheeler, 1972)

This suggested that despite increasing personal mobility and service decentralization a significant distance constraint upon shopping behaviour remains, while the C.B.D. retains a significant link with virtually all parts of the city and to no particular area exclusively. The evidence of these studies might be considered to provide additional support for the applicability of the behavioural norms of spatial interaction theory for consumer behaviour in the North American situation.

However, in city-wide sample surveys of shopping behaviour, variability is the prime feature of both the socioeconomic characteristics of the population and of the spatial patterns of available shopping opportunities. Behavioural variations which emerge might be related to variations in socioeconomic characteristics, to variations in shopping opportunities, or to a complex combination of both. Thus, it is usually only possible to describe and to explain tentatively the behavioural variations which occur. It is not possible to isolate the independent effect of specific factors as determinants of shopping behaviour. To overcome this problem, the third category of studies has been developed. In the British literature, a research design has been adopted whereby survey areas are designated which have access to similar shopping opportunities and, as far as possible, only differ with respect to the factors being investigated.

Most research has concentrated on the clarification of the combined influence of variations in income, social status and personal mobility. Davies (1969) conducted a survey in a high income and a low income area in suburban Leeds covering fourteen separate goods and services representing all levels of specialization. Shopping journeys were divided into those internal and external to the residential areas and considerable differences between the behaviour of the residents of the areas were demonstrated for all the convenience goods.

The low income shoppers were significantly more dependent upon the low-order local facilities, while the high income shoppers tended to concentrate more shopping in a greater variety of centres outside their residential area, although the effect did not extend as far as the C.B.D. In fact, the C.B.D. was patronized slightly more frequently by the low income group. The differences were considered to reflect the desire of the higher income groups for a greater choice of convenience goods combined with a greater ability to overcome the friction of distance, while journeys from the low income area were restricted to local facilities, except for specific trips to the C.B.D. by public transport. Similar findings were not reported for durable shopping. The superior facilities of the C.B.D. tended to dominate shopping for these goods from both areas.

The evidence of this study has subsequently been supported by Thomas (1974). Six survey areas were designated in Greater Swansea, each comprising two spatially juxtaposed but socially different residential areas (e.g. the Sketty high status sample included 55 per cent. of the heads of households in social classes I and II, compared with 3.9 per cent. for the low status sample, while car-owning households were 72 per cent. and 44 per cent. respectively). The shopping opportunities available to the different status groups of any one area were reasonably similar in each case. Again, significant differences between

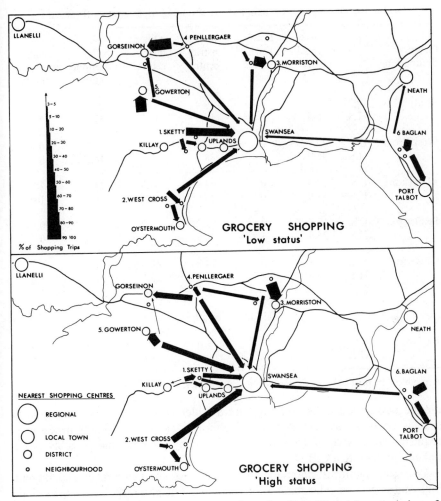

FIGURE 1.9   Greater Swansea: grocery shopping trips (Reproduced by permission of *Cambria*, from C. J. Thomas, 1974, Figure 2, p. 109)

the patterns of behaviour of the high and low status consumers were illustrated for grocery shopping (Figure 1.9). The high status groups tended to travel further to higher hierarchical levels than their low status counterparts (Table 1.6), a fact directly related to a much greater dependence upon car-borne shopping trips. However, this tendency was not apparent in every case. A number of alternative district centres were located reasonably near to the Sketty and Penllergaer survey areas. In these cases, the high status groups displayed more variable behaviour at the district level, while the less mobile groups made more use of Swansea (Sketty sample) or the nearest district centre (Penllergaer sample), both easily accessible by public transport. A similar tendency was noted by Davies (1969) and it seems to suggest that an increasingly

Table 1.6 Destinations of main grocery shopping trips: Greater Swansea

Grocery destinations (%)		Swansea regional centre	Local town centres	Nearest district centre	Other district centres	Nearest Neigh-bourhood centre	Other neigh-bourhood centres
Sketty	L.S.	46.7	0	19.4	3.9	27.2	1.3
	H.S.	26.4	0	19.5	16.0	32.1	5.7
West Cross	L.S.	32.7	0	32.7	0	32.7	0
	H.S.	46.9	0	38.7	0	14.2	0
Morriston	L.S.	18.0	0	64.0	2.3	11.2	2.3
	H.S.	18.0	0	80.0	0	0	1.0
Penllergear	L.S.	18.5	0	72.2	3.7	5.5	0
	H.S.	25.9	1.8	33.3	18.5	20.3	0
Gowerton	L.S.	12.1	0	74.3	10.8	1.3	1.3
	H.S.	30.5	2.7	58.3	5.5	1.3	1.3
			Port Talbot	Neath			
Baglan	L.S.	5.4	38.1	9.0	0	43.6	3.6
	H.S.	11.2	30.6	0	1.6	53.6	3.0

Reproduced by permission of *Cambria* from C. J. Thomas, 1974, Table 4, p. 108.

mobile population is likely to require a wider choice of convenience goods than is normally available at the neighbourhood level, but not necessarily requiring the degree of specialization offered by a longer and possibly more difficult journey to a C.B.D.

The only significant anomalies were noted for the Penllergaer and Baglan high status groups, who made more use of the neighbourhood facilities than expected (Table 1.6). This was related to the problem of maintaining strictly similar shopping opportunities between the groups at the local level. In both cases, the high status group lived significantly closer to the neighbourhood facilities. However, like Davies' study, similar behavioural variations were not noted for clothing and furniture shopping. For these purchases, the influence of Swansea was overridingly dominant irrespective of variations in either social class or car ownership.

There is also some evidence to suggest the relative significance of the influence of social status and personal mobility on the behavioural variations noted. Thomas (1974). disaggregated grocery shopping trips for car-owning and non-car-owning households within each of the two status categories. The within-group significance of car ownership and the greater importance of social class than car ownership as an explanation of between-group variations was demonstrated. This suggests the need to disaggregate shopping trips with respect to car ownership within status groups, if an understanding of consumer shopping behaviour is to be enhanced.

The only additional factor which has been considered is the effect of variations in age-structure upon shopping behaviour, although the evidence is both sparse and inconclusive. Davies (1969) concluded that no significant behavioural variations could be related to age-structure, although Thomas (1974) suggested that an imbalance of families of pre-school age might be partly responsible for unexpectedly high allegiances to local facilities. A more comprehensive analysis of the influence of age-structure was undertaken by Raybould (1973), although the evidence relates to a different environmental context. The sample population was drawn from the small towns of Pontypridd and Bridgend, located within the regional spheres of influence of Cardiff and Swansea. Grocery shopping was not significantly affected, but a discernible influence was noted for durable shopping. It appeared that the 21–30 age group displayed above-average orientation to the regional centres, while the over 61 age groups was significantly more orientated to the local town centres. In both cases the effect was small, ranging from 5–10 per cent., and appeared to be explained by the style and choice consciousness of the younger group and by the lower levels of personal mobility and lower incomes of the older group. Clearly, there appears to be scope for further investigation of the influence of this factor.

To date, the empirical behavioural approach has achieved a number of results. Evidence has been presented which sheds further light upon the general validity of the normative models, differentiating between the North American and British situations. It was also apparent that a substantial distance constraint upon behaviour can be discerned whatever the degree of specialization of the shopping trip. However, it might be suggested that the most significant result is the demonstration of the importance of the influence of the socioeconomic status of consumers, their personal mobility and, possibly, their age characteristics upon their spatial behaviour. This strongly suggests that further advances in the understanding of intra-urban consumer behaviour is likely to require the disaggregation of behaviour patterns with respect to social differentiation in the city.

The cognitive behavioural approach

This concentrates upon the clarification of the perceptual aspects of consumer decision-making. The majority of the work derives from Isard's (1956) concept of individual space preferences and rests on the assumption that the most important behavioural stimulus to decision-making is the individual's perception of the alternatives available to him. Huff (1960) argued that this assumption was applicable to consumer spatial behaviour and considered that an understanding of the perceptual basis of the decision-making process was essential to an understanding of consumer shopping behaviour. This forms the central theme of the cognitive behavioural approach, but substantiative work has been slow to materialize. Thompson (1966) and Marble (1967) were still calling for investigations of this type and the view has been reiterated more recently by Harvey (1969). The slow start can be related to the fundamental question raised by the implicit assumption of this approach: 'Can it be demonstrated that consumer spatial behaviour is determined by the individual's knowledge levels (both fact and fiction) and the way in which this information is evaluated' (Downs, 1970, p. 16).

This question has yet to be precisely answered, one assumes because of the inherent difficulty of distinguishing whether an individual's perception of alternative shopping opportunities determine spatial behaviour or is the result of spatial behaviour caused, in part, by intervening stimuli. Consequently, recent research has less ambitiously attempted to provide additional information which might eventually be used to illuminate the relationship between the image of the shopping environment and behaviour. Three foci of attention can be recognized: studies have been made of the manner in which consumers acquire knowledge of the shopping opportunities; and the amount of knowledge of the urban environment which consumers possess; while attempts have also been made to clarify the structure of the image that consumers have of specific shopping centres. Each of these will be briefly examined.

Golledge and Brown (1967) and Golledge (1969) consider that the market-decision process can be likened to a learning procedure whereby a newly arrived household in a city initially looks to its immediate neighbourhood to meet its shopping requirements, but eventually widens its search before ultimately developing habitual response patterns. This procedure is considered an important facet of shopping behaviour in North America, where moving house between cities is a relatively frequent occurrence. Therefore, it is considered that explanations of consumer behaviour should subsume a range of behaviour from an initial search stage to habitual responses. However, this approach is still at an exploratory stage. Its degree of explanatory importance has yet to be demonstrated, while the several alternative mathematical models have still to be empirically tested.

The work of Horton and Reynolds (1969, 1971) is not specifically related to studies of consumer behaviour, but it has considerable relevance. They were primarily concerned with the measurement of the part of the urban environment which was most familiar to an individual (action space). This was assumed likely to encompass the majority of his day-to-day spatial behaviour (activity space). An attempt was also made to determine whether definable sub-groups of the urban population shared a similar knowledge of the urban environment. No attempt was made to distinguish whether an individual's behaviour was determined by his action space perception or whether his behaviour created his action space. Nevertheless, the relevance of the action space concept to an understanding of consumer behaviour is clear. A knowledge of individual or group action spaces provides an indication of the area in which consumer search behaviour is likely to be constrained.

An individual's action space was conceptualized as being formed by the interaction of the social, economic and psychological attributes of the individual with the objective spatial characteristics of the urban environment. However, it was suggested that the most important single influence upon an individual's environmental perception was his residential location. It was considered that by a learning process similar to that outlined by Golledge and Brown (1967) that an individual's familiarity with the urban area was likely to decline with distance from his residence, while social interaction at the residential site tended to reinforce this spatial familiarity bias. Therefore, it was hypothesized that individual images and the resultant action spaces are to a large extent shared by groups of people in close geographical and social propinquity.

This was tested by illustrating the aggregate action spaces of the residents of two socially contrasting residential areas in Cedar Rapids, Iowa. Each person in the two sample populations was asked to indicate their degree of familiarity, measured on a five-point scale, with twenty-seven sub-areas of the city. The ordinal response data was transformed into an interval scale by a multidimensional scaling procedure and a mean scaled familiarity response was determined for each of the sample areas (Figure 1.10). The low income group indicated a pronounced familiarity with the home area and the adjacent C.B.D. but elsewhere familiarity declined with distance, while the middle income group demonstrated a similar pattern, although a greater overall familiarity and a significantly greater knowledge of the major outlying shopping plaza was apparent. This evidence suggested a positive relationship between the areal extent of action space and socioeconomic status and a strong residential location bias in the patterns of familiarity.

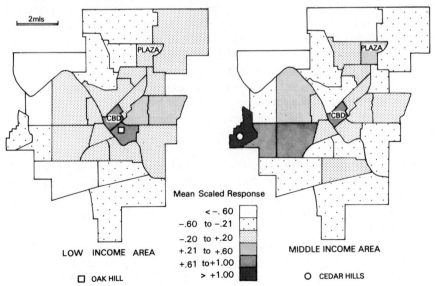

FIGURE 1.10   Familiarity—mean scaled responses: Cedar Rapids, Iowa (After Horton, Reynolds 1971) Reproduced by permission of *Economic Geography*, from F. E. Horton and D. R. Reynolds, 1971, Figures 2 and 3)

However, it did not indicate whether the action spaces of the individuals within each of the sample areas were sufficiently similar for geographical propinquity to be considered the most important determining influence. Consequently, the degree of variation in familiarity within each of the two sample populations was tested by Varimax principal component analyses of the matrices of correlations representing patterns of familiarity between *areas*. The resulting factor structures for both the low and middle income groups indicated that each of the twenty-seven areas had a high factor loading on only one spatial dimension of familiarity. This suggested that each dimension was the result of systematic covariations in familiarity with clusters of areas, and this implied that the individual patterns of familiarity of each of the sample populations did not vary markedly.

In addition, for the low income area six dimensions of variability in familiarity accounted for 67 per cent. of the total variance, while in the middle income samples even dimensions accounted for 69 per cent. of the variance. The relatively high levels of 'explained' variation were considered to support the hypothesis that individuals sharing similar residential locations share similar images of spatial structure. However, this conclusion cannot be drawn directly from the evidence presented on this particular point. The dimensions extracted from the principal component analysis represent specific familarity dimensions such as 'home area' or 'area of moderate familiarity', but it is difficult to see how this information supports the contention that individuals sharing similar residential locations share similar environmental perceptions. To test the degree of individual variation in familiarity patterns within each sample area more directly, it would have been more suitable to have undertaken a principal component analysis of matrices of correlation representing familiarity patterns between *individuals*. The nature and number of dimensions to emerge from such an analysis would have provided a much clearer idea of the degree of variation in the action spaces of individuals in each sample area. Thus, the degree of internal uniformity of the perceptions of a geographically defined social group remains to be completely clarified.

The manner in which consumers perceive the attractions of a specific shopping centre has been most comprehensively investigated by Downs (1970). An attempt was made to describe the structure of the perceptual image of a downtown shopping centre, specifically excluding the influence of distance between the consumers and the centre, in order to determine how the relative attractions of shopping opportunities are likely to be evaluated. Such information was considered an essential prerequisite for model- or theory-building.

It was hypothesized that the image is based upon the interaction of nine cognitive components, which were derived from a literature review and from interviews with shoppers. These were arbitrarily listed as: (a) price, (b) structure and design, (c) ease of internal movement and parking, (d) visual appearance, (e) reputation, (f) range of goods, (g) service, (h) shopping hours and (i) atmosphere.

The research attempted to determine whether these categories existed in the

TABLE 1.7 Cognitive factor dimensions: Bristol, Broadmead Centre

Factor		Original variance extracted (%)
I	Service quality	21.9
IV + IX	Shopping hours	8.1
II	Price	7.4
III	Structure and design	5.8
V	Range of goods	4.0
VIII	Visual Appearance	3.5
XI	Traffic conditions	2.8

This table is reprinted from 'The cognitive structure of an urban shopping center' by Roger M. Downs, from *Environment and Behavior*, vol. **2**, No. 1 (June 1970), p. 34 by permission of the Publisher, Sage Publications, Inc. (Beverly Hills, California, U.S.A. and London).

perceptions of consumers and, if so, their relative importance. Four seven-point semantic differential scales for each of the nine components were constructed and a sample population of shoppers were asked to indicate their evaluation of the centre on each of the thirty-six scales. The responses of each interviewee were summed for each of the scales, creating a data matrix of thirty-six scales by seven evaluation categories. Each of these scales was correlated with every other and subjected to a Varimax principal component analysis. If the nine cognitive categories existed, they would be expected to appear as independent factor dimensions. In fact, nine interpretable factors accounted for 57.8 per cent. of the variance. Seven of the hypothesized categories could be recognized (Table 1.7); ease of internal movement and parking was split into two more specific factors III and XI; and reputation and atmosphere were not recognized as distinct facets of the image. Thus, it was concluded that the image of the downtown shopping centre was a complex construct composed of at least eight cognitive categories, in order of importance indicated by Table 1.7.

This study has initiated an interesting line of research, but further investigation of the possibility of additional categories or of the stability of images in relation to social sub-groups in the city and to various types of shopping centre would considerably consolidate Downs' work.

From the preceding discussion, it is apparent that the cognitive behavioural approach is at an exploratory stage and is still concentrating upon the clarification of partial aspects of shopping behaviour. However, an alternative approach has been suggested which is capable of utilizing concepts developed in both perceptual and empirical investigations. This has been termed the study of 'trip motivations' (Davies, 1973). Consumers were provided with a list of possible reasons for shopping in a particular centre. This was composed of the three major categories of economic, perceptual and personality factors, derived from the marketing literature. Respondents were required to indicate any of the reasons they considered important in their selection of a particular shopping centre. The data was aggregated for the sample population and this indicated the most important factors presumed to be determinants of behaviour. The list of reasons used by Davies was not exhaustive and his analysis was essentially introductory, but, nevertheless, the general approach promises to produce interesting additional insights into the determinants of shopping behaviour.

CONCLUSIONS

A generalized knowledge exists of the manner in which the spatial structure of shopping facilities develops in Western cities, and a close relationship is also apparent between detailed hierarchical variations and residential differentiation. However, the interrelationship between the spatial structure of shopping centres and consumer behaviour is not completely clear, and a refined theory capable of either describing the present relationship or of predicting a future situation does not exist. A number of alternative approaches have been developed to rectify this deficiency and these are interrelated in a complex manner. Central place theory provided an early focus, but its initial behavioural postulates have proved too simple and have not been modified sufficiently to accord with reality. Spatial interaction theory shows considerable potential and versions which have already been suggested seem to provide close approximations of existing behavioural interaction, but problems of practical application and explanation at the intra-urban scale remain.

The limitations of the normative models have generated detailed behavioural investigation and a number of additional foci have emerged. A significant part of the North American literature has concentrated upon the development of an alternative to the existing normative models—the theoretical behavioural approach—but this also contains problems of explanation which have yet to be solved. Empirical studies have concentrated more specifically upon the factors which underlie shopping behaviour, with the principal aim of clarifying the behavioural aspects of the theoretical formulations. The cognitive behavioural approach has more recently attempted to elucidate the perceptual basis of the consumer decision-making process for the same reason, but here substantiative work is still at an exploratory stage. In addition, it was suggested that a combination of the perceptual and empirical viewpoints might ultimately result in the development of the investigation of trip motivations, which could. be of relevance to the theoretical alternatives.

A number of approaches to the study of intra-urban consumer behaviour can, therefore, be recognized, although a comprehensive theory has yet to be synthesized from the available information (Figure 1.11). This awaits the resolution of some of the outstanding issues raised in this chapter.

The literature also suggests additional conclusions of fundamental importance to the development of a theory of consumer behaviour. It was evident from both the normative and behavioural approaches that despite the profusion of alternative shopping opportunities available to increasingly mobile urban consumers, the residential location of the consumer was still a significant influence upon behaviour patterns. Whatever the degree of specialization of the shopping trip, a significant distance constraint upon behaviour could be noted,

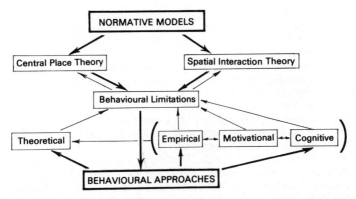

FIGURE 1.11 Interrelationships between the alternative approaches to the study of intra-urban consumer shopping behaviour

albeit far less significant than that assumed by central place theory. A possible reason for this was provided in the cognitive behavioural concept of action space, which demonstrated a significant residential location bias in consumers' familiarity with the urban environment.

In addition, the empirical investigation of specific factors influencing shopping behaviour indicated the importance of spatial variations in the socioeconomic characteristics of consumers to the development of an explanation of behavioural variations. Also, it was suggested that some of the existing limitations of spatial interaction theory, the theoretical behavioural studies and cognitive behavioural investigations were related to a failure to take sufficient account of this feature. These findings strongly suggest that existing theoretical approaches to the study of intra-urban consumer behaviour pay insufficient attention to the undoubted importance of the influence of socio-spatial differentiation in the city. It might, therefore, be suggested that future behavioural analysis should be disaggregated with respect to both social and spatial segregation, if future research effort is to be maximized and the development of theory advanced.

Finally, it is apparent that most studies of services in cities have concentrated on the shopping situation. This has traditionally been the main focus of attention of geographers. Nevertheless, it was also demonstrated that patterns of medical services and patient spatial behaviour are significantly similar to the shopping situation, which indicated that each might benefit from an examination of the methods of analysis and findings of the other. This suggests that the extensive literature on the geography of retailing should, in the future, form the basis of a common research methodology for a range of additional urban services.

REFERENCES

Ambrose, P. J. (1967–68). 'An analysis of intra-urban shopping patterns'. *Town Planning Review*, **38**, 327–334.

60

Ardell, D. B. (1970). 'Public regional councils and comprehensive health planning: a partnership?'. *Journal of the American Institute of Planners*, **36**, 393–404.

Babson, J. H. (1972). *Health Care Delivery Systems: A Multinational Survey*, Pitman Medical, London.

Berry, B. J. L., and Garrison, W. L. (1958). 'Recent developments of central place theory'. *Papers and Proceedings of the Regional Science Association*, **4**, 107–120.

Berry, B. J. L., Parsons, S. J., and Platt, R. H. (1968). *The Impact of Urban Renewal on Small Business*, Center for Urban Studies, University of Chicago, Chicago.

Berry, B. J. L., assisted by Tennant, R. J., Garner, B. J., and Simmons, J. W. (1963). *Commercial Structure and Commercial Blight*, Research Paper No. 85, Department of Geography, University of Chicago, Chicago.

Boal, F. W., and Johnson, D. B. (1965). 'The functions of retail and service establishments on commercial ribbons'. *Canadian Geographer*, **9** (3), 154–169.

Brush, J. E., and Gauthier, H. L. (1968). *Studies on the Philadelphia Metropolitan Fringe*, Research Paper No. 113, Department of Geography, University of Chicago, Chicago.

Buchanan, C. D., and Partners (1968). *The Cardiff Development and Transportation Study*, Cardiff City Council, Cardiff, pp. 63–74.

Buttimer, A. (1971). 'Health and welfare: whose responsibility?'. *Antipode*, **3**, (1), 31–45.

Christaller, W. (1966). *Central Places in Southern Germany* (Translated from the 1933 German version by C. W. Baskin), Prentice-Hall, Englewood Cliffs, New Jersey.

Clark, W. A. V. (1967). 'The spatial structure of retail functions in a New Zealand city'. *New Zealand Geographer*, **22**, 23–34.

Clark, W. A. V. (1968). 'Consumer travel patterns and the concept of range'. *Annals of the Association of American Geographers*, **58**, 386–396.

Clark, W. A. V., and Rushton, G. (1970). 'Models of intra-urban consumer behaviour and their implications for central place theory'. *Economic Geography*, **46**, 486–497.

Cohen, S. B., and Lewis, G. K. (1967). 'Form and function in the geography of retailing'. *Economic Geography*, **43**, 1–42.

Davies, R. L. (1968). 'Effects of consumer income differences on the business provision of small shopping centres'. *Urban Studies*, **5**, 144–163.

Davies, R. L. (1969). 'Effects of consumer income differences on shopping movement behaviour'. *Tijdschrift voor Econ. en Soc. Geografie*, **60**, 111–121.

Davies, R. L. (1972). 'Structural models of retail distribution: analogies with settlement and urban land use theory'. *Transactions of the Institute of British Geographers*, **57**, 59–82.

Davies, R. L. (1973). *Patterns and Profiles of Consumer Behaviour*, Research Series No. 10, Department of Geography, University of Newcastle-Upon-Tyne, Northumberland.

Davies, R. L. (1974). 'Nucleated and ribbon components of the urban retail system in Britain'. *Town Planning Review*, **45**, 91–111.

Dawson, J. A. (1974). 'The suburbanization of retail activity'. In J. H. Johnson (Ed.), *Suburban Growth: Geographical Processes at the Edge of the Western City*, John Wiley, London. Chap. 8, pp. 155–176.

Dawson, J. A., and Murray, I. D. (1973). *Aspects of the Impact of Karrinyup Shopping Centre, Western Australia*, Geowest Working Paper No. 1, Department of Geography, University of Western Australia, Perth.

Day, R. A. (1973). 'Consumer shopping behaviour in a planned urban environment'. *Tijdschrift voor Econ. en Soc. Geografie*, **64**, 77–85.

Department of Health and Social Security (1971). *The N.H.S. Reorganisation* (Consultative Document), D.H.S.S., London.

Downs, R. (1970). 'The cognitive structure of an urban shopping centre'. *Environment and Behaviour*, **2**, 13–39.

Earickson, R. (1970). *The Spatial Behavior of Hospital Patients*, Research Paper No. 124, Department of Geography, University of Chicago, Chicago.

61

Frieden, B. J., and Peters, J. (1970). 'Urban planning and health services: opportunities for cooperation'. *Journal of the American Institute of Planners*, **36**, 82–95)

Gantvoort, J. T. (1971). 'Shopping centre versus town centre'. *Town Planning Review*, **42**, 61–70.

Garrison, W. L., Berry. B. J. L., Marble, D. F., Nystuen, J. D., and Morrill, R. L. (1959). *Studies of Highway Development and Geographic Change*, University of Washington Press, Seattle.

Golledge, R. G. (1969). 'The geographical relevance of some learning theories'. In K. R. Cox and R. G. Golledge (Eds.), *Behavioural Problems in Geography: A symposium*, Research Studies No. 17, Department of Geography, Northwestern University, Evanston, Illinois. pp. 101–145.

Golledge, R. G., and Brown, L. A. (1967). 'Search learning and the market decision process'. *Geografiska Annaler*, **49B**, 116–124.

Greater London Council (1969). *Greater London Development Plan Statement*, G.L.C., London.

Harvey, D. W. (1969). 'Conceptual and measurement problems in the cognitive-behavioural approach to location theory'. In K. R. Cox and R. G. Golledge (Eds.), *Behavioural Problems in Geography: A Symposium*, Research Studies No. 17, Department of Geography, Northwestern University, Evanston, Illinois. pp. 35–68.

Holly, B. P., and Wheeler, J. O. (1972). 'Patterns of retail location and the shopping trips of low-income households'. *Urban Studies*, **9**, 215–220.

Horton, F. E., and Reynolds, D. R. (1969). 'An investigation of individual action spaces'. *Proceedings of the American Association of Geographers*, **1**, 70–75.

Horton, F. E., and Reynolds, D. R. (1971). 'Effects of urban spatial structure on individual behaviour'. *Economic Geography*, **47**, 36–46.

Hotelling, H. (1929). 'Stability in competition'. *Economic Journal*, **39**, 41–57.

Hoyt, H. (1939). *The Structure and Growth of Residential Neighborhoods in American Cities*, Federal Housing Administration, Washington, D.C.

Huff, D. L. (1960). 'A topographical model of consumer space preferences'. *Papers and Proceedings of the Regional Science Association*, **6**, 159–174.

Huff, D. L. (1971). 'Ecological characteristics of consumer behaviour'. *Papers and Proceedings of the Regional Science Association*, **7**, 19–28.

Huff, D. L. (1963). 'A probabilistic analysis of shopping centre trade areas'. *Land Economics*, **39**, 81–90.

Isard, W. (1956). *Location and Space-economy*, The M.I.T. Press, Cambridge, Massachusetts.

Jensen-Butler, C. (1972). 'Gravity models as planning tools: a review of theoretical and operational problems'. *Geografiska Annaler*, **54B**, 68–78.

Jensen-Butler, C., and Petersen, V. C. (1973). 'Aarscal One, Aarscal Two: two nonmetric multidimensional scaling programs'. *Computer Applications*, **1**, 1–50.

Johnston, R. J. (1966). 'The distribution of an intra-metropolitan central place hierarchy'. *Australian Geographical Studies*, **4**, 19–33.

Johnston, R. J. (1968). 'Railways, when growth and central place patterns'. *Tijdschrift voor Econ. en Soc. Geografie*, **59**, 33–41.

Johnston, R. J., and Rimmer, P. J. (1967). 'Some recent changes in Melbourne's commercial landscape'. *Erkunde*, **21**, 64–67.

Johnston, R. J., and Rimmer, P. J. (1969). *Retailing in Melbourne*, Research School of Pacific Studies Publication HG/3, Department of Human Geography, Australian National University, Canberra.

Kivell, P. T. (1972). 'Retailing in non-central locations'. *Institute of British Geographers*, *Occasional Publication No. 1*, 1972, 49–58.

Lakshmanan, T. R., and Hansen, W. G. (1965). 'A retail market potential model'. *Journal of the American Institute of Planners*, **31**, 134–144.

Marble, D. F. (1967). 'A theoretical exploration of individual travel behavior'. In W. L.

Garrison and D. F. Marble (Eds.), *Quantitative Geography Part 1*, Research Studies No. 13, Department of Geography, Northwestern University, Evanston, Illinois. pp. 33–53.

Ministry of Health (1962). *A Hospital Plan for England and Wales*, H.M.S.O., London.

Morrill, R. L., and Earickson, R. (1968a). 'Variations in the character and use of hospital services'. Reprinted in L. S. Bourne (1971). *Internal Structure of the City*, Oxford University Press, Oxford. pp. 391–399.

Morrill, R. L., and Earickson, R. (1968b). 'Hospital variation and patient travel distances'. *Inquiry*, **5** (4), 26–34.

Morrill, R. L., and Earickson, R. J. (1969). 'Problems in modelling interaction: the case of hospital care'. In K. R. Cox and R. G. Golledge (Eds.), *Behavioral Problems in Geography: A Symposium*, Research Studies No. 17, Department of Geography, Northwestern University, Evanston, Illinois. pp. 254–276.

Morrill, R. L., Earickson, R. J., and Rees, P. (1970). 'Factors influencing distances traveled to hospitals'. *Economic Geography*, **46**, 161–171.

Morrill, R. L., and Kelley, M. B. (1970). 'The simulation of hospital use and the estimation of location efficiency'. *Geographical Analysis*, **2**, 283–300.

Mottershaw, B. (1968). 'Estimating shopping potential'. *Planning Outlook*, **5**, 40–68.

National Economic Development Office (1971). *The Future Pattern of Shopping*, H.M.S.O., London.

Office of Health Economics (1974). *The N. H. S. Reorganisation*, Studies of Current Health Problems No. 48, O.H.E., London.

Pred, A. (1967). 'Behaviour and Location Part I'. *Lund Studies in Geography*, Series B, No. 27, Gleaup, Lund, Sweden.

Raybould, A. R. (1973). *A Geographical Analysis of the Effects of Socio-economic Class on Consumer Movements*. Unpublished M. A. Thesis, University of Wales, Cardiff.

Rees, P. H. (1970). 'The urban envelope: patterns and dynamics of population density'. In B. J. L. Berry and F. E. Horton (Eds.), *Geographic Perspectives on Urban Systems*, Prentice-Hall, Englewood Cliffs, New Jersey. Chap. 9, pp. 276–305.

Reilly, W. J. (1931). *The Law of Retail Gravitation*, Putman and Sons, New York.

Rushton, G. (1969a). 'Analysis of spatial behavior by revealed space preference'. *Annals of the Association of American Geographers*, **59**, 391–400.

Rushton, G. (1969b). 'The scaling of location preferences'. In K. R. Cox and R. G. Golledge (Eds.), *Behavioral Problems in Geography: A Symposium*, Research Studies No. 17, Department of Geography, Northwestern University, Evanston, Illinois. pp. 197–227.

Rushton, G. (1971). 'Behavioral correlates of urban spatial structure', *Economic Geography*, **47**, 49–59.

Rushton, G., Golledge, R. G., and Clark, W. A. V. (1967). 'Formulation and test of a normative model for the spatial allocation of grocery expenditures by a dispersed population'. *Annals of the Association of American Geographers*, **57**, 389–400.

Ryan, M. (1968). 'Health centre policy in England and Wales'. *British Journal of Sociology*, **19**, 34–46.

Schiller, R. K. (1971). 'Location trends of specialist services'. *Regional Studies*, **5**, 1–10.

Shannon, G. W., and Dever, G.E.A. (1974). *Health Care Delivery: Spatial Perspectives*, McGraw-Hill, New York.

Simmons, J. W. (1964). *The Changing Pattern of Retail Location*, Research Paper No. 92, Department of Geography, University of Chicago, Chicago.

Simmons, J. W. (1966). *Toronto's Changing Retail Complex: A Study in Growth and Blight*, Research Paper No. 104, Department of Geography, University of Chicago, Chicago.

Simon, H. A. (1957). *Models of Man*, Wiley, New York.

Smith, B. A. (1973). 'Retail planning in France'. *Town Planning Review*, **44**, 279–306.

Stouffer, S. R. (1940). 'Intervening opportunities: a theory relating mobility and distance'. *American Sociological Review*, **5**, 845–867.

Sumner, G. (1971). 'Trends in the location of primary medical care in Britain: some social implications'. *Antipode*, **3** (1), 46–53.

Symons, J. G. (1971). 'Some comments on equity and efficiency in public facility'. *Antipode*, **3** (1), 54–67.

Thomas, C. J. (1974). 'The effects of social class and car ownership on intra-urban shopping behaviour in Greater Swansea'. *Cambria*, **1**, 98–126.

Thompson, D. L. (1966). 'Future directions in retail area research'. *Economic Geography*, **42**, 1–19.

Thorpe, D., and Kivell, P. T. (1971). *Woolco, Thornaby*, Report No. 3, Retail Outlets Research Unit, Manchester Business School, Manchester.

Thorpe, D., Kivell, P. T., Pratley, D. R., and Andrews, M. (1972). *The Hampshire Centre, Bournemouth*, Report No. 6, Retail Outlets Research Unit, Manchester Business School, Manchester.

Vance, J. E., Jr. (1962). 'Emerging patterns of commercial structure in American cities'. *Proceedings of the I. G. U. Symposium of Urban Geography, Lund Studies in Geography*, Series B, No. 24. pp. 485–518.

Vise, P. de (1971). 'Cook County Hospital: bulwark of Chicago's apartheid health system and prototype of the nation's public health hospitals'. *Antipode*, **3** (1), 9–20.

Waide, L. (1971). 'Where retail planning takes over'. *Official Architecture and Planning*, 1971, 116–119.

Webber, M. J. (1972). *The Impact of Uncertainty on Location*, The M.I.T. Press, Cambridge, Massachusetts.

Wilson, A. G. (1970). *Entropy in Urban and Regional Modelling*, Pion, London.

Wilson, A. G. (1974). *Urban and Regional Models in Geography and Planning*, John Wiley, London.

Chapter 2

Political Behaviour and the Residential Mosaic

R. J. Johnston

Of the many types of political behaviour which occur in a democracy, the present essay focuses on those which can involve a majority of the adult residents. Three types are identified, although not all are relevant parameters of political behaviour in all countries and some cannot be investigated because of data limitations. The first involves the decision to register as a voter, in countries where this act is not compulsory. The second is the decision to exercise the right to vote at an election or referendum, though again this act may be compulsory, as in Australian Federal elections. Finally, there is the voting act itself, the expression of support for a given candidate, party or issue.

A great number of investigations, covering a wide range of locales, has indicated strong and consistent correlations between each of these political acts and various characteristics of the actors. In many elections, especially those fought on partisan lines, a large number of people will vote from positions of self-interest, which leads to strong correlations between 'social class' and patterns of party support. Thus, the relatively well-off will tend to vote for the free-enterprise parties and the less well-to-do for parties with stronger beliefs in equitable distributions of society's resources and rewards, though the strength of this relationship varies from country to country (Alford, 1963; Rowley, 1969). Since, as was shown in the first volume of this book, people of different socioeconomic levels tend to occupy separate parts of an urban area, this class/voting correlation produces a clearly defined spatial pattern of party support differences. This occurred in the voting for the Leeds Metropolitan District Council in the area of the then City of Leeds in May 1973 (Figure 2.1), when the Conservative Party won all of the seats for the wards in the more 'desirable' areas to the north whereas the 'working class' wards in the Aire Valley and South Leeds mostly returned Labour representatives.

Elections which are non-partisan also often produce spatial patterns of voting which can be interpreted in the light of corresponding maps of the social environment. Thus, the three main candidates for Toronto's mayoralty in 1972 drew their support from different parts of that city (Figure 2.2). O'Donohue's particular appeal was to many of the recent European immigrants to

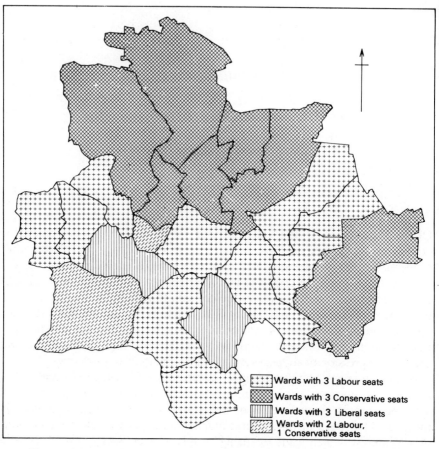

Wards with 3 Labour seats
Wards with 3 Conservative seats
Wards with 3 Liberal seats
Wards with 2 Labour, 1 Conservative seats

FIGURE 2.1 Results by wards, Leeds metropolitan district elections, 1972

Toronto, especially those of the Roman Catholic faith, and he won most booths in the areas both west and east of the city centre, where those people are concentrated. Rotenberg gained most support from the Jewish community and most of the polls he topped were in the main Jewish residential areas, particularly the higher income ones in the north of the city. (The outlines of the immigrant and Jewish areas in Figure 2.2 are taken from Murdie, 1969.) Finally, Crombie, the victor, drew support from a wide range of neighbourhoods in north, central and east Toronto in his 'anti-developer' campaign; he also polled well in part of south-west Toronto, arround his former home.

Voting turnout rates can also be associated with social characteristics of areas. Kaufman and Greer (1960) classified each of 207 districts of metropolitan St. Louis according to the three Shevky–Bell indices of social rank, urbanization and segregation and correlated these values with four measures of local political behaviour:

1. The percentage of the population who voted in the 1952 Presidential election.

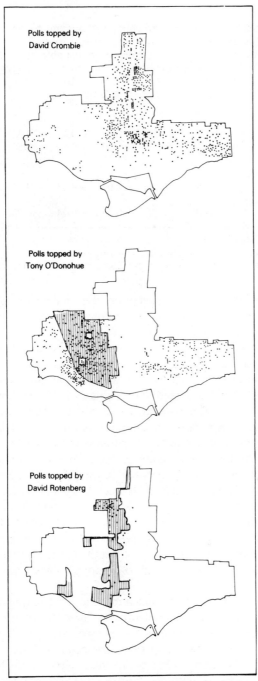

Polls topped by
David Crombie

Polls topped by
Tony O'Donohue

Polls topped by
David Rotenberg

FIGURE 2.2 The Toronto mayoralty election, 1972, showing the booths where each of the three main candidates topped the poll. The shaded areas on O'Donohue's map show the main Italian areas (after Murdie, 1969, p. 99), those on Rotenberg's map show the main Jewish areas (after Murdie, 1969, p. 70)

TABLE 2.1 Social area indices and voting patterns: metropolitan St. Louis

| Dependent variable | Independent variable | | | | | | Multi-ple correlation |
| | Social rank | | Urbanization | | Segregation | | |
	A	B	A	B	A	B	
% Turnout, 1952 Presidential	0.32	0.26	−0.27	−0.18	−0.32	−0.21	0·44
% Democrat 1952	−0.74	−0.79	0·50	0·55	0·50	0·43	0·88
% Turnout, 1950 metropolitan sewer district	0·52	0·50	−0·64	−0·63	−0·39	−0·18	0·78
% Favourable, sewer district	0·40	0·51	0·24	0·24	0·23	0·31	0·56

ColumnA—zero-order correlation.
Column B—partial correlation, holding other two variables constant.
Reproduced by permission of *Social Forces* from W. Kaufman and S. Greer, vol. **38**, 1960, Table 1, p. 201.

2. The percentage of the voters who supported the Democrat candidate.
3. The percentage of the population who voted in a 1950 referendum on the creation of a metropolitan sewer district for St. Louis.
4. The percentage of the voters who favoured creating the district.

Higher social rank was shown to be associated with greater voter turnout, with greater support for the metropolitan sewer scheme and with lower support for the Democrat Presidential candidate (Table 2.1). An increasing score on the urbanization dimension was associated with greater Democrat support, with lower turnout rates, especially on the metropolitan referendum (suggesting that mobile persons consider such a local issue irrelevant to them), and with greater support for the metropolitan project. The last finding suggests that suburbanites were more 'locally-oriented' in their political behaviour. Finally, segregation was positively related to Democrat support. Thus, all three of the major dimensions of the residential mosaic were found relevant in accounting for spatial variation in various political acts. Uyeki (1966) also found this for metropolitan Cleveland, where Negro areas meant strong Democrat support, high income areas were nodes of Republican support and the 'urbanized' districts of the central city voted on cosmopolitan lines, supporting metropolis-wide projects

These conformities between the social maps and the voting maps of the city are persistent over time, with parameters of the latter changing as do those of the former. Tryon (1967), for example, has shown voting stability among San Francisco's social areas paralleling their 'biosocial' stability (but see Norris and Barnett, 1975). When an area's social characteristics do change, so might its political behaviours, as with the upsurge in Democratic support in areas of Flint, Michigan, occupied by Negroes (Lewis, 1965) and the swing towards the Republican party in Miami neighbourhoods 'invaded' by Cubans (Salter and Mings, 1972).

Identification of the spatial relationships and patterns just discussed requires a sound data base. Because of the almost universal secret ballot, individual data are never available, although sample surveys and opinion polls provide some cross-classifications of value. In some countries, notably Great Britain of those discussed here, votes are counted by constituency only, which precludes much fine-grained intra-urban study. For others, however, votes are counted and published by polling booth, although in only some (Australia, for example, but not New Zealand) does the elector have to cast his vote at a particular booth, thereby allowing detailed study of turnout rates. Correlation of these, and of results, with population characteristics further requires conformities between the areas served by polling booths and those for which census and other data are collected (Prescott, 1972). In many cases, some of these criteria are not met, requiring either the abandonment of certain lines of enquiry or the adoption of certain behavioural assumptions, such as that most voters use the closest polling booth to their home if they have a choice.

SPATIAL VARIABLES AND POLITICAL BEHAVIOUR

The various relationships outlined above suggest that political behaviours are further characteristics of social areas which could be added to the range of indices used to denote neighbourhood features. As there is no complete correlation between social characteristics—of individuals, of groups and of district populations—and political behaviour, it may be that inclusion of measures of voter turnout and party support would introduce noise to the delimitation of social areas, and perhaps further confuse the technical problems involved. There would, however, be little need for a separate study of political behaviour.

Such a conclusion assumes that location is a passive variable, which in no way influences an individual's attitudes and behaviour. There is evidence, however, that the pattern of a city's residential mosaic may considerably 'warp' the voting patterns which could be predicted from knowledge of, for example, the general correlation between social rank and political action. This warping can be produced in a number of ways, which may be subsumed within Harvey's (1973) threefold typology of locations:

1. Absolute locations, which are the division of an area into territories, such as local government areas, that for certain purposes may be considered dimensionless. In the political context, constituencies are prime examples of absolute locations.
2. Relative locations, in which the location of one phenomenon is expressed vis-à-vis another. The support for Crombie in the Toronto mayorality election in the area around his former home (see Figure 2.2) exemplifies the role of relative locations in warping voting maps.
3. Relational locations, the spatial positions of certain phenomena with regard to all members of a given population. The spatial concept of population potential indexes such locations.

The remainder of this essay looks at the effects of these three types.

NEIGHBOURHOOD EFFECTS AND VOTING

The existence and strength of structural effects is a research focus common to several of the social sciences. These suggest that attitudes and actions are influenced by two major variables: (a) the characteristics of the individual actor and (b) the characteristics of the social environment in which he interacts (Blau, 1960). In the context of geographical enquiries, the latter variable is the social area, so that the type of structural effect being studied may be termed a neighbourhood effect. The neighbourhood may be a very localized environment—the home, perhaps, or the workplace—or it might be the block or district in which the person lives. Each of these acts as a mediator between the individual and society; the focus here is on the local area as the mediator, suggesting that individuals vote not only on their perceptions of their best interests but also on the attitudes and perceptions of local people with whom they discuss political matters.

Work on such neighbourhood effects was pioneered in the United States by Lazarsfeld and his associates (see Berelson, Lazarsfeld and McPhee 1954; Campbell and coauthors, 1960, 1966; Lazarsfeld, Berelson and Goudet, 1954), especially at the University of Michigan's Survey Research Center. Most of their findings have supported the general notion. For some people, the influence may be non-local, such as a religious group, but Segal and Meyer (1969, p. 220) have claimed that 'all other things being equal, people will tend to vote for the party supported by the climate of opinion of the communities in which they live'. This conclusion was drawn from survey data analysis which indicated that people of low socioeconomic status were much more likely to vote Republican if they lived in a high rather than low status district, and especially if they lived in a town where status and attitudes differed considerably among the population. Somewhat similar findings were reported by Foladare (1968) regarding the effects of occupation and religion on voting.

Segal and Meyer (1969) proposed a mechanism for the production of neighbourhood effects. Assuming random contacts and choice of partners for political discussions within a given area, with each person having an equal chance of meeting every other, they used binomial probabilities to produce the contact patterns listed in Table 2.2. These indicate that 'the likelihood that

TABLE 2.2 Random probabilities of meeting and party domination of groups

| | | Percentage party X supporters in area | | | | | |
	20	30	40	50	60	70	80
Three-person group	10	22	35	50	65	78	90
Five-person group	6	16	32	50	68	84	94

Values in the cells of the matrix are the percentages of groups in which a majority of members support party X.

Reproduced by permission of the M.I.T. Press from D. R. Segal and M. W. Meyer, 1969, p. 223.

primary groups will be dominated by members of the majority party is higher than the proportion of adherents to that party in the community . . . the majority sentiment in the community is accentuated in primary groups' (Segal and Meyer, 1969, p. 223), especially larger groups. If neighbourhood effects operate, therefore, and political discussions occur within groups which are random samples of the local population, the mechanism is the exaggerated strength of the majority party in a small group and its converting power on the 'deviants'.

Structural effects and voting maps

The general hypothesis of neighbourhood effects suggests that knowledge of the individual characteristics of an area's population is insufficient to predict their political behaviour, and thus the political complexion of the area. As well as the mechanisms which allocate people to different neighbourhoods, it is also necessary to investigate those which influence the flow of political information within neighbourhoods (Reynolds and Archer, 1969, p. 17). Each individual is located in a network of persons who are receiving, processing and emitting politically relevant information (Cox, 1969a). His resistance to information of various types and his selectivity in processing and propagating it are, in part, influenced by his personal characteristics; his connectivity within a social network determines what information he receives, and who from, and who in turn he can pass it to. His group membership will also influence the social norms which govern his predisposition towards various pieces and types of information.

This communications model was used as a study of Columbus, Ohio (Cox, 1969b). The dependent variable was the individual's party identification; the major independent variable was the political complexion of his neighbourhood, indexed by the percentage of its residents voting Democrat at the 1964 election. Further independent variables were introduced through four hypotheses suggestive of neighbourhood effects:

1. That members of local informal social groups are more influenced by their party identification than are those people, most of whose friends live outside their home district. The evidence did not support this contention.
2. That members of local formal organizations (such as those associated with schools and churches) will be more influenced by local milieu than people who are primarily members of non-local organizations (such as trade unions). The hypothesis was validated, especially when a further variable, whether or not politics was discussed in those groups, was controlled for.

Combining the tests for these first two hypotheses, Cox suggested a continuum of influences towards neighbourhood effects. The strongest was membership of local organizations, followed by friends in the area; friends outside the local area ranked third, and membership of non-local organizations the fourth, and weakest influence. This stronger influence of formal associations is supposedly because these are more likely than informal social groups to bring together people of opposing political views (Putnam, 1966).

3. That recent movers to an area will more likely be influenced by neighbourhood opinion than those who have lived there for a longer period.

This was a valid proposition, especially for recent immigrants who had joined
local formal organizations. (Elsewhere, Cox, 1970, has shown that, among
the same sample of Columbus residents, long-term residents were more stable
in their voting habits over the 1960 and 1964 Presidential elections than
were recent immigrants; party identification was a better indicator of voting
behaviour for the long-term residents; and there was less consistency between
the individual's vote and his sociopolitical milieu for the shorter-period
residents).

4. That neighbourhood effects have their strongest influence on persons who
are neither strongly committed to any party nor are apathetic towards
political issues, a hypothesis which was confirmed, again especially for the
members of local formal organizations.

In sum, Cox's findings are consistent with the notions of a neighbourhood
effect. Those most affected by their local political milieu participate in local
activities, discuss political issues with neighbours, are relatively 'open' to
influence (the 'floating voters') and presumably seek local approval through
their political actions.

Predicting neighbourhood effects

Large social surveys are expensive to undertake, so few comparable attempts
have been made by geographers to match Cox's study. Instead, most seek
methods which predict a spatial pattern of voters which, because of the internal
logic of the related model, are indicative of a neighbourhood effect. Such an
approach must compound the problems of inferring processes from patterns.
Cox's survey data themselves did not directly identify neighbourhood effects
and, as pointed out later, other plausible hypotheses can be suggested for the
observed patterns.

Neighbourhood effects can be modelled as the residuals from a predicted
voting pattern based on known characteristics of an area's residents and general
data on, for example, income levels and party choices. For example, if survey
or poll data indicate the proportion of adults of each income level who vote
Labour, then there should be a clear relationship (presumably a negative one)
between the income levels of an area's population and the percentage of its
residents voting Labour. If, in addition, there is a neighbourhood effect, the
regression should be S-shaped (Figure 2.3), indicating lower proportions than
expected voting Labour in areas where that party is weak, and higher than
expected proportions where it is strong. (In Figure 2.3, it is suggested that the
independent variable could be a score on a socioeconomic status component,
obtained from a factorial ecology.) Kory (1972) has tested such a notion
demonstrating a relationship between racial homogeneity and Democrat
support in Pittsburgh. Unfortunately, his use of rank correlations obscured
some of the possible relationships which might have been uncovered by his

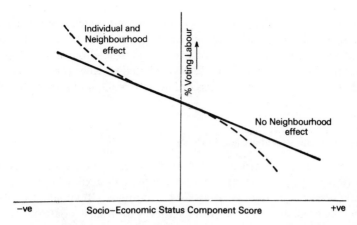

FIGURE 2.3 Hypothetical relationship between socioeconomic status (indexed by a principal component score) and percentage voting Labour, with and without a neighbourhood effect

index of racial homogeneity (Lieberson, 1969), which is probably a better measure than a component score.

Factorial ecologies have been used in studies of neighbourhood effects, such as Reynolds and Archer's (1969) of an Indianapolis mayoralty contest. Five components were extracted to represent nineteen variable distributions over 125 areas of the city, and together these five accounted for 82 per cent. of the areal variation in the percentage support for the Republican candidate. The residuals from the multiple regression were spatially autocorrelated, suggesting the operation in certain areas of the process which would produce neighbourhood effects. A somewhat similar approach was used by Cox (1968) in a study of both voter turnout and Conservative support in Greater London at the 1950 and 1951 general elections. Four components—labelled social rank, suburban location, importance of out-commuting and age-structure— were used as non-orthogonal, independent variables in regressions from which Cox (1968, p. 121) concluded that:

Suburban location affects directly both participation and party preference when other contexts are taken into account . . . it is also related to the political behavioural variables by causal links of an indirect nature.

This 'firm conclusion' (Cox, 1968, p. 127) was contested by Taylor (1969, p. 404), who reworked Cox's causal model and claimed that:

. . . we can explain London's 1951 voting behaviour reasonably well without postulating a direct causal link between suburban location and party preference. We have not proved that such a link does not exist but Cox . . . places far too much weight on the validity of his accepted model.

Cox (1969c) briefly argued against this criticism. Biel reworked the data and concluded that (Biel, 1972, p. 43) 'the suburban context clearly exerts a statistically significant effect upon Conservative vote, even after the consideration of socio-economic considerations', which suggests a neighbourhood effect in a certain spatial context. Kasperson (1969a) debated whether this was a function of conversion through local discussion, which point is discussed in a later section.

Changing votes and neighbourhood effects

Cox (1972) has presented a threefold classification of approaches to the identification of neighbourhood effects: contextual studies based on survey data (Cox, 1969b); contiguity analysis of residuals (Reynolds and Archer, 1969); and the prediction of local voting patterns from survey data (an approach favoured by French sociologists). He finds all three lacking on two evaluative criteria: scale of study and static evaluations of dynamic, learning processes.

On the spatial scale criterion, Cox argues that the areas used by, for example, Reynolds and Archer are too large for the detection of 'true neighbourhood effects'. Quoting evidence that most variance is very local (Kish, 1961), he claims that wards and precincts are too large and that 'any clustering of residuals should be attributable to a spatial clustering of relevant within-individual or aggregate-level variables that have been overlooked in the research design'. This is a criticism which applies to all three approaches. Its validity may depend on the homogeneity of the areas used. One that is socially heterogeneous, containing blocks housing people of different types, should not produce patterns that can be inferred as neighbourhood effects, but one that is homogeneous may comprise a number of districts of similar character, in each of which the anticipated effect operates. In the former case, effects in different directions should counterbalance each other, whereas in the latter they should be additive.

To overcome the static representation of a dynamic process, Cox has amalgamated survey data and aggregate voting patterns in a predictive model. The survey data represent the learning process by a transition probability matrix of the form:

	Party voted for at t_2	
	X	Y
Party Voted for at t_1	$X\ P_{11}$	P_{12}
	$Y\ P_{21}$	P_{22}

in which P_{11}, for example, is the probability that a person who supported X at the first election would also do so at the second. Assuming that this matrix is applicable to all areas within the population sampled, the percentage voting X at t_2 in place i can be predicted by

$$\hat{X}_{it_2} = P_{21} + (P_{11} - P_{21})\, X_{it_1} \qquad (2.1)$$

where

X_i = observed vote for X at place i

P = probability defined in transition matrix

$\hat{X}_i$ = predicted vote for X at place i

Application of this equation also assumes that the electorate does not change between contests. Cox (1971, p. 32) notes that 'this is admittedly a restrictive assumption, but we have as yet no reason to believe that it critically invalidates the model's predictions'. As long as the contests are separated by only a few years, this is probably an acceptable qualifying statement. It is supported by Tryon's (1967) findings of the stability of area characteristics despite changing membership, though Prescott (1972) and Rowley (1970) dispute this. In any case, it would be desirable to have a more complete matrix, with extra rows for those who abstained at t_i or who were ineligible to vote then, and extra columns for those dying by t_2 and those abstaining then, plus a provision for 'minor parties' (Butler and Stokes, 1971, pp. 335–367).

It is the residuals from equation (2.1) predictions, the under- and over-estimations of X's vote, which depict possible neighbourhood effects. Areas of overestimation, for example, should be where X is already strong (Figure 2.3), through there is the problem of accounting for abstentions (A. H. Taylor, 1973). The following regression model:

$$\mathrm{Dev}\ (\hat{X}_{it_2} - X_{it_2} = a + b\, X_{it_1} \qquad (2.2)$$

in which the residuals from the dependent variable and, voting at the first date, the independent should identify the effect. For Columbus, Ohio, it accounted for 25 per cent. of the variation in the 1964 Presidential voting, which was not already accounted for by a 1960–64 transition matrix (Cox, 1971, 1972). This suggests that (Cox, 1972, p. 168): 'In the highly Republican areas the strength of the Republican party was eroded much less than in the Democratic strongholds', with a similar effect for Democrats in their strongholds. The residuals from this regression—equation (2.2)—were also spatially clustered (Figure 2.4), indicating to Cox areal variations in the relevance of the transition matrix. The Democrat vote, for example, was still considerably underpredicted in the black ghetto in north-east Columbus. On average, Negroes were stronger Democrat supporters than were whites; on the other hand, whites living near the ghetto were less strongly Democrat than predicted by equations (2.1) and (2.2), presumably through dislike of that party's civil rights and open housing policies.

The neighbourhood effects analysed by equation (2.2) accounted for 11 per cent. of the Democrat's 1964 vote there. But is this finding typical of all places? Smaller places might have weaker effects, because of less social segregation, greater city-wide rather than local identification and the prevalence of

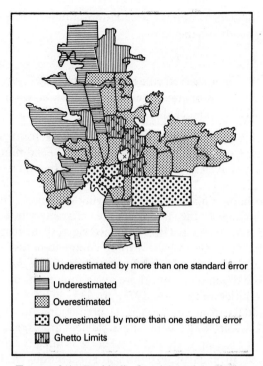

FIGURE 2.4   Residuals from equation (9.2)—see text—predicting 1964 presidential election voting in Columbus, Ohio. (Reproduced by permission of Lexington Books, from Cox, 1972, p. 170)

city-wide formal organizations. Cox (1971) investigated this possibility for a selection of Ohio towns, using a 1948–52 transition matrix, with the following findings:

City size (inhabitants)	b coefficient, equation (9.2)	1952 voting accounted for by neighbourhood effect (%)
Less than 5 000	0.056	7.7
5 000–15 000	0.138	5.1
More than 15 000	0.265	24.3

These clearly suggest that neighbourhood effects were both stronger and more intensive in the larger places.

Mapping the strength of neighbourhood effects

A consequence of the neighbourhood effect, if it is shown to be valid, would be a greater polarization of votes than of the underlying class support for those votes. But this assumes that neighbourhood effects apply equally in all parts of the city. Cox's (1969a, 1969b) work suggests that the effects are most likely where residents participate in local formal and informal social organizations; his London study (Cox, 1968) suggests that this is most likely in suburban areas. Hence equation (2.2) might be rewritten as:

$$\text{Dev} \ (X_{i_2} - X_{i_2}) = a + b_1 X_{i_1} + b_2 U_{i_1} \qquad (2.3)$$

where U_{i_1} = the score for place i or an urbanization or family status component derived from a factorial ecology

which suggests that local political activity and conversion are greatest where the suburban life-style is strongest. Residents of different areas may also vary in their attitudes to their locale (Orbell and Uno, 1972) and perhaps their response to its political activity.

Support for the hypothesis of equation (2.3) comes with survey data from St. Louis. Several types of political actor were defined by Greer (1960) according to their degree of political activity and level of political competence, of which the main ones are:

1. Isolates, who participate in neither local neighbourhood nor wider community affairs.
2. Neighbourhood actors, who participate only in the local area.
3. Community actors, who participate only at that level.

According to Greer's hypotheses, the third type should be politically the most active and competent, with the first type the least so; data from 983 St. Louis residents validated these suggestions (Table 2.3). High family status areas, with high levels of local interaction, produce the most active and competent political actors. A number of other independent variables were also significant (community actors were on average older and better educated, for example, and males were over-represented among the isolates), but area of

TABLE 2.3 Population types, residential areas and political behaviour

	Type		
	Isolate	Neighbourhood actor	Community actor
Percentage of residents of high family status areas	29	18	47
Percentage of residents of low family status areas	36	18	38
Percentage who voted in local municipal elections	44	41	71
Percentage who could name local leaders	33	42	62

Reproduced by permission of the Rural Sociological Society from S. Greer, vol. 27, 1962, Tables 4 and 5, and pp. 447 and 449.

residence was the most consistent predictor of behaviour (Greer, 1962). Neighbourhood effects, therefore, are most likely to occur in suburbia.

The causes of neighbourhood effects

The discussion so far has interpreted observed voting patterns in the context of the structural effects hypothesis, which suggests that discussion of political issues in the neighbourhood will lead to the conversion of some people to that district's majority view. As already stressed, however, this discussion has been based on the inference of processes from patterns, which is not a satisfactory way to validate process theories. Two alternative hypotheses can be presented to account for the same patterns.

The first of these alternatives expresses local deviations from voting patterns, predicted from resident characteristics as consequences of differential canvassing activity by participants or other groups with interests in the election. This assumes both that such ·campaigning influences voting decisions and that where a party does very well is indicative of active canvassing. Evidence would support the former assumption, at least, but there are several suggestions from studies in the United States that intense campaigning is not the only cause of extra success. There is evidence, for example, of neighbourhood effects when such campaigning activities have been held constant (Cutright, 1963); of the impact of party activity tending to vary inversely with voters' perceived salience of the issue (Wolfinger, 1963); and of the impact of a strong local leader on the vote in his neighbourhood (Katz and Eldersveld, 1961). Further, parties are unlikely to devote scarce resources (money and canvassers, in many cases) to areas where they will probably either win substantially or lose to a large majority (Cox, 1972); rather they are likely to concentrate on marginal areas, where swings from one party to another often are greatest (Rowley, 1971).

The second alternative concerns voters self-selection. It suggests that people who live in an X-dominated area and vote X, when from their individual characteristics a vote for Y would be predicted, do so not because they have been converted by X's supporters but because their attitudes and aspirations are pro-X. External characteristics (age, income, etc.) suggest support for Y; individual norms and aspirations are better met by a vote for X, and may also be reflected by choosing to live in an area where such norms and attitudes prevail and X is generally supported. Thus, voting for X is not a consequence of residence in the area, but is a function of a general characteristic, of which voting is a part. Testing the validity of this hypothesis requires detailed survey data. Cox (1972, p. 162) concludes that 'the issue has been so little researched that it cannot be discussed at any length'. It is intuitively appealing, however, and could be considered part of a general tendency to use choice of residential area as an expression of both social norms and social mobility expectations (see Duncan and Duncan, 1955).

On balance, majority support would seem to be for the 'conversion' hypothesis of neighbourhood effects. Nevertheless, in two contemporaneous papers, Greenstein and Wolfinger (1958) concluded, from a national survey, that neighbourhood effects tend to emphasize and reinforce 'self-selection', but Manis and Stine (1958) found no evidence of much neighbourhood political discussion, let alone of a structural effect, among homeowners in a Kalamazoo suburb. Social participation is generally greater in suburban areas, however (Tomeh, 1964).

Some critics have questioned the proposed mechanism behind the neighbourhood effect. Kasperson (1969a, p. 409) has quoted literature that suggests little political discussion among suburban neighbours and that what discussion does occur tends to be between people of known similar views, which is another example of self-selection (see also Fitton, 1973; and Norris, 1970). In reply, Cox (1969c) claimed that Kasperson was selective in his literature review. Prescott (1972, p. 87) writes that

> My own experience in talking to individuals about the way they voted in particular elections, is that many do not know exactly why they voted as they did. Certainly in rationalizing their decision, no one has ever explained their votes in terms of the flow of information or the political complexion of the area in which they live.

He cites Butler and Stokes' (1971, p. 271) finding that persons least exposed to information are the most likely to change their views and voting behaviour, but not their later statement (Butler and Stokes, 1971, p. 272): 'the correlations adduced to show that the poorly informed are most likely to change their votes have been fairly weak ones'. Butler and Stokes' own work produced similar correlations, but there are doubts as to the marginal utility of a large proportion of the information, much of which comes from the mass media and not local sources (Janowitz and Marwick, 1956). And in a series of instructive interviews with Melbourne suburbanites, Davies (1972) was given several examples of behaviour consistent with the neighbourhood effects hypothesis.

Further hypotheses can be derived which, if validated, would enhance the support for that of neighbourhood effects. One was tested in Cox's (1971) study of different sized cities. Another relates to the degree of an area's social homogeneity on the predictor criterion. Butler and Stokes (1971, pp. 182–189) demonstrated for British parliamentary constituencies that the greater the percentage of their population in a given socioeconomic class, the larger the proportion of its members voting for a single party (Conservative for the middle class and Labour for the working class). Because of the size of these constituencies, it cannot be assumed that these are neighbourhood effects, but their findings add to the general body of evidence which gives strong intuitive support to the neighbourhood conversion notions (Green, 1971, 1972).

RELATIVE SPACE AND VOTING PATTERNS

The neighbourhood effects model investigates individual voting behaviour in its relational space by postulating an elector influenced by a field of locational stimuli. As a special case of this, a model based on relative space propounds a single locational stimulus, from which information emanates that is relevant to the voting decision. The basic hypothesis of this model is that the further a voter lives from such a stimulus, the lower is the probability that his decision will be influenced by its information. Thus, it was suggested that the further a person lived from the black ghetto in Flint, Michigan, the lower the likelihood that he would have hostile attitudes to blacks and fear their competition in the housing market. A consequence of this should be a positive relationship between distance from the ghetto's edge and support for an open housing referendum, but in fact the reverse pattern was found. (see Brunn, and Hoffmann, 1970; Brunn, Hoffmann and Romsa, 1969; see also Berry, 1973. One problem with this study was undoubtedly its use of 1960 census data to define the ghetto; the referendum was held in 1968.)

The relative space model is frequently referred to as a 'friends-and-neighbours' model in which (Reynolds, 1969, p. 82) 'the individual's voting decision is to some extent dependent upon his access to information regarding the candidate or issue, which in turn is partially dependent upon his relative location in a communications network within social groups'. The definition clearly suggests some of the influences—political conversion by social interaction—which characterize the neighbourhood effects model. From it can be deduced the proposition that the closer a voter lives to a candidate's home, the more likely it is that both persons are members of common formal and informal social organizations and the more likely it is that the voter will support the candidate. Since most individual interaction fields have small radii, few people will get to know a candidate and come to support him as a result of social contact, though an active seeker of office may seek to extend his interaction field as part of his vote-winning drive. (There is, of course, always the possibility of a negative effect, converting voters against the candidate.) Usually, such conversion effects would be spatially too attenuated to be visible in available data (Cox, 1972). Interpersonal contact and knowledge is only one possible mechanism for the friends-and-neighbours effect, however; it could arise (Reynolds, 1969, p. 186):

> (1) when the voting decision is predicated upon close personal interaction between the voter and the candidate or friends of the candidate, or (2) when the voting decision is predicated upon a real or imagined bond between the individual voter and the candidate, exemplified by responses such as '1 voted for X because he understands the problems of our area.'

Alternatively, the mechanism may simply be 'loyalty to the local boy' (Johnston, 1974; Key, 1949).

The friends-and-neighbours effect should be indicated by a candidate polling better close to his home than elsewhere. Most empirical tests of this have been for rural areas, where Cox (1969b), quoting Key, suggests that the effect is most likely to appear because of greater 'in-group' solidarity in those areas and relative weakness of other 'divisive' forces. McCarty (1960), for example, has shown that, over and above his general rural support, Senator Joseph McCarthy polled much better near to his eastern Wisconsin home, and Reynolds (1969) isolated a similar pattern in support for Linder, a candidate in a Georgian Democratic gubernatorial contest. Key (1949) has produced a number of maps strongly suggestive of this effect in the southern States. Within urban areas, Reynolds suggests, the friends-and-neighbours effect will be spatially more attenuated and thus harder to isolate, because of greater population densities and the wider range of appeals to voters.

Testing the friends-and-neighbours model involves a difficult problem of predicting what a candidate's support at any place would be without such an effect. In many elections of the 'one man—one vote' type, and especially partisan elections, voters may be reluctant to base their choice on local and personal grounds rather than the more widely based partisan issues. In consequence, the model can perhaps best be tested in elections which give each person several votes. In these, a voter may be prepared to transfer some of his partisan support to a local candidate, without any feeling of serious injury to the party he gives major support to. Thus, in a partisan, across-the-board election, each candidate of a particular party might (a) obtain about the same number of votes at each booth, plus (b) do slightly better than his colleagues in areas close to his home.

These two propositions have been tested for several New Zealand local body elections. Christchurch City Council, for example, has nineteen members and each resident has nineteen votes at the triennial elections, which in recent years have been dominated by partisan issues, with each of two main parties offering a full slate of nineteen candidates. Inductive analysis of the 1968 election (Johnston, 1972) showed that the first proposition—termed the party effect—accounted for some 80 per cent. of the pattern of votes of the forty-one candidates over the 119 polling stations. This party effect was delimited by a principal components analysis, from which the scores were used to predict the performances of individual candidates over the 119 stations. Major residuals from these regressions indicate where there are considerable deviations between the performances of the candidate and his party; if the second proposition—of individual effects—is valid, the positive residuals (where the candidate's performance exceeded his party's) should be clustered around his home. Of the thirty-four candidates to whom this test could be applied, twenty-six had a greater proportion of large positive residuals within one mile of their homes than might have been expected; thirty-two of thirty-seven had a greater proportion within a two-mile radius. (The number of candidates varies because some lived beyond the city boundary.)

Only individual effects centred on the candidate's home can be identified by the above method. An inductive search for all clusters of residuals of similar magnitude fitted conical trend surfaces to the map of residuals (Casetti and Semple, 1968). If the friends-and-neighbours effect dominates, the major cones should be centred close to the candidate's home, and this proved to be so with fourteen of the twenty-eight city residents (Johnston, 1973). With this method, it is also possible to assess the strength of the individual effects. On average, they accounted for only 3 per cent. of the spatial variation in candidates' performance, though the value ranged up to 30 per cent. In the slightly less partisan Dunedin City Council election of 1971, the party effect accounted for 70 per cent. and the individual effect averaged 8 per cent. (Forrest and Johnston, 1973). Of the nineteen major party candidates contesting that election, however, the trend surfaces suggested a home-based individual effect for only seven; for two others there was a similar effect centred on their workplace, the university.

Neighbourhood effects, it was suggested earlier, should be most likely in suburban areas dominated by a family-centred life-style, although the recent growth of community associations in many cities may be presaging a wider spatial base. A similar suggestion can be made for the friends-and-neighbours effect. Residents of many non-family-centred areas are highly mobile, have few local ties, are unlikely to know local candidates and are unlikely to put local interests foremost when deciding how to vote—if indeed they do vote. Suburban residents, on the other hand, display life-styles closer to the rural 'norm' for friends-and-neighbours effects, and a map of the parts of Christchurch City where individual effects were apparent in the 1971 election can be interpreted as supporting this hypothesis (Johnston, 1974). In addition, the parameters of such a map depend on the distribution of candidates' homes, especially of those who win an individual effect. Of the contestants in the Christchurch 1971 election, the following appeared most likely to attract an individual, or local, vote (Johnston, 1974):

1. Independent candidates, most of whom have no city-wide basis on which to campaign.
2. Those who live in 'opposition territory', since candidates living in their own party's stronghold probably get most of the votes there in any case.
3. Those living apart from other candidates, since a cluster of candidates could produce competition for, and attenuation of, the local vote.
4. Candidates standing for the first time, who are not well known to the electorate and could be 'dropped' by their party's supporters elsewhere, when they transfer some of their votes to local candidates of other parties.

A candidate's home need not be the only locational stimulus for a voting pattern conforming to the relative space model. Another stimulus might be a local issue. The 1971 Christchurch City mayoralty election, for example, was fought partly about the attitudes of the sitting mayor and partly about two local issues: (a) a proposal for a motorway through a large central park; and (b) rival proposals for location of the facilities for the 1974 British Commonwealth Games. The personality issue should have produced a uniform swing against Guthrey, the sitting mayor; the local issues should have warped that swing in areas close to the proposals. A regression model tested this. Its general form:

$$G_{71} = 0.069 + 0.86G_{68} \qquad (r^2 = 0.76) \qquad (2.4)$$

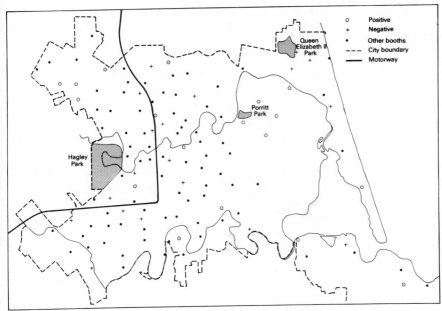

FIGURE 2.5 Residuals from equation (9.4)—see text—predicting the vote for Guthrey in the 1971 Christchurch City mayoralty election. The large residual identified exceed one standard error of the regression line

where G_{71} and G_{68} are the percentage votes for Guthrey in 1971 and 1968 respectively at each of the 119 polling stations, clearly indicates a city-wide swing against Guthrey. The map of residuals (Figure 2.5) shows no local effect around the proposed motorway through Hagley Park. A cluster of positive residuals suggests that the swing was much less severe around Porritt Park, where the incumbent Guthrey's party intended to build the Games stadium; negative residuals suggested a stronger-than-average swing around Queen Elizabeth II Park, the site of the opposition's proposed stadium. Of two additional clusters of major residuals, one was a discontinuous string of considerable overpredictions of Guthrey's 1971 performance (negative residuals), which roughly follows the line of a proposed motorway that, although not an obvious campaign issue, could have swung votes against the tenant mayor where it threatened properties. The other, a cluster of positive residuals in the north-west, suggests that the swing against Guthrey was less in one of the areas of his strongest support, in which he lives.

ABSOLUTE SPACES

Two prime methods exist for the division of an area into territories, whose form influences political behaviour. The first creates a mosaic of independent local government areas; the second organizes its electoral system through an areal division. Most countries comprise a spatial hierarchy of governments and use a constituency system to elect representatives, so an area may be part of both an independent unit for some functions and a contributing unit to administration of other functions. The various boundaries may coincide, as in metropolitan Britain: Greater London's boroughs are both independent units and constituences for the Greater London Council and constituencies for the House of Commons. This may produce commonalities of interest and stronger partisan organization, which are not as apparent if boundaries do not relate, but produce a chaotic assemblage of overlapping areas.

The ease with which a population may constitute their own territorial unit varies by time and place. In any case, this ability may only give local control over 'bread and butter' issues such as street maintenance, garbage collection and library provision. Such functions are little desired, and few populations will fight to retain them unless they carry other advantages, such as lower property taxes. On the other hand, if municipalities control functions usually perceived as more important to local well-being, such as provision of education, building standards and land use zoning, municipal status will probably be keenly sought and stoutly defended. Of the countries considered here, the United States has been most liberal in allowing local autonomy for small territories which choose to adopt the relevant status and powers. The result is often a plethora of units and clear delineation of their boundaries in social and physical landscapes. An extreme example of this was the decision of a group of dairy farmers on the Los Angeles periphery to incorporate their land into three separate municipalities. Two of them zoned all, and the other two-thirds, of their land for agriculture, thereby preventing land value speculation and consequent property tax increases (Fielding, 1962).

Since political behaviour is commonly predicted on self-interest, there are frequent strong fights to retain urban and suburban 'municipal ghettos'. Thus Wilson and Banfield (1965) hypothesized that high income suburban residents would not vote favourably on referenda for metropolitan-wide projects carrying financial implications; the more valuable a person's home, the more he will be taxed and the less benefit he will get, per dollar invested, from the project, relative to the occupant of a lowly rated property. Their hypothesis was not confirmed, however; such voting against self-interest may have reflected a cosmopolitan orientation (Kaufman and Greer, 1960; and Uyeki, 1966, present an opposite view), a decreasing marginal utility of the dollar or, in Wilson and Banfield's (1965) view, inter-cultural differences, since many European immigrant groups were strongly against such expenditures.

Large cities are often divided into wards for electoral purposes (Kasperson, 1969b, discusses the American literature). These have advantages over at-large electoral systems by bringing elector and elected into relatively close contact and by giving minority groups greater chances for representation. Their disadvantages include the possible dominance of local over city-wide issues in council debate and policy, the greater potential for patronage and 'graft', especially if wards are also financial units with their own budgets, and the possibility of ineffective city-wide control, unless a handful of councillors can gain the upper hand (Kasperson, 1965). As with the use of constituencies for elections to national parliaments, wards can lead to serve imbalances between the proportion of the total poll obtained by a party and its proportion of elected representatives (P. J. Taylor, 1973). Without careful safeguards, this can produce electoral malpractices, such as the gerry-mandering of boundaries in order to minimize one party's representation and maximizing another's (Morrill, 1973); according to Kasperson (1969b), the Los Angeles City Council has the power to redistrict its city every four years.

Finally, the existence of absolute spaces, particularly independent territorial units, in political systems encourages self-interested acts which prolong and exacerbate social inequalities and injustices. These have been described recently at macrospatial scales (Coates and Rawstron, 1971; Smith, 1973); undoubtedly they are just as marked within urban areas. Residents of suburban municipalities may vote for metropolitan-wide projects, thereby promising to subsidize the central-city 'poor', but they also provide better school facilities, for example, to which residents of other territories may be denied access and whose development may, by their capture of limited resources such as good teachers, further disadvantage the 'outsiders'. Political parties, too, may determine locational strategies for their expenditure to woo voters or to thank them (Glassberg, 1973).

CONCLUSION

The theme of this chapter, like the others in this volume, is the salience of the residential mosaic as an influence on social activity—in this case political behaviour. In particular, various parameters of voting maps have been related to the spatial patterns of social areas; to local relational spaces in terms of the conversion effect of neighbourhood political discussion; to local relative space, with the importance of local issues and candidates to behaviour; and to the creation, operation and defence of local absolute spaces. One as yet unanswered question in all of the literature on these topics concerns the role of these spatial variables as determinants of election results, which must be a major concern of electoral investigations. In one case, Cox (1971) has indicated that neighbourhood effects were responsible for 11 per cent. of the Democrat vote; it may be, however, that a similar proportion of the Republican vote could be accounted for in this way, suggesting that neighbourhood effects are self-correcting. Only detailed empirical study and simulation will show whether, indeed, the various effects discussed here are interesting but irrelevant processes in the final division of political power, or whether in certain instances they are potent determinants of the outcomes of democracy.

A final qualification of most of the work discussed here is that the generalization reached are essentially speculative, being based on behavioural inferences from aggregate patterns and the relative merits of rival hypotheses tested with ecological correlations. Even the so-called behavioural studies tend to make inferences about the processes of political learning and decision-making. Yet the general conclusion remains clear; maps of political behaviour, such as voter turnout and, in particular, voting choice, apparently are warped by aspects of the sociospatial enironment to which they refer.

REFERENCES

Alford, R. (1963). *Party and Society*, Rand McNally, Chicago.

Berelson, B., Lazarsfeld, P. F., and McPhee, W. N. (1954). *Voting*, University of Chicago, Chicago.

Berry, B. J. L. (1973). 'A paradigm for modern geography'. In R. J. Chorley (Ed.), *Directions in Geography*, Methuen, London. pp. 3–22.

Biel, H. S. (1972). 'Suburbia and voting behaviour in the London metropolitan area: an alternative perspective'. *Tijdschrift voor Economische en Sociale Geografie*, **62**, 39–43.

Blau, P. M. (1960). 'Structural effects'. *American Sociological Review*, **25**, 178–193.

Brunn, S. D., and Hoffman, W. L. (1970). 'The spatial response of Negroes and whites towards open housing: the Flint referendum'. *Annals, Association of American Geographers*, **60**, 18–36.

Brunn, S. D., Hoffman, W. L., and Romsa, G. H. (1969). 'Some spatial considerations of the Flint open housing referendum'. *Proceedings, Association of American Geographers*, **1**, 26–32.

Butler, D. E., and Stokes, D. E. (1971). *Political Change in Britain*, Penguin Books, Harmondsworth, Middlesex.

Campbell, A., Converse, P. E., Miller, W. E., and Stokes, D. E. (1960). *The American Voter*, John Wiley, New York.

Campbell, A., Converse, P. E., Miller, W. E., and Stokes, D. E. (1966). *Elections and the Political Order*, John Wiley, New York.

Casetti, E., and Semple, R. K. (1968). *A Method for the Stepwise Separation of Spatial Trends*, Discussion Paper No. 11, Michigan Inter-University Community of Mathematical Geographers, Michigan.

Coates, B. E., and Rawstron, E. M. (1971). *Regional Variations in Britain*, Batsford, London.

Cox, K. R. (1968). 'Suburbia and voting behavior in the London metropolitan area'. *Annals, Association of American Geographers*, **58**, 111–127.

Cox, K. R. (1969a). 'The voting decision in a spatial context'. *Progress in Geography*, **1**, 81–117.

Cox, K. R. (1969b). 'The spatial structuring of information flow and partisan attitudes'. In M. Dogan and S. Rokkan (Eds.), *Quantitative Ecological Analysis in the Social Sciences*, The M.I.T. Press, Cambridge, Massachusetts. pp. 157–185.

Cox, K. R. (1969c). 'Comments in reply to Kasperšon and Taylor'. *Annals, Association of American Geographers*, **59**, 411–415.

Cox, K. R. (1970). 'Residential relocation and political behavior: conceptual model and empirical tests'. *Acta Sociologica*, **13**, 40–53.

Cox, K. R. (1971). 'The spatial components of urban voting response surfaces'. *Economic Geography*, **47**, 27–35.

Cox, K. R. (1972). 'The neighbourhood effect in urban voting response surfaces'. In D. C. Sweet (Ed.), *Models of Urban Structure*, D. C. Heath, Lexington, Massachusetts. pp. 159–176.

Cutright, P. (1963). 'Measuring the impact of local party activity on the general election vote'. *Public Opinion Quarterly*, **27**, 572–586.

Davies, A. F. (1972). *Essays in Political Sociology*, Cheshire, Melbourne.

Duncan, O. D., and Duncan, B. (1955). 'Occupational stratification and residential distribution'. *American Journal of Sociology*, **50**, 493–503.

Fielding, G. J. (1962). 'Dairying in cities designed to keep people out'. *The Professional Geographer*, **14** (1), 12–17.

Fitton, M. (1973). 'Neighbourhood and voting: a sociometric examination'. *British Journal of Political Science*, **3**, 445–472.

Foladare, I. S. (1968). 'The effect of neighbourhood on voting behavior'. *Political Science Quarterly*, **83**, 516–529.

Forrest, J., and Johnston, R. J. (1973). 'Spatial aspects of voting in the Dunedin city council elections of 1971'. *New Zealand Geographer*, **29**, 166–181.

Glassberg, A. (1973). 'The linkage between urban policy outputs and voting behavior: New York and London'. *British Journal of Political Studies*, **3**, 341–361.

Green, B. S. R. (1971). 'Social area analysis and structural effects'. *Sociology*, **5**, 1–19.

Green, B. S. R. (1972). *Social Areas and Social Participation: Some Explanatory Models.* Unpublished Paper, Department of Sociology, York University.

Greenstein, F. I., and Wolfinger, R. E. (1958). 'The suburbs and shifting party loyalties'. *Public Opinion Quarterly*, **22**, 473–482.

Greer, S. (1960). 'The social structure and political process of suburbia'. *American Sociological Review*, **25**, 514–520.

Greer, S. (1962). 'The social structure and political process of suburbia: an empirical test'. *Rural Sociology*, **27**, 438–459.

Harvey, D. W. (1973). *Social Justice and the City*, Edward Arnold, London.

Janowitz, M., and Marwick, D. (1956). 'Competitive pressure and democratic consent'. In H. Eulau, S. J. Eldersfeld and M. Janowitz (Eds.), *Political Behavior*, The Free Press, Glencoe, Illinois. pp. 275–286.

Johnston, R. J. (1972). 'Spatial elements in voting patterns at the 1968 Christchurch city council election'. *Political Science*, **24**, 49–61.

Johnston, R. J. (1973). 'Spatial patterns and influences on voting in multi-candidate elections: the Christchurch city council election, 1971'. *Urban Studies*, **10**, 69–82.

Johnston, R. J. (1974). 'Local effects in voting at a local election'. *Annals, Association of American Geographers*, **64**.

Kasperson, R. E. (1965). 'Towards a geography of urban politics: Chicago, a case study'. *Economic Geography*, **41**, 95–107.

Kasperson, R. E. (1969a). 'On suburbia and voting behavior'. *Annals, Association of American Geographers*, **59**, 405–411.

Kasperson, R. E. (1969b). 'Ward systems and urban politics'. *The Southeastern Geographer*, **9**, 17–25.

Katz, D., and Eldersveld, S. J. (1961). 'The impact of local party activity upon the electorate'. *Public Opinion Quarterly*, **25**, 1–24.

Kaufman, W. C., and Greer, S. (1960). 'Voting in a metropolitan community: an application of social area analysis'. *Social Forces*, **38**, 196–204.

Key, V. O. (1949). *Southern Politics*, A. A. Knopf, New York.

Kish, L. (1961). 'A measure of homogeneity in areal units'. *Bulletin de l'Institut International de Statistique*, **39**, 201–210.

Kory, W. B. (1972). 'Political significance of population homogeneity: a Pittsburgh example'. *The Professional Geographer*, **24**, 118–122.

Lazarsfeld, P. F., Berelson, B., and Gaudet, H. (1944). *The People's Choice*, Columbia University Press, New York.

Lewis, P. F. (1965). 'Impact of Negro migration on the electoral geography of Flint, Michigan, 1932–1962: a cartographic analysis'. *Annals, Association of American Geographers*, **55**, 1–25.

Lieberson, S. (1969). 'Measuring population diversity'. *American Sociological Review*, **34**, 850–862.

McCarty, H. H. (1960). 'McCarty on McCarthy'. Referred to in E. N. Thomas (1967),

'Maps of residuals from regression'. In B. J. L. Berry and D. F. Marble (Eds.), *Spatial Analysis*, Prentice-Hall, Englewood Cliffs, New Jersey. pp. 326–352.

Manis, J. G., and Stine, L. C. (1968). 'Suburban residence and political behavior'. *Public Opinion Quarterly*, **22**, 483–489.

Morrill, R. L. (1973). 'Ideal and reality in reapportionment'. *Annals, Association of American Geographers*, **63**, 463–477.

Murdie, R. A. (1969). *Factorial Ecology of Metropolitan Toronto 1951–1961*, Research Paper No. 116, Department of Geography, University of Chicago, Chicago.

Norris, R. E. (1970). *Spatial Interaction and the Politicization of Individuals*. Ph.D. Thesis, University of Iowa.

Norris, R. E., and Barnett, J. R. (1975). *Migration and Political Change in Californian Cities* (forthcoming).

Orbell, J. M., and Uno, T. (1972). A theory of neighborhood problem-solving; political action versus residential mobility'. *American Political Science Review*, **66**, 471–489.

Prescott, J. R. V. (1972). *Political Geography*, Methuen, London.

Putnam, R. D. (1966). 'Political attitudes and the local community'. *American Political Science Review*, **60**, 640–654.

Reynolds, D. R. (1969). 'A "friends-and-neighbours" voting model as a spatial interactional model for electoral geography'. In K. R. Cox and R. G. Golledge (Eds.), *Behavioral Problems in Geography: A Symposium*, Studies in Geography No. 17, Northwestern University, Evanston, Illinois. pp. 81–100.

Reynolds, D. R., and Archer, J. C. (1969). *An Inquiry into the Spatial Basis of Electoral Geography*, Discussion Paper No. 11, Department of Geography, University of Iowa.

Rowley, G. (1969). 'Electoral behavior and electoral behaviour: a note on certain recent developments in electoral geography'. *The Professional Geographer*, **21**, 398–400.

Rowley, G. (1970). 'Elections and population changes'. *Area*, **2** (3), 13–18.

Rowley, G. (1971). 'The Greater London Council elections of 1964 and 1967: a study in electoral geography'. *Transactions, Institute of British Geographers*, **53**, 117–132.

Salter, P. S., and Mings, R. C. (1972). 'The projected impact of Cuban settlement on voting patterns in metropolitan Miami, Florida'. *The Professional Geographer*, **24**, 123–131.

Segal, D. R., and Meyer, M. W. (1969). 'The social context of political partisanship'. In M. Dogan and S. Rokkan (Eds.), *Quantitative Ecological Analysis in the Social Sciences*, The M.I.T. Press, Cambridge, Massachusetts. pp. 217–232.

Smith, D. M. (1973). *The Geography of Social Well-being in the United States*, McGraw-Hill, New York.

Taylor, A. H. (1973). 'Variation in the relationship between class and voting in England, 1950 to 1970'. *Tijdschrift voor Economische en Sociale Geografie*, **64**, 164–169.

Taylor, P. J. (1969). 'Causal models in geographic research'. *Annals, Association of American Geographers*, **59**, 402–404.

Taylor, P. J. (1973). 'On some implications of the spatial organisation of elections'. *Transactions, Institute of British Geographers*, **60**, 121–136.

Tomeh, A. K. (1964). 'Informal group participation and residential patterns'. *American Journal of Sociology*, **70**, 28–35.

Tryon, R. C. (1967). 'Predicting group differences in cluster analysis: the social area problem'. *Multivariate Behavioural Research*, **2**, 453–475.

Uyeki, E. S. (1966). 'Patterns of voting in a metropolitan area, 1938–1962'. *Urban Affairs Quarterly*, **1** (4), 65–77.

Wilson, J. Q., and Banfield, E. C. (1965). 'Voting behavior on municipal public expenditures: a study in rationality and self-interest'. In J. Margolis (Ed.), *The Public Economy of Urban Communities*, Resources for the Future, Washington. pp. 72–92.

Wolfinger, R. E. (1963). 'The influence of precinct work on voting behaviour'. *Public Opinion Quarterly*, **27**, 387–398.

Chapter 3

Social Deviance in the City:
A Spatial Perspective

D. T. Herbert

INTRODUCTION

Deviance as a societal concept implies that there are individuals with characteristics which are not those of the large majority of any given population group; most definitions of social deviance refer to normative rules (Cohen, 1966; Phillipson, 1971). In some forms of deviance, such as mental illness, an individual may have no control over the qualities which make him deviant; in others, such as crime or delinquency, he may through choice be infringing the rules or norms of the wider society. Most classifications of social deviance are based upon attitudes and forms of behaviour (Clinard, 1968; Merton and Nisbet, 1971). Research in the social sciences has recognized the importance of isolating specific forms of deviance, but has also demonstrated the fact that there are characteristic features which tend to recur over the field as a whole. While it must be acknowledged that the precise causes of deviance are often highly individual, there are consistent variations in the incidence rates of deviance which are related to the social environment of which the individual is part. Deviant sub-groups within a society, when identified, are very frequently found to possess other common characteristics such as low socioeconomic status, weak social integration, mobility and substandard living conditions. Whereas such correlates can be measured in fairly unambiguous terms, the meaning of any relationship in a causal sense is much more difficult to establish. Those theories of deviant behaviour which are conceptually attractive can rarely be verified in empirical terms. One result, common to all forms of social deviance research, is an abandonment of single-stranded theories and the acceptance of multi-factor solutions. An understanding both of individual deviant acts and of the societal conditions in which they are most liable to occur is likely to require the analysis of many factors and their interrelationships.

A significant fact for geographical research is that these systematic variations in the occurrence of deviance within society are paralleled by variations in spatial distributions within cities. When deviance data are mapped, the revealed patterns are rarely random or haphazard, but take the form of well-defined

89

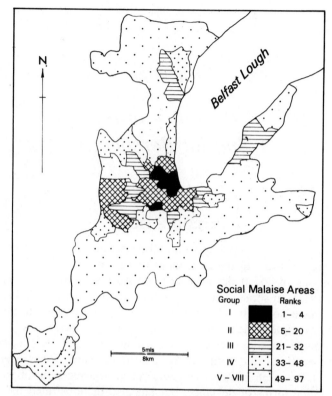

FIGURE 3.1 Social malaise areas in Belfast. The classification of areas is based upon ranks on seven measures of malaise: highest ranks (1–4 in Group I) indicate multiple deprivation. (Reproduced by permission of the Northern Ireland Department of Education, from F. W. Boal, P. Doherty and D. G. Pringle, 1974, Figure 10, p. 65)

clusters. Further, when these distributions are examined in closer detail, it is apparent that they show consistent associations with particular attributes of the sociospatial environment. These facts are important in themselves in that they indicate the validity of residential area as an indicator of societal groups. Evidence does exist, however, to suggest that spatial distributions of deviance are not merely those which could be predicted from a knowledge of the deviancy rates of various social groups and the spatial arrangements of those groups. Spatial qualities, of location, contiguity and environment, are themselves of relevance in the comprehension of the geographical distribution of deviance. An example drawn from a study of delinquency (Herbert, 1976) will be used to demonstrate some aspects of these spatial qualities.

While it can be shown that some forms of deviance have separate and individually distinctive spatial expressions, there does tend to be a concentration in particular districts of the city. Experiments with a large number of territorial indicators (Boal, Doherty and Pringle,1974; Smith, 1973) have demonstrated the clustering of many types of deviance in similar areas (Figure 3.1). Exercises of this kind have been developed in statistically sophisticated ways and have considerable practical value, in that they allow general social malaise areas to be identified. This discussion will refer to several types of deviance, but will be mainly concerned with crime and delinquency and is not therefore a comprehensive overview of the subject. Those forms of deviance which are given scant treatment here are discussed in greater detail in the more specialized texts (e.g. Clinard, 1968). It is suggested, however, that the forms of deviant behaviour which are discussed are in many ways indicative of the whole field and that the research methodologies to which reference is made have wider application.

The general approach which is adopted in this chapter emphasizes the spatial qualities of deviance data. Although some spatial studies of deviance have been content to depict patterns (Harries, 1971), most have adopted an ecological approach and, through its emphasis upon relationships, have been drawn into consideration of cause and effect (Wallis and Maliphant, 1967). Detailed mapping of the incidence of deviance has allowed spatial generalizations to be made, the best known of which suggests zonal arrangements with progression from high central-city to low peripheral scores. (Shaw and McKay, 1942, revised 1969), and also has enabled the calculation of deviance rates for small areas within the city which may be tested for statistical association with other variables derived from available aggregate data. Much of this work has remained descriptive, in that it has simply revealed patterns of geographical distribution and statistical association and has not probed more deeply into the questions of cause and effect. This is not in itself a criticism, as in a field of study such as deviance a perspective which adopts a scale larger than the individual is unlikely to provide precise causal explanation. A more realistic aim is to extend the investigation of the incidence of deviance and of the social environmental qualities which are associated with it. While this aim will not provide individual aetiologies, it may well identify the external circumstances in which deviance may be precipitated.

The question of scale is, of course, important. Most studies which use aggregate data have, to varying extents, acknowledged the dangers of ecological fallacy which accompany any attempt to make inferences on individual behaviour. Analyses of this kind need not be unnecessarily denegrated, however, and the individualistic fallacy (Berry, 1971) is no less real. The individual is rarely divorced from the social groups of which he is part and the residential social group may well be the key reference group (Hyman and Singer, 1968) to which he belongs. Statistical analysis of aggregate data can form the bases for probablistic statements on individual behaviour. Established concepts and methodologies in the study of residential differentiation and ecological statistical association are in themselves capable of enlargement and further application. They may also, however, provide frameworks from which new directions in analysis concerned with underlying attitudes and forms of behaviour may proceed (Herbert and Evans, 1974). There seem clear ways in which studies at the ecological scale may continue and also provide a link with analyses at more individual scales (Dogan and Rokkan, 1969).

Although four categories of deviance are discussed in this chapter, crime and delinquency receive most attention. Studies of physical health, which is the first category considered, marginally warrant the description of deviance, but they do identify the same basic spatial qualities as social deviance data and also provide a context in which causal relationships can be seen in a comparatively unambiguous way. Consideration of mental illness and of suicide provide a rational progression from this first category of studies to the analysis of crime and delinquency. The aim in consideration of each of these themes will be to identify the evidence for spatial and ecological generalizations and to consider the contributions which an emphasis upon spatial qualities has to offer.

STUDIES IN URBAN MEDICAL GEOGRAPHY

The incidence of disease has been studied by geographers over a long period of time, though most research has concentrated upon spatial variation at the regional scale of analysis (McGlashan, 1972). Spread of contagious diseases obviously lends itself to spatial interpretation and simulation techniques have been used to good effect in the analysis of diffusion patterns (Pyle, 1968). Information upon temporal change is obviously of great value, but where the detailed distribution of any form of ill health is known its associated environmental conditions can be investigated.

Empirical evidence from British industrial cities in the nineteenth century often suggested that much ill health was highly localized in the housing environments of poor quality. Perhaps the best-known study from this period was concerned with the outbreak of cholera in London in the early 1850s (Snow, 1964). Mapping of the residences of those individuals struck down by the disease in central parts of the city showed a close coincidence with a source of contaminated water; the causal relationship could be clearly identified. Although advances in medical science have virtually eliminated a whole range of diseases and have reduced the effects of others, recent researchers suggest that forms of ill health over which less control has been achieved are still concentrated in particular parts of the city. Pyle (1968) and Pyle and Rees (1971) adopted a factor analytic approach to the study of a set of small area statistics in Chicago which included measures of health, social composition and housing. The dimensions which were identified indicated a typology of diseases and their social environmental correlates. A range of health measures, including tuberculosis and infant mortality, were linked with a leading dimension which was labelled the 'poverty syndrome'. When the scores for this factor were mapped, the poorest communities of the city were delineated. The second dimension linked population density with infectious diseases such as mumps and whooping cough—these having high scores in overcrowded districts. Although the third and fourth factors showed no distinctive geographical

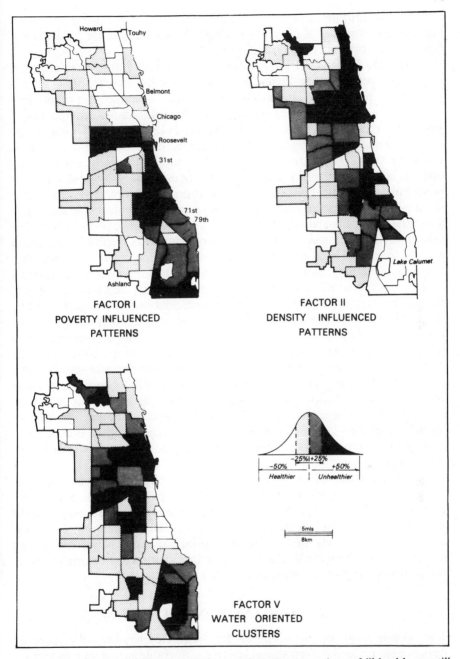

FIGURE 3.2 Death and disease in Chicago, 1965. Concentrations of ill-health are still evident in Chicago with clusters associated with poverty and high population density. Particular diseases are associated with the spatial distribution of rivers and other water surface (factor V). (Reproduced by permission of G. F. Pyle and P. H. Rees and *Economic Geography*, vol. **47** (1971), Figure 2, p. 477)

patterns, the fifth demonstrated a spatial correspondence between infectious hepatitis and stretches of open water. Figure 3.2 shows these three patterns of factor scores for Chicago (Pyle and Rees, 1971).

Despite the findings of Pyle and Rees, which rest upon statistical inference, causal links between ill health and environmental conditions are often difficult to establish in modern Western cities. Spatial analyses at the intra-urban scale which successfully demonstrate such relationships are, in fact, comparatively few and a recent study of leukaemia (Dever, 1972) highlighted some of the problems which are involved. Dever analysed the distribution of leukaemia in Buffalo with a set of variables calculated at the geographical scales of tax district, census tract, block and individual housing unit. Normal statistical procedures to investigate patterns of association did not reveal positive results when variables were calculated in terms of census tracts or blocks. At the largest aggregate level of analysis (the tax district which contained an average of five census tracts), a statistically significant set of results was obtained. Regression analysis suggested that increasing rates of leukaemia were associated with fewer rooms in both owner-occupied and rented housing units and revealed a clear connection with levels of overcrowding. These facts were taken as support for the theory of a viral aetiology for this particular disease and high and low risk areas in the city could be identified. Using housing units as the scale of analysis, crowding as a variable again appeared relevant as incidence rates were higher in apartments. Dever's findings could not be conclusive. His data set was not large and had not been replicated over several time periods; again, he was dealing with a disease which was not fully understood in terms of its causation. His summary of achievements was suitably cautious (Dever, 1972, p. 245): 'The significant finding of this paper is the identification of spatially high and low risk areas in the intra-urban setting of Buffalo. It is evident that causation has not been established but association was definitely determined.'

It is the experience of research in medical geography that the spatial analysis of many forms of physical disease offers valuable perspectives. Because many diseases have direct links with facets of the environment, clues to the explanation may be evident. With contemporary medical and public health services, however, it is unlikely that consistent spatial variations will occur to any marked extent within the Western city. The focus for further research is likely to be outside the Western world and at the regional scale.

MENTAL ILLNESS IN THE CITY

The various forms of mental illness fall more closely within the scope of deviance studies as it is likely that at least a considerable part of the explanation for their occurrence lies in the social environment of the individual. Studies of mental illness indices have shown for some time that there are both distinctive spatial patterns and consistent variations with the form of urban ecological structure. It is also apparent, however, that some types of mental illness display very distinctive spatial characteristics while others appear to be aspatial. In a well-known study of Chicago in the 1930s, Dunham (1937) analysed the distributions of schizophrenia and manic depression. His sample of schizophrenics consisted of 7 253 cases, recorded in terms of the 120 community areas which comprised the city, and incidence rates were found to vary from 111 per 1 000 on the periphery to 1 195 near the centre. The community areas with high incidence rates were all in the central city and corresponded with districts such as hobohemia, the rooming house district and the ethnic quarters. A regular gradient, with scores decreasing from centre to periphery, was found to exist even when race was held constant, when sexes were distinguished and when different types of schizophrenia were mapped separately.

Dunham (1937) also analysed the incidence of manic depression using two samples, the largest of which consisted of 2 311 cases, but in this instance failed to identify a spatial pattern which could be described as other than random. Whereas, therefore, schizophrenia bore strong spatial relationships to the underlying pattern of residential differentiation, being concentrated in underprivileged and substandard districts of Chicago, manic depression had no such simple geographical pattern and appeared to be more explicable in terms of personality and psychological factors. Some confirmation of these findings was provided by Mintz and Schwarz (1964) in a more recent study of an American city. They established a typology of ecological areas and examined the associational patterns between these and the two categories of mental disorder. Whereas schizophrenia could be shown to possess an ordered spatial pattern and to be associated with levels of neighbourhood stability, manic depression was again characterized by a random distribution.

Analyses of the spatial qualities associated with mental disorder are not limited to American cities and there are several studies which show a marked concentration of some types of disorder in the substandard inner-city districts (Castle and Gittus, 1957). A further characteristic of the distribution of mental illness in British cities, however, is its association with municipal housing estates (Timms, 1971). This finding has led to the suggestion that mental deviance (which is amenable to ecological scale analysis) is more likely to be related to the social milieu rather than to the physical or built urban environment. British public sector housing policy has had the effect of transferring population groups from old central to new peripheral residential districts and has effected a redistribution of some deviance patterns in the process. Research in Nottingham by Giggs (1973), however, which was only concerned with schizophrenia, has tended to confirm the established patterns for this type of mental disorder.

Giggs (1973) collected information on the 444 individuals classed as schizophrenics who were admitted to hospital from an address in Nottingham for the first time during the years 1963–69. A gradient analysis—based upon one-kilometre zones—showed that most of the schizophrenics were first admitted from addresses in or near to the city centre and that 68 per cent. of all patients came from addresses within four kilometres of the city centre. There

Table 3.1 Factor analyses of schizophrenic and census variables, Nottingham

Variables	Loadings, Primary	Varimax	Pattern coefficients, Promax $(K = B)$			
	I	I	I	III	IV	VI
Schizophrenics						
1. Percentage total	836	952	1038			
2. Percentage male	750	878	1002			
3. Percentage female	647	675	662			473
4. Percentage males, aged 15–44	672	793	922			
5. Percentage males, aged 45	551	613	651			
6. Percentage females, aged 15–44	532	535	498			379
7. Percentage females, aged 45	310	283	271			369
8. Percentage single	803	854	901			
9. Percentage married	535	713	828			
10. Percentage foreign-born	259	367	451	316		
11. Percentage native-born	733	802	841			251
12. Percentage chronic cases	688	874	994			
Population structure						
13. Percentage males, aged 15–44					290	
14. Percentage males, aged 45						
15. Percentage females, aged 15–44					440	
16. Percentage females, aged 45						
17. Percentage single persons	652	297		435		634
18. Percentage married persons	661	296		448		636
19. Percentage divorced persons	521	281		557	428	
20. Percentage single mobile	555			737		
21. Percentage married mobile						
22. Percentage foreign-born, 'white'	623	313		265	433	
23. Percentage foreign-born, 'coloured'	587			539	270	
Socioeconomic						
24. Percentage males in Classes I/II					251	
25. Percentage males in Class V	403				557	
26. Percentage unemployed	536	405	335		507	
27. Percentage households with car	545				497	
Household tenure						
28. Percentage owner occupied	402					
29. Percentage from Local authority	459				811	
30. Percentage rented, furnished	639			997		
31. Percentage rented, unfurnished	511				1102	

Households and housing

32. Percentage households sharing amenities	613			<u>1019</u>
33. Percentage outside W.C.	490		338	<u>1056</u>
34. Percentage households sharing a dwelling	647		1058	
35. Percentage multi-dwellings	529	278	334	
36. Average rooms per dwellings	561		<u>905</u>	
37. Percentage households in 1–3 rooms	645		1102	302
38. Average persons per room				296
39. Average persons per household	380	260	<u>597</u>	
40. Percentage single-person households	767	329	513	<u>248</u>

Location

41. Distance from Market Square	<u>701</u>	<u>336</u>		623

Note. Factors II and V have been omitted from the Promax solution.
Reproduced by permission of the Institute of British Geographers from J. A. Giggs, 1973, Table 2, p. 64.
Significant loadings and pattern coefficients are shown (1.0 per cent. level); negative values are underlined.

was, however, some variation by sub-group and the figures for foreign-born and married patients were 99 per cent. and 64 per cent. respectively. These sub-group variations do, of course, reflect general ecological structure; a very small proportion of the foreign-born population, for example, would live more than four kilometres from the city centre. Concluding that the regular spatial patterns could not have occurred by chance, Giggs examined the relationships between twelve schizophrenic variables and a set of social environmental variables (all except one of the latter abstracted from the 1966 census), all of which were recorded by enumeration districts. Giggs used factor analysis in a manner which has become typical of most ecological studies of deviance data. His justification for this approach was that his objective was to identify the underlying structure from the relationships among many variables, that the investigation was exploratory and that it allowed common variance to be isolated. Table 3.1 summarizes the main results from this approach for Primary, Varimax and Promax factors.

The leading factor shows (from Primary through Varimax to Promax solutions) an increasingly simple structure, in which relationships between measures of schizophrenia and other variables in the input are polarized. In the Primary factor solution, the twenty-seven variables with positive loadings include the set of twelve schizophrenic variables and fifteen social-environmental attributes which have been shown (either singly or in groups) to have significant association with the disorder in previous studies. A Varimax rotation, which kept the constraints of orthogonality while retaining the twelve schizophrenic variables, reduced the significant loadings on the other set to eight. The Promax solution again retained the initial twelve variables but only two other variables (percentage unemployed and average persons per household) were associated with the factor. This was described as a schizophrenic dimension *par excellence*. Mapping of factor scores allowed spatial patterns to be identified and enumeration districts with high schizophrenic rates were mainly concentrated in a single region of central Nottingham.

From the evidence of the pattern coefficients (Table 3.1), the schizophrenic variables have little direct involvement in the remaining factors, which are dimensions of more general ecological structure. Schizophrenic variables only load significantly onto factor III (described as an urbanism/familism dimension) and factor VI, in which several schizophrenic variables load negatively as does the percentage of married persons. As the Promax solution allows inter-correlations between factors to be identified, however, strong associations between factor I and factor III and between factor I and factor IV (rented housing/housing amenities) were evident. The oblique solution therefore isolated the key variables on each factor and showed which factors were highly correlated.

This analysis of schizophrenia in Nottingham provides an example of recent research by geographers based upon aggregate statistics for deviance. Its findings were not novel, but served to confirm established generalizations on the spatial patterning of incidence rates and their statistical associations. It is unlikely that analyses of this kind can proceed much further in terms of the investigations of the causal bases of the form of deviance being studied; to this extent the factor analytic model limits us to the more basic geographic roles of identifying patterns. Factor analysis as a set of techniques may be most appropriate at an initial stage of analysis, when broad patterns of association can be identified. The more detailed specification of relationships requires other statistical models, such as regression, perhaps proceeding from the factorial ecological stage at which an orthogonal set of independent variables had been identified. Examples of these alternative, or complementary, statistical strategies will be given in the context of delinquency studies, but some comments on the scope of spatial analysis of mental illness may be appropriate.

Schizophrenia is an example of a psychotic form of mental disorder for which no clear causal explanation exist. Although the social environment of the individual may be shown to form part of an explanation, the more traditional view would suggest that genetic and biological factors are responsible. It is upon the validity of the social environmental factors that an analysis of spatial qualities rests. A substantial amount of research of the kind described for Nottingham has identified patterns of association at the aggregate scale and, more recently, access to case histories has allowed some of the generalizations to be tested at the micro-scale (Taylor, 1974). The stance adopted by Giggs (1973, p. 60) is probably correct: 'Our field of enquiry is necessarily confined to the analysis of potential relationships between variations in the incidence of schizophrenia and attributes of the social environmental milieu since the role of constitutional factors cannot yet be assessed.' If this contribution is limited, it is nevertheless valuable, as the aggregate scale is that at which policies have to be formed and administrative decisions have to be made. Giggs (1975) has argued that 'good' social and urban environments reduce the incidence of psychoses and urban renewal may be a form of preventive medicine. Spatial analyses of many forms of mental illness have not been made and the extent to which other disorders resemble the ecological features of schizophrenia is not known.

SUICIDE

Suicide has clear behavioural connotations, although it often may be linked with some kind of mental disorder. As a form of deviance, therefore, it provides a point on the continuum between what might be termed 'involuntary' and 'voluntary' characteristics. Most work in the social sciences on suicide still takes as a point of reference the treatise of Durkheim (1951), in which he formed a theory which rested upon the role of social factors. The argument advanced in support of this theory has wide relevance. An essential distinction was suggested between the explanation of variations in suicide *rates*, expressed for groups or areas, and the aetiology of any individual act. Individual case histories allow specific causes to be identified, but these do not necessarily allow statistical distributions of suicide to be explained. Empirical facts which were known about incidence rates allowed greater probabilities to be attached to the occurrence of acts of suicide in particular population sub-groups and particular areas. Henry and Short (1957, p. 63), for example, stated:

> The suicide rate is higher in the central disorganized sectors of cities than in outlying residential areas; it is higher in cities than in rural areas; it is higher for the single, widowed, and divorced than for the married; and, finally, it is higher for the old than for the young.

Suicide as a form of deviance, therefore, has an ecological basis for which spatial and social correlates can be identified.

As with several types of deviance, causes of suicide are imperfectly understood and a multi-factor solution is likely; main texts review a wide range of theories (e.g. Douglas, 1967). Attempts to identify social factors which are associated with suicide are particularly hazardous; low socioeconomic status and poverty which frequently correspond with incidence rates for deviance are much more ambiguous in the suicide case. Sainsbury (1955) analysed suicide rates and a range of social characteristics for the London boroughs, or their near equivalents, and found that highest suicide rates tended to occur in middle-class areas. Maris (1969) found that Chicago's high rate areas were typically populated by slightly more educated and higher income inhabitants, and were over-represented in white-collar workers. An early survey by Stearns (1921) found that 65 per cent. of suicides were well-to-do. Sainsbury (1955) did, however, investigate the actual economic status of suicides at the time of their death and found that the proportion in poverty was much higher. Status change or loss of status might therefore have been a more meaningful indicator than objective social class position (Douglas, 1967; Sainsbury, 1955).

Attempts to relate unemployment levels to suicide rates have been inconclusive. Maris (1969) found fewer unemployed in high suicide rate areas; Sainsbury (1955) identified a much higher suicide rate amongst the unemployed than amongst the corresponding employed population, but thought that economic upheaval was the common factor to both unemployment and suicide. As a concept, isolation has been an attractive potential correlate of suicide; studies have frequently linked high suicide rates to lodging house areas with their transient, lone occupants (Cavan, 1928). Sainsbury (1955) developed an index of solitary living and showed that, in London, high suicide rates corresponded with those boroughs in which the most opportunities for solitary living occurred. Other studies have linked social isolation with the problems of the elderly (Batchelor, 1957). Mobility is also viewed as a factor which promotes social and cultural isolation and links between suicide and mobility were hypothesized in Minneapolis (Schmid, 1939) and in London (Sainsbury, 1955).

Most studies of suicide rates in large cities have demonstrated a clustering of high scores in parts of the central city—a pattern reminiscent of many other forms of deviance. 'Besides suicide, rates of divorce, delinquency, drug addiction and certain forms of mental illness tend to find a peak in such areas' (Giddens, 1971, p. 243). Maris (1969) was able to depict the spatial patterning of suicide for Chicago from 1959 to 1963, and to compare it with the earlier work of Cavan (1928). A concentration of high rates in the Loop and the central-city areas of North and West Side has persisted over time; by 1959 sectors were discernible, particularly along Lake Michigan. Near South Side, which had high scores in 1928, had much lower rates in 1959, a decrease which Maris attributed to greater numbers of Negro population. Sainsbury's (1955) study of London allowed spatial patterns to be identified for three time periods in the first half of the twentieth century. Figure 3.3 shows the distribution of high suicide rates, taken as those more than one standard deviation above the mean, for 1919–23, 1929–33 and 1940–44. Five central-city districts to the north of the Thames obtain high scores for each time period; these are City, Holborn, Westminster, Paddington and Hampstead. St. Marylebone scored highly in 1919 to 1923 but not subsequently, while Chelsea obtained a high score in the last period. Taking suicide rates over all the boroughs, correlation coefficients showed a high level of stability in the spatial pattern. Between 1919–23 and 1929–33, the coefficient was 0.91; between 1929–33 and 1940–44, it was 0.84. In both cases, therefore, a highly significant relationship could be identified but one which had diminished over time. This latter fact was confirmed by a coefficient between 1919–23 and 1940–44 of 0.77. A detailed exposition of the social characteristics of high suicide rate areas is provided by Sainsbury (1955), but there is good evidence that suicide rates are amenable to analysis in spatial terms.

CRIME AND DELINQUENCY

Crime and delinquency are perhaps the most obvious examples of deviance. An individual becomes deviant because he disregards a set of rules for behaviour

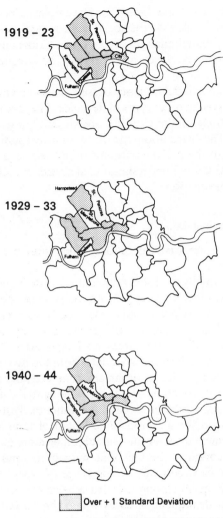

FIGURE 3.3 Suicide in London, 1919–44. At each of three time periods the above average rates of suicide occur in closely similar parts of the city. (Reproduced by permission of P. Sainsbury and the Institute of Psychiatry, from Sansbury, 1955)

which society has prescribed. Any general consensus about the explanation for these forms of deviance is conspicuously absent in the very considerable literature (e.g. Mannheim, 1965). The main dichotomy is between theories based upon genetic factors and those based upon the social environment. Both sets of theories must continue to be regarded as tenable and the recent support for a multi-factor theory of causality would provide sufficient flexibility to accommodate them (Wilkins, 1961–62). The emphasis has shifted, however, to those theories which relate to the social environment, and it is only in the context of these that spatial analyses are credible. Crime and delinquency are legally defined forms of deviance and can only be adequately studied in a societal context.

Most types of crime and delinquency possess the same kind of spatial order which has been observed in other types of deviance. They are highly concentrated in particular districts of the city, but are virtually absent in the majority of residential areas. The distributions also have persistent statistical associations with other qualities of the social environment and once again the evidence of spatial order suggests that an understanding of spatial qualities will contribute towards a broader explanation.

Problems of definition and data

There are several general considerations which must preface any study of crime and delinquency.

1. The distinction normally made between crime and delinquency is in terms of the age of offenders; delinquency refers to adolescent offenders and groups under the age of twenty are usually discussed. Differences between crime and delinquency may be particularly relevant to spatial analyses, as it has been contended that crime areas no longer exist (Mack, 1964). The assumption here is that the adult criminal is both too diverse and too mobile to be associated with particular urban environments, but this may be over-generalized and for petty criminals, at least, the spatial clusters may persist. Juvenile delinquents, on the other hand, are more likely to have lived in the same neighbourhood for a considerable length of time and the effects of the social environment upon the individual can be more realistically studied. A related point concerns the fact that both crime and delinquency are general terms and each contains a wide range of types of offence. Studies of both must distinguish among these various categories, but the problem is less pressing in delinquent offences where the range is less and many forms of misbehaviour are relatively minor.

2. A further important distinction must be made between delinquency occurrence—the locations at which offences occur—and delinquency residences—the places where offenders live. There are spatial qualities attached to both occurrence and residence which, although not mutually exclusive, have significant differences between them. Delinquency occurrence can be analysed in terms of factors such as opportunities, access and observability; delinquency-prone environments are those in which there are high numbers of accessible targets. Delinquency residence studies emphasize the social environments and neighbourhoods which may be delinquency-producing or-conditioning. The delinquency area concept is better understood in the context of residence of offenders; delinquency areas are identified through spatial concentrations of residence and the hypothesis must be that the individual in these areas is more likely to turn to delinquent behaviour than

in other areas. Some would argue that delinquency areas are best regarded as clusters of both offences and offenders (Schmid, 1960), but it is contended here that occurrence and residence are best viewed—at least initially—as separate fields of study.

3. The reliability of available data is a problem in all studies of deviance and is particularly so in the context of delinquency and crime. Data bases are certainly not complete and the working assumption of studies—that they possess a representative sample—is certainly open to question. One problem for delinquency residence studies is that police detection rates are comparatively low, the average being about 40 per cent. (McClintock and Avison, 1968), and analyses are thus based upon partial information. An advantage of delinquency occurrence studies is that the data base is more complete, as the police know a great deal more about the location of offences than of offenders. Added to the loss of information through non-detection is what criminologists (McClintock and Avison, 1968) have termed the 'dark area', which affects knowledge about both occurrence and residence. This term describes offences which either never come to the notice of the police or are not officially proceeded with, Estimates of the dimensions of this 'dark area' are, of course, very difficult to form with any accuracy. Problems with data discussed so far indicate a reduction in the information upon which analyses may be based; the remaining key problem is whether the available information can be regarded as representative. The view that police-reporting of delinquency is biased against the children of lower income groups finds strong support in the literature (Mays, 1968). The evidence cannot be regarded as conclusive, but it is a credible proposition that middle-class parents would be more readily regarded as being capable of imposing their own sanctions for misbehaviour. If the evidence was conclusive, it would indicate that official statistics provide a biased sample, but the case for strong bias likely to give misleading results is not substantiated and analyses can justifiably proceed with the data which is available.

Patterns of crime occurrence

Crime or delinquency occurrence has received limited attention in the established literature and the tendency has not been to distinguish it as a separate field of study. Schmid (1960, p. 657) took the view that, 'In defining delinquency or crime areas, it is important to know not only where offenders live but also where crimes are committed'. There is a case to the effect that occurrence and residence may coincide (areas of delinquency residence are also those in which most delinquent acts are committed), but exceptions are frequent; the central business district (C.B.D.), for example, with very high rates of offences against property is a non-residential area. It is suggested, therefore, that initially separate analyses offer a better research strategy. Spatial analyses concerned specifically with occurrence rates have demonstrated variations amongst categories of offence.

Schmid (1960) looked at cheque fraud and female drunkenness offences in

Seattle and found that the C.B.D., was the locus for the former and Skid Row for the latter. Schmid (1960, p. 676) interpreted this as a contrast between offences against property and offences against morality and concluded that 'The higher frequency of certain types of crime in one milieu than in another may be merely a reflection of greater opportunities, profitableness and other conditions favourable for committing such crime'. Schmid calculated occurrence rates against the resident populations in small areas, but Sarah L. Boggs (1965) has argued that these are better calculated against the number of targets at risk. Using the example of St. Louis in 1960, she showed that rates specific to opportunities revealed marked differences from those calculated on a population base. A factor analytic procedure identified several dimensions of crime occurrence which included familiarity between offenders and their targets and the profitability of particular target areas. Boggs also showed that for some offences—homicide, aggravated assault and residential burglary—occurrence did coincide closely with known delinquency residence.

Several recent research projects by geographers in American cities have been concerned with occurrence rates and with the analysis of the identified spatial patterns (e.g. Phillips, 1972). In general terms, most studies have tended to confirm the broad spatial pattern of high central-city and low periphery scores. The pattern varies with type of offence, however, and Cybriwsky and Ley (1973) have attempted to explain rather than to describe the spatial qualities of one specific occurrence rate. Their main argument was that the types of spaces in which offences were most likely to occur could be defined in a systematic way: (Cybriwsky and Ley, 1973, p. 7):

> The stronger the territorial control of the local society, the more completely will non-social and criminal behaviour be confined to spaces where there is no surveillance. Deviant behaviour makes its own bid for space and this bid, we hypothesise, finds its location in the power vacua of socially claimed space.

Using the example of cars which had been abandoned and subsequently stripped of useful parts, Cybriwsky and Ley (1973) found that they occurred in specific types of location. Their typology of spaces for this offence included institutional land and vacant lots and other spaces which were unclaimed, often at the interstices of local control systems. Although the example could be regarded as a statement of the obvious, the approach has conceptual merit and demonstrates ways in which the susceptibility of areas to offences may be systematically analysed.

Other recent studies have examined the relationship between location of offence and offender's residence. This places the emphasis upon spatial interaction and accessibility between delinquency-prone and delinquent-producing environments. It has been suggested in a study of Phoenix (Haring, 1972), for example, that the average distance from residence to the point of crime commission differed significantly over types of offence. Further, where barriers such as rivers or freeways intervened, the patterns were significantly affected.

A different type of study by Ley (1972) in North Philadelphia examined individuals perceptions of unsafe parts of the city and the effects of these upon travel patterns. People tended to make considerable detours to avoid unsafe areas, depending upon the way in which they perceived them. It is clear that there is considerable scope for the spatial analyses of crime occurrence and that delinquency- or crime-prone environments can be defined. While the literature on residential differentiation is not directly relevant to occurrence patterns, there are types of offence where occurrence and residence do coincide spatially, and also approaches which examine the links between offender and offence.

Crime and delinquency residence: development of studies and some aspects of theory

Most of the available analyses of delinquency residence data were produced by social ecologists, and criminologocal studies formed an important facet of the work on Chicago in the 1920s and 1930s. Shaw and McKay (1942, revised 1969) provided systematic frameworks for the ecological study of crime and delinquency patterns and formalized basic techniques such as delinquency rates and concepts such as the gradient principle. Major empirical observations from their work were that crime and delinquency rates declined in a regular progression from city centre to periphery and that concentric zonal generalizations could be made of the spatial form of the distributions. In the American cities which they studied, Shaw and McKay observed a recurrent set of crime correlates which included substandard housing, poverty, foreign-born population and mobility. Crime rates were highest in the central districts of poverty and physical deterioration (often with transient populations) and were the lowest in the stable, family suburbs. To a considerable extent, both the spatial generalizations and the ecological correlates of crime and delinquency residence which were identified by Shaw and McKay have remained stable over time in American cities (Schmid, 1960). That they are culture-specific and reflect a particular form of urban ecological structure is shown by the divergences from the American prototype which occur in other parts of the world. Distribution of crime and delinquency residence in Britain, for example, reveal clusters in peripheral as well as in central districts of the city (Morris, 1957); neither simple gradients nor zonal generalizations have any useful application. The basic distorting factor would appear to be the public sector intervention in the British housing market, which in the process of transferring population groups from city centre to periphery has also transferred their behaviour patterns (see Figure 3.4). This evidence suggests that it is not urban environments *per se* but social characteristics of the group which are the 'real' correlates of delinquent behaviour. Beyond a few Western countries, the extent to which cross-cultural comparisons can be made in limited because of the lack of basic data and detailed analyses do not exist for many parts of the world.

Shaw and McKay (1942) recognized that the identification of statistical correlates did not necessarily imply a causal relationship. They concluded that

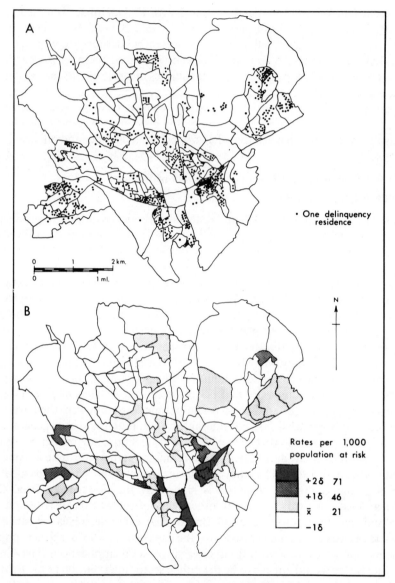

FIGURE 3.4   Rates of delinquency residence in Cardiff, 1971. Data from the Social Services Department has been used to show: A. the distribution of delinquents and B. the rates of delinquency by enumeration districts. (Reproduced by permission of the Editor *Town Planning Review*)

the correlates were symptomatic, as was delinquency itself, of an underlying state of disorder. Their concept of social disorganization suggested that the absence of a stable social group, with legalistically based behaviour codes and established norms and values, promoted the conditions under which crime and delinquency thrived. As a theory, social disorganization lacked generality, as it failed to account for the fact that there may well be social order in central-city slums and cohesion within delinquent groups. The deviant sub-culture theory, which is particularly associated with Cohen (1955) and Mays (1963), suggested that within population sub-groups there were accepted norms of behaviour which were at odds with those of society as a whole. Delinquency may typify the members of some groups to the extent that it is a normal form of activity and part of the internal social system. Although there is no theoretical reason why a deviant sub-culture of this type should be defined in spatial terms, major studies have inevitably been concerned with particular districts of the city. It is therefore one of the principal derivative theories from criminology which may be employed in a spatial analysis.

A persistent difficulty with the deviant sub-culture concept and, indeed, with all theories which rest upon the social environment, is that they cannot easily be used to explain individual differences. The worst social environments will contain individuals, usually a significant proportion of the total adolescent population, who never become delinquent. Group-based theories are thus susceptible to criticism and must always be stated in terms of probabilities. A rejoinder, nevertheless, can be made in terms of the quality of data on 'known' offenders. Comparatively low detection rates and a certain amount of un-reported delinquency may contribute to the fact that high rates of delinquency are hidden and the exceptions may be much fewer than is apparent. An example of an approach which has flexibility to allow for individual differences was that advanced by Cloward and Ohlin (1960). They argued that the situation in which the individual had to react was multi-faceted; discontent might spring from restricted access to normal and legal avenues of progress, but delinquent behaviour would also be influenced by the availability of illegal opportunities. Within each of the sets of influences, legitimate and illegitimate, there were a number of key elements such as family, neighbourhood and school, each of which is variable and any one may become the dominant influence. A strong parent, for example, may act as a socializing force to offset the deleterious effect of a bad neighbourhood.

Although criminological studies have produced many theories of explanation for delinquent behaviour (Mannheim, 1965), none of these have been universally accepted and relatively little consensus of opinion exists. In common with other fields of deviance study, the recent trend has been to suggest that explanations are not single-stranded and a multi-factor solution should be preferred. In its broadest form, a multi-factor explanation would include measurement of the physical and mental makeup of the individual as well as of the social environ-ment of which he is part (Glueck and Glueck, 1950, 1952). Individual physical traits and somato-types cannot easily be part of any spatially organized theory of delinquent behaviour, which rests upon the assumption that the observed spatial order of delinquency patterns is paralleled by systematic variations of key elements in the social environment. Acceptance of a multi-factor solution implies that no general theory is adequate and where partial explanations are required a spatially based perspective is as attractive as any other.

Analyses of aggregate statistics

Most criminological studies which include an analysis of spatial patterns of crime and delinquency residence data have been based upon aggregate statistics for small areas. These studies have varied considerably in terms of levels of statistical sophistication and rigour. A basic approach involving the calculation of relationships between delinquency rates and other individual variables was followed in a study by Wallis and Maliphant (1967). Their data set comprised 350 delinquent boys and rates per 1 000 male population aged 17 to 20 years were calculated for forty-six areas in Greater London; for the main correlative analysis, these were reduced to twenty-nine boroughs in order to compare directly with census data. There are obviously considerable hazards in basing a statistical analysis upon data of these qualities; use of boroughs as a territorial base must inevitably have obscured many details of the spatial pattern. Rank-order correlation coefficients were calculated between the delinquency rate and each of the other variables; highest correlations were with overcrowding, substandardness, population decline, increasing numbers of non-whites and a predominance of manual workers.

Simple correlative exercises of this kind, particularly when based upon such a thin data base, are as likely to produce misleading results as they are to provide positive guidelines. Most analyses have turned to multivariate techniques and to more suitable statistical models. Schmid (1960) provided an example of a factor analytic model which incorporated crime variables with a set of census variables. This approach closely resembled that used by Giggs (1973) in his analysis of schizophrenia and will not be described in further detail. Schmid (1960) collected data for the city of Seattle in the period 1949–51 and the crime set comprised 35 000 offences and 30 000 arrests. There were twenty crime variables and eighteen measures of demographic, socioeconomic and housing characteristics. Results which were discussed were obtained from an orthogonal rotation of the eight leading factors derived from a principal axes factor analysis. The leading three factors were described successively as 'low social cohesion and low family status', 'low social cohesion and low occupational status' and 'low family and economic status'. Factor 3 which had high loadings on many crime variables (Table 3.2) was described by Schmid as a crime dimension *par excellence*. Schmid (1960, p. 678) concluded that 'Urban crime areas, including areas where criminals reside and areas where crimes are committed, are generally characterised by all or most of the following factors: low social cohesion, weak family life, low socio-economic status, physical deterioration, high rates of population mobility and personal disorganization'. He recognized the fallabilities of available crime data and stressed that ecological analysis was designed to demonstrate statistical association rather than causality.

Factor analytic techniques were used by Lander (1954) in his well-known study of Baltimore, but he also employed partial correlation and regression techniques. Partial correlation coefficients allow the effects of each independent variable to be measured while others are held constant. Potentially, therefore, this approach provides stronger support for any inferences drawn

TABLE 3.2 Urban crime dimensions in Seattle

Variable name	No.	Reactor			
		I	II	III	IV
Crime					
Suicide, attempted	1	0.426		0.565	0.633
Suicide, completed	2	0.593		0.325	
Drunkenness	3			0.932	
Drunkenness, common	4			0.937	
Disorderly conduct, lighting	5		0.328	0.906	
Disorderly conduct, other	6		0.313	0.904	
Vagrancy	7			0.936	
Lewdness	8			0.932	
Indecent exposure	9	0.476			
Larceny, petty	10			0.917	
Shoplifting	11	0.386		0.438	0.748
Bicycle theft	12				
Automatic theft	13	0.591			0.551
Theft from automobile	14	0.498		0.648	0.483
Fraud, cheque	15	0.319		0.430	0.828
Burglary, residence, day	16			0.744	0.580
Burglary, residence, night	17			0.644	0.706
Burglary, non-residential	18		0.315		
Robbery, highway and car	19		0.312	0.905	
Robbery, non-residential	20	0.349			
Social, economic and demographic					
Population change, 1940–50	21	−0.777			
Sex, percentage male	22		0.514	0.782	
Percentage 60 years and over	23	0.873			
Percentage foreign-born, white	24	0.650	0.322		
Percentage Negro	25		0.535		
Percentage married	26	−0.909		−0.375	
Fertility ratio	27	−0.930			
Median income	28	−0.755	−0.531		
Percentage of dwellings with television	29	−0.806	−0.490		
Median grade completed (education)	30	−0.349	−0.872		
Percentage professional workers	31		−0.943		
Percentage proprietors, managers, etc.	32	−0.320	−0.851		
Percentage labourers	33		0.959		
Percentage females in labour force	34	0.938			
Percentage unemployed	35	0.498	0.519	0.647	
Mobility, in different country, 1949–50	36	0.546			0.460
Housing, percentage owner-occupied	37	−0.798			
Housing, percentage built before 1920	38	0.886	0.378		

Orthogonal rotation solution: only loadings $\geq$ 0.3 are shown for the leading four factors.
Reproduced by permission of the American Sociological Association, from C. F. Schmid, *American Sociological Review*, vol. **25** (1960), p. 536.

TABLE 3.3 Statistical correlates of delinquency rates in Baltimore

	Zero-order correlation	Partial correlation	Index of partial correlation
Median school years completed	−0.51	0.0055	0.0370
Median monthly rent	−0.53	0.0003	0.0109
Percentage overcrowded homes	+0.73	0.0079	0.0090
Percentage non-white	+0.70	0.0086	0.1229
Percentage substandard homes	+0.69	0.0052	0.0000
Percentage foreign-born	−0.16	0.0213	0.0000
Percentage owner-occupiers	−0.80	0.1764	0.2438

Reproduced by permission of the Columbia University Press, from B. Lander, 1954, Tables IX and X, p. 46.

in causal terms. Lander was also concerned with procedures for testing the linearity of the relationship between each pair of variables and with correcting for non-linear patterns. His pairwise measures of associations comprised zero-order correlations, partial correlations and indices of partial correlation which were corrected for non-linearity. There are marked differences in apparent levels of association over the three measures in Table 3.3, and Lander regarded the index of partial correlation as the most accurate. As shown by scores in the last column in Table 3.3, overcrowding, substandardness and foreign-born variables are left with little or no influence and non-white and owner-occupiers form the most influential variables.

Lander (1954) also calculated regression coefficients which allowed measures of the extent to which delinquency rates were dependent on, controlled by or a consequence of other variables. Beta coefficients, the final indices adopted, included a correction for variation in the initial units of measurement. Again only two variables, the percentages of non-white and owner-occupiers, held statistically significant relationships with the rates of juvenile delinquency. The index of determination indicated that 72 per cent. of the variance in delinquency rates could be accounted for on the basis of these two variables.

From the evidence of his statistical analysis, Lander (1954, p. 89) was able to proceed to the hypothesis that an explanation of the variation in delinquency rates was found in the concept of anomie: 'When the group norms are no longer binding or valid in an area or for a population sub-group in so far is individual behaviour likely to lead to deviant behaviour.' In Baltimore, Lander found that the delinquency rate increased as the percentage of Negro residents approached 50 per cent., but declined thereafter. In completely Negro areas, the delinquency rates were no higher than in white areas, and maximum social instability occurred in areas in which the two racial groups approached equality in numbers. This he took as empirical evidence for the validity of the anomie hypothesis. Lander's work has been quoted principally as a methodological example, but it should be noted that the Baltimore study has been criticized both on the grounds of numerical accuracy and also in terms of the validity of its anomie hypothesis (Chilton, 1964). There was some doubt regarding the allocation of signs in the factor analysis stage of Lander's study; Chilton suggested that the signs of the loadings for four of the eight variables—delinquency, overcrowding, non-white and substandard housing—were incorrectly listed. Again, Lander had argued that variables measuring proportions of owner-occupance and non-white population in census tracts could be used as indicators of anomie; whether such a complex sociological concept can be approximated in terms of these variables is doubtful.

A further example of a multivariate procedure which may provide a better statistical model than factor analysis is given by Elizabeth Gittus and C. J. Stephens (1973) in their application of canonical analysis to Schmid's (1960) data set for Seattle. Schmid's purpose had been to identify the underlying social-demographic dimensions in the distribution of crime, and he processed his twenty crime and eighteen social–economic–demographic variables in a single principal axes factor analysis. While the Varimax rotation was intended to enhance the interpretability of the dimensions, it had the effect of separating the two data sets used in Schmid's case study, rendering the designation of crime areas a hazardous procedure. Gittus and Stephens (1973) argued that canonical analysis might have been used in order to maximize the correlations between the canonical Y (crime) and X (social–economic–demographic) variates. Canonical analysis has the over-riding advantage of preserving the distinction between the two data sets; it may be likened to multiple regression as a procedure, but with canonical analysis the dependent variable is no longer a single index but a linear combination of indices from the dependent set.

The procedure adopted by Gittus and Stephens (1973) involved separate factor analyses of each data set and a canonical analysis which used factor scores as input. This had the advantages of reducing the dimensions of the analysis, allowing control over the data set and—because of the orthogonality constraint on factors—removing the problems caused by intercorrelations among the origin of variables. Table 3.4 summarized the results from this application of canonical analysis to Schmid's data using scores from the leading five crime factors and the leading eight social–economic–demographic factors. The dominance of the first pair of canonical variates, as evidenced by the percentage of variance accounted for, is striking, but the remaining less important pairs cannot be dismissed in any interpretation.

From Table 3.4, the character of the canonical variates can be interpreted in terms of the original input variables. Most of the crime variables are highly associated with the first canonical variate and the social dimension is highly positively linked with males and unemployed. This is described as a persistent correlation of high crime rates with low socioeconomic status and low family status. The second pair of canonical variates shows for crime a moderate positive correlation with completed suicides, car thefts, bicycle thefts and violations of non-residential property and low correlations on all arrests excepting indecent exposure. Social variables involved suggested low family status and the run-down areas of poor housing on the edge of the C.B.D. The third pair of canonical variates linked violations of non-residential property

TABLE 3.4 Canonical analysis of Schmid's Seattle data. Correlations in each set between canonical variates and input indices

Index No.	Crime $Y(c)_k$ $K=1$	2	3	4	Index No.	Social-economic-demographic $(X(c)_k$ $K=1$	2	3	4
1	0.81	−0.02	−0.08	0.47	21	−0.25	−0.58	−0.44	0.10
2	0.79	0.32	−0.14	−0.01	22	0.83	−0.42	0.08	0.04
3	0.86	−0.41	0.11	−0.17	23	0.68	0.41	0.02	−0.21
4	0.76	−0.49	0.14	−0.31	24	0.55	0.41	0.07	−0.01
5	0.85	−0.38	0.23	−0.08	25	0.26	−0.01	0.78*	−0.08
6	0.86	−0.37	0.19	−0.17	26	−0.80	−0.35	0.02	−0.01
7	0.81	−0.45	0.17	−0.24	27	−0.40	−0.70	0.06	−0.10
8	0.86	−0.41	0.15	−0.08	28	−0.73	−0.36	−0.18	0.05
9	0.11	0.58*	0.18	−0.07	29	−0.60	−0.44	−0.21	0.06
10	0.88	−0.35	0.09	−0.16	30	−0.64	−0.15	−0.40	0.19
11	0.60	0.09	0.12	0.54	31	−0.36	−0.32	−0.28	0.20
12	−0.31	0.22	0.14	−0.12	32	−0.39	−0.28	−0.03	0.21
13	0.73	0.40	−0.24	0.24	33	0.43	0.24	0.42	−0.13
14	0.91*	0.03	−0.05	0.28	34	0.38	0.77*	−0.22	0.00
15	0.64	0.03	−0.15	0.68*	35	0.94*	−0.01	0.13	−0.18
16	0.75	−0.27	0.05	0.46	36	0.45	0.18	−0.27	0.68*
17	0.68	−0.20	0.03	0.60	37	−0.73	−0.48	0.08	0.01
18	−0.11	0.43	0.71	−0.02	38	−0.57	−0.49	−0.27	−0.14
19	0.88	−0.34	0.16	−0.05					
20	0.26	0.20	0.79*	−0.08					

	Y 1	2	3	4	5	1–5	X 1	2	3	4	5	1–5
Percentage variation within set	52	11	8	10	8	89	35	18	8	4	6	71
Percentage variance between sets	45	4	3	1	1	55	31	7	3	0.5	0.5	41

Correlations ρ between $Y(c)_k$ and $X(c)_k$
$K = 1$ (0.935); 2 (0.617); 3 (0.611); 4 (0.403).
*Highest correlation with each variate.
Reproduced by permission of E. Gittus and C. J. Stephens, 1973.

with Negroes and labourers; the fourth pair associated cheque fraud, shoplifting and residential burglary with high levels of mobility in the population group. Although Gittus and Stephens (1973) had reservations on the value of this type of statistical analysis, their claim that canonical analysis provided a clearer, more coherent and consistent picture of Schmid's data set has considerable strength. The procedure allows the systematic investigation of relationships between dimensions of crime and urban social structure. Whereas a mixed input of crime and other variables to single-factor analyses may reveal patterns of association, the amount of control given by canonical analysis is a major advantage. A disadvantage of the procedure is that interpretation of results can be difficult, particularly if the initial factors are not simply structured.

The series of methodologies which have been discussed illustrate ways in which the ecological correlates of deviance can be identified. Such procedures provide valuable guidelines for more detailed research and for public policy, but, although having intrinsic value, they are formed upon inferential statistics. Most studies of this kind depend upon available published sources of data which contain no information upon attitudes or forms of behaviour. While the statistical models can be improved by more sophisticated use of regression techniques, for example, which allow specific relationships to be investigated, they can also be linked in a systematic way to research at other scales. This last objective may be achieved by using aggregate analysis as a framework from which to proceed to more detailed study at the scale of the individual. A recent research project in Cardiff (Herbert and Evans, 1973) will be used as an example of this latter approach.

Area sampling frameworks and analyses of attitudes and behaviour

The well-established methodologies in social geography for social area analysis and factorial ecology have provided the bases for many detailed studies of residential differentiation in cities (Herbert, 1972; Johnston, 1971). An original objective of social area analysis, in particular, was that it should form a framework of areas from which particular types could be selected for more detailed study. There is a literature which provides examples of this type of approach both in general behavioural studies (Bell and Boat, 1957; Bell and Force, 1956) and in the field of deviance (Polk, 1967; Quinney, 1964). In the Cardiff study, a number of standard procedures, principal components analysis and cluster analysis, were used to establish an area sampling framework. Forty variables calculated from the 1966 census were recorded for 119 enumeration districts in the city; scores from the five leading components, which could be labelled as social class, life-cycle and tenure, substandardness, tenure and housing quality, formed the input to a cluster analysis program. The classification of enumeration districts so obtained formed one basis for the selection of six districts in which detailed social surveys could be conducted. A second basis was obtained by calculating the delinquency residence rates for each enumeration district of the city using data from the local authority (Herbert and Evans, 1974). By this area sampling procedure, therefore, aggregate data could be used as an initial stage and the areas selected for survey could be seen in a comparative framework of residential differentiation in the city (Figure 3.5).

Six enumeration districts were selected for detailed investigation; these formed convenient statistical units and were representative of neighbourhood types. Three of the selected districts had high rates of delinquency residence and were regarded as 'delinquency areas'; they comprised one terraced row district near the city centre and two peripheral local authority estates. The other three districts had low rates of delinquency residence and comprised one terraced row district, a local authority estate and a private suburb. Figure 3.5 shows the location of these selected districts in the city. The two terraced row districts were similar in all measurable qualities from the cluster analysis classification based upon census data, but were contrasted in terms of the

114

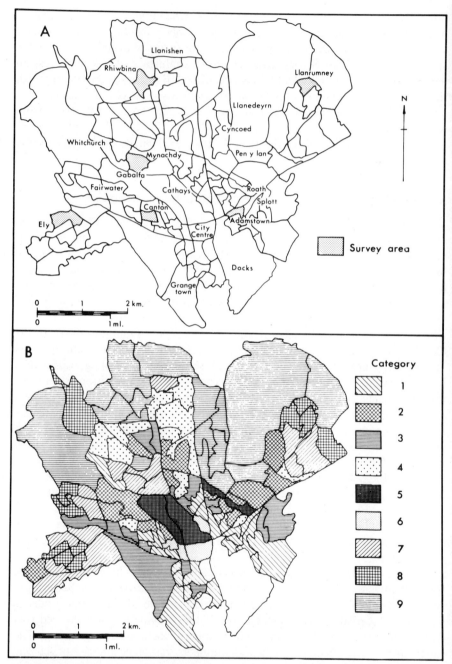

FIGURE 3.5 Survey areas and urban-social structure in Cardiff. A. Six areas chosen by area sampling procedures are identified, three of which had high delinquency rates. B. Cluster analysis has been used to classify enumeration districts on the bases of social, economic and demographic variables (see D. T. Herbert and D. J. Evans, 1974)

incidence of delinquency; the three local authority estates fell within the same cluster analysis group, but one was non-delinquent; the non-delinquent private suburb provided a contrast in terms of social class. Within each of the selected enumeration districts, a random sampling procedure was followed to choose individual dwellings, though the sample was controlled for family type. Total sample size was 500 households with fifty in the private suburb and ninety in each of the other districts.

The area sampling procedure which was followed in Cardiff provided a framework for testing the differences between delinquent and non-delinquent areas as matched samples. More than one research strategy is possible in adopting social survey procedures (Herbert, 1976), but this particular strategy focused upon area differences, using area as a surrogate for territorial group. Information was obtained from individual households within each area, but was largely interpreted in aggregate form. The singular advantage of the original individual base, in this instance, was that it allowed the collection of data on attitudes and behaviour which are not normally obtainable from published sources. One hypothesis was that significant differences would exist between delinquent and non-delinquent areas in certain attitudes and forms of behaviour. A further hypothesis was that these attitudinal and behavioural differences would support some aspects of sub-cultural theory. Delinquent sub-culture concepts have been developed mainly in relation to teenage gangs and could not be tested in the traditional way in a research format which did not identify individual offenders. The best-known studies, however, have been concerned with groups in particular districts of the city (Mays, 1972), and the widening of the concept to include the broader societal context within which the known offenders live was judged a desirable extension. Implicit in these hypotheses was the assumption that there would be a neighbourhood effect (Cox, 1969) which operated through the fact of territorial contiguity to influence patterns of attitude and behaviour. This idea of neighbourhood effect has been otherwise described as consensus and the product of relational space (Harvey, 1973). Its advocacy does not imply that other reference groups, such as those provided by work, school or specialized interests are unimportant, but merely that one significant reference goup is locality-based.

The results from this survey are stated in detail elsewhere (Herbert, 1976); here some of the main findings are reported in summary form. Neighbourhood, in itself a multi-stranded concept, was being used as a reference point in a behavioural study; it was important initially, therefore, to establish the reality of neighbourhood to the sample populations. Questions relating to local social interaction, to assessment of neighbourhood quality and to spatial images, allowed this to be analysed. It was also important to establish the reality of the dichotomous classification of delinquent and non-delinquent areas in the minds of the areas' inhabitants. Respondents were asked to compare their own district with others in Cardiff as a place where offenders lived and as a place where offences were committed. The delinquency areas were perceived as such by their occupants, while non-delinquent areas were viewed in more favourable terms;

it seemed, therefore, that official statistics had served as reliable indicators. These themes will be used to illustrate the results relevant to the stated hypotheses; these are parental attitudes towards educational attainment, definitions of delinquent behaviour and parental sanctions on misbehaviour.

Several important theories of delinquent behaviour have emphasized the importance of aspirations, achievements and a wide range of attitudes related to occupation and education (Hargreaves, 1967). Assumptions have often been that homes with high aspirations are likely to be 'good' influences, that educational attainment is a useful indicator and that aspirations may be related to the amount of encouragement which children receives and the kinds of opportunities which are made available to them (Cloward and Ohlin, 1960). These were several questions on attitudes towards education which failed to reveal significant patterns of variation either by areas or by other parameters such as social class or age. Among these were questions on parental attitudes to advice from teachers, encouragement in schoolwork and aspirations. Very high levels of affirmative answers suggested idealistic rather than realistic responses. Questions on actual behaviour, however, were more discriminating. In delinquency areas, less parents attended evening classes or had any contact with their children's schools. It was also possible to test the responses to the question on aspirations, as in each survey area a sizeable number of households recorded children past school-leaving age, so actual attainment could be measured. Table 3.5 summarizes the information on attainment for the two terraced row districts, the delinquent member of which had recorded highest aspirations. The actual record of attainment is significantly higher in the non-delinquent area, despite the fact that almost three-quarters of respondents in the delinquent area had aspirations of college education for their children.

An attempt was made to examine ways in which delinquent behaviour was defined by the sample populations; in common with other questions which explicitly investigated delinquency, questions were posed in terms of a hypothetical fourteen-year-old boy in an attempt to obtain a uniform and maximal response. Respondents were shown a card containing a range of offences from trivial to serious and were asked to nominate those which would lead them to think that a boy was a real problem and should be reported. Table 3.6 summari-

TABLE 3.5 Educational aspiration and attainment, Cardiff

	Hopes for qualifications		Actual qualifications			Age left school	
	A	B	A	B		A	B
					Years		
None	3	2	45	73	15	52	67
C.S.E.	6	10	3	4	16	18	23
G.C.E./trade	45	15	34	19	17	7	6
Higher	41	71	10	1	18+	23	2
Technical	5	2	10	2			

A = non-delinquent area; B = delinquent area. All figures are percentages.
Chi-square tests showed significant (1 per cent level) differences between A and B on each column.

TABLE 3.6 Acts which should be reported, Cardiff

Offence	Non-delinquent			Delinquent		
	M	C	R	A	E	L
Drink under age	36	54	26	31	47	32
Take money from child	50	56	20	21	40	31
Take from school	57	51	26	26	31	28
Travel without ticket	38	38	10	23	17	13
Damage public property	80	74	84	67	73	69
Take drugs	91	97	84	82	94	90
Take from cars	82	84	84	86	85	61
Open meters	86	89	90	92	90	76
Break into shop	88	92	88	91	92	77
Attack strangers	89	97	94	93	97	86

All figures are percentages.
Chi-square tests:
  34.1: significant at 1 per cent. level when M and C compared with A, E, L.
    3.7: no significant difference between M and C.
  13.4: no significant difference among A, E and L.

zes the results from this question. The private suburb (R) was anomalous to the extent that it recorded the lowest scores on several of the offences; presumably middle-class parents thought these to be too trivial for anything but sanctions in the home. The three delinquent areas showed significantly more tolerant attitudes over most of the less serious offences; this fact was taken as substantial evidence in support of the original hypotheses. For the more serious offences, condemnation became more general and there was little differences between areas, though some individual variations did occur.

The theme of parental sanctions and controls has an established place in the criminological literature (e.g. Andry, 1960) and is implicit, for example, in the theories of social disorganization and delinquent sub-culture; a working hypothesis, in its simplest form, might be that those circumstances in which control is firm, consistent and comprehensible to a child would be most likely to deter misbehaviour. Table 3.7 summarizes responses to a question on parental

TABLE 3.7 General reaction to misbehaviour, Cardiff

Sanction	Non-delinquent			Delinquent		
	M	C	R	A	E	L
Physical punishment	19	17	6	38	21	24
Verbal solution	51	64	70	48	23	48
Withdraw privileges	28	48	20	12	43	52
Report/institutional sanction	6	0	0	2	15	3
Ignore	8	0	16	10	21	7

All figures are percentages; respondents were not limited to one reaction.
Chi-square tests:
  22.9: significant (1 per cent. level) difference between M, C, R and A, E, L.
  15.3: significant (1 per cent. level) difference between M, C and A, E, L.
    2.7: no significant difference between M and C.
  42.5: significant (1 per cent. level) difference among A, E and L.

reaction to general misbehaviour. Response patterns between delinquent and non-delinquent areas were significantly different, and remained so when the private suburb was omitted from the comparison. Whereas parents in non-delinquent areas favoured a verbal sanction, reasoning with a child or 'telling-off', parents in delinquent areas leaned more towards physical punishment. When specific types of misbehaviour were nominated, the same contrast persisted in many cases. There were some interesting variations; in the instance of truancy, for example, parents from delinquent areas were much more inclined to report the child to school and use an institutional sanction.

This example of research into delinquency residence, through area-sampling and detailed social survey, has shown that the spatial order which can be identified by mapping where delinquents live is underlain by systematic variations in related attitudes and forms of behaviour. It has produced evidence which suggests that territorially based sub-cultures occur and, in a related way, suggests that the geographical distribution of delinquency residence does not merely reflect the characteristics of social groups but also shows an accumulation in particular areas which may be the result of a neighbourhood effect. Both these findings are worthy of further research in a greater variety of urban contexts. Although data was collected on an individual basis, it has been analysed in aggregate form as part of a particular research strategy. This procedure has, however, allowed a shift in emphasis from analysis of the basic facts of population composition, based primarily on census data, to the study of attitudes and behaviour; similarly, the emphasis is moved from statistical inference to direct survey. With these additional dimensions to its normal modes of analysis, a more searching geographical perspective may be attainable.

CONCLUSIONS

Most forms of social deviance display qualities of spatial order which cannot be dismissed as chance and which warrant detailed investigation. The development of such lines of investigation in the past have concentrated upon the identification of geographical distributions of deviance and have used available sources of aggregate statistics to demonstrate patterns of correlation with other qualities of the social environment. Studies of this kind have intrinsic value insofar as they are able to show the disproportionate incidence of social malaise. What exercises in statistical association have revealed is the fact that the worst areas are often typified by a whole variety of forms of deviance and constitute problem areas in a full sense. As territorial indicators and as guides to public policy which must operate at this aggregate level, such studies have practical value. If geographical perspectives simply indicate the extent to which deviance is only a feature of some districts, showing that it is a multi-stranded phenomenon which may influence public policy, they already fulfil valuable functions. The need to make the step from problem-identification to involvement in problem-solving processes has become a priority in the more recent contributions of social geographers (Harvey, 1973).

An over-reliance upon official sources of statistical data for crime and delinquency does present some problems for geographical analysis; if there is bias in the information source, for whatever reason, this will be reflected in the spatial distribution and will affect any interpretation of that set of findings in policy-making or problem-solving terms. As Pahl (1975, p. 387) has suggested, 'There may be more poverty among certain categories of workers which are not geographically concentrated and certain crimes such as tax evasion and fraud may be more damaging to the economy than inner city crimes against property. Politicians are often anxious to limit the size of the problem with which they have to deal. Geographers would surely not wish to collude unwittingly by focusing only on those problems which have the most obvious spatial manifestations'.

There are no persuasive reasons why analyses of the spatial qualities of social deviance should adopt limited roles. Statistical analyses of aggregate data can approach the questions of cause and effect, albeit from an inferential basis. Use of official statistics does incur limitations but this can be followed and complemented by in-depth studies at an individual scale, perhaps incorporating a temporal dimension. If such studies are not limited to officially designated offenders, then a more realistic perspective may be obtained. An approach which rests upon the significance of spatial qualities cannot claim to offer a full comprehension of delinquency or of any other form of deviance. It must of necessity refer to those theories of deviant behaviour which are derived from other branches of the social sciences. Such an approach, however, may fairly claim to offer a partial contribution to the understanding of a form of behaviour which clearly needs a broadly based and multi-faceted approach.

REFERENCES

Andry, R. (1960). *Delinquency and Parental Pathology*, Methuen, London.
Batchelor, I. R. C. (1957). 'Suicide in Old Age', in E. S. Schniedman and N. L. Farberow (Eds.) *Clues to Suicide*, McGraw Hill, New York, 143–151.
Bell, W., and Boat, M. D. (1957). 'Urban neighbourhoods and informal social relations'. *American Journal of Sociology*, **62**, 391–398.
Bell W., and Force, M. T. (1956). 'Urban neighbourhood types and participation in formal associations'. *American Sociological Review*, **21**, 345–350.
Berry, B. J. L. (1971). 'The logic and limit of comparative factorial ecology'. *Economic Geography*, **47**, 209–219.
Boal, F. W., Doherty, P., and Pringle, D. G. (1974). *The Spatial Distribution of Some Social Problems in the Belfast Urban Area*, Northern Ireland Community Relations Commission, Belfast.
Boggs, Sarah L. (1965). 'Urban crime patterns'. *American Sociological Review*, **30**, 899–908.
Castle, I., and Gittus, E. (1957). 'The distribution of social defects in Liverpool'. *Sociological Review*, **5**, 43–64.
Cavan, R. S. (1928). *Suicide*, University of Chicago Press, Chicago.
Chilton, R. J. (1964). 'Continuity in delinquency area research: a comparison of studies for Baltimore, Detroit, and Indianapolis'. *American Sociological Review*, **29**, 71–83.
Clinard, M. B. (1968). *Sociology of Deviant Behaviour*, Holt, Rinehart and Winston, New York.

120

Cloward, R. A., and Ohlin, L. E. (1960). *Delinquency and Opportunity: A Theory of Delinquent Gangs*, The Free Press, Glencoe, Illinois.

Cohen, A. (1955). *Delinquent Boys: The Culture of the Gang*, The Free Press, Glencoe, Illinois.

Cohen, A. (1966). *Deviance and Control*, Prentice Hall, Englewood Cliffs, New Jersey.

Cox, K. R. (1969). 'The voting decision in a spatial context'. In C. Board, R. J. Chorley, P. Haggett and D. R. Stoddart (Eds.), *Progress in Geography*, 1, 96–112.

Cybriwsky, R., and Ley, D. (1973). *The Spatial Ecology of Stripped Cars*. Unpublished discussion paper, Temple University, Philadelphia.

Dever, G. E. A. (1972). 'Leukaemia and housing: an intra urban analysis'. In N. D. McGlashan (Ed.), *Medical Geography*, Methuen, London. pp. 233–245.

Dogan, M., and Rokkan, S. (Eds.) (1969). *Quantitative Ecological Analysis in the Social Sciences*, The M.I.T. Press, Cambridge, Massachusetts.

Douglas, J. D. (1967). *The Social Meanings of Suicide*, Princeton University Press, Princeton, New Jersey.

Dunham, H. W. (1937). 'The ecology of functional psychoses in Chicago', *American Sociological Review*, 2, 467–79.

Durkheim, E. (1951). *Suicide: A Study in Sociology*, The Free Press, Glencoe, Illinois.

Giddens, A. (Ed.) (1971). *The Sociology of Suicide*, F. Cass, London.

Giggs, J. A. (1973). 'The distribution of schizophrenics in Nottingham'. *Transactions of the Institute of British Geographers*, 59, 55–76.

Giggs, J. A. (1975). 'The distribution of schizophrenics in Nottingham: a reply'. *Transactions of the Institute of British Geographers*, 64, 150–156.

Gittus, E., and Stephens, C. J. (1973). *Some Problems in the Use of Canonical Analysis: An Example from Urban Sociology*. Discussion paper, University of Newcastle-upon-Tyne, Northumberland.

Glueck, S., and Glueck, E. (1950). *Unravelling Juvenile Delinquency*, Commonwealth Fund, New York.

Glueck, S., and Glueck, E. (1952). *Delinquency in the Making*, Harper, New York.

Hargreaves, D. (1967). *Social Relations in a Secondary School*, Routledge and Kegan Paul, London.

Haring, L. L. (Ed.) (1972). *A Summary Report of Spatial Studies of Juvenile Delinquency in Phoenix, Arizona*, Arizona State University.

Harries, K. D. (1971). 'The geography of American crime'. *Journal of Geography*, 70, 204–213.

Harvey, D. (1973). *Social Justice in the City*, Edward Arnold, London.

Henry, A. F., and Short, J. (1957). 'The sociology of suicide'. In E. S. Shneidman and N. L. Farberow (Eds.), *Clues to Suicide*, McGraw-Hill, New York. pp. 58–69.

Herbert, D. T. (1972). *Urban Geography: A Social Perspective*, David and Charles, Newton Abbott.

Herbert, D. T. (1976). 'The study of delinquency areas: a geographical approach'. *Transactions, Institute of British Geographers*, 1:4 New Series (forthcoming).

Herbert, D. T., and Evans, D. J. (1973). *Urban Environments and Juvenile Delinquency: A Study of Cardiff*, Report to Home Office Research Unit, London.

Herbert, D. T., and Evans, D. J. (1974). 'Urban sub-areas in sampling frameworks for social survey'. *Town Planning Review*, 45, 171–188.

Hyman, H. H., and Singer, E (Eds.) (1968). *Readings in Reference Group Theory and Research*, The Free Press, New York.

Johnston, R. J. (1971). *Urban Residential Patterns: An Introductory Review*, G. Bell, London.

Lander, B. (1954). *Towards an Understanding of Juvenile Delinquency*, Columbia University Press, New York.

Ley, D. (1972). *The Black Inner City as a Frontier Outpost: Images and Behaviour of A Philadelphia Neighbourhood*. Ph.D. Dissertation, Pennsylvania State University, Philadelphia.

McClintock, F. H., and Avison, N. H. (1968). *Crime in England and Wales*, Heinemann, London.

McGlashan, N. D. (Ed.) (1972). *Medical Geography*, Methuen, London.

Mack, J. (1964). Full-time miscreants, delinquent neighbourhoods, and criminal networks'. *British Journal of Sociology*, 15, 38–53.

Mannheim, H. (1965). *Comparative Criminology*, Routledge and Kegan Paul, London.

Maris, R. W. (1969). *Social Forces in Urban Suicide*, Dorsey Press, Illinois.

Mays, J. B. (1963). 'Delinquency areas: a re-assessment'. *British Journal of Criminology*, 3, 216–230.

Mays, J. B. (1968). 'Crime and the urban pattern'. *Sociological Review*, 16, 241–255.

Mays, J. B. (Ed.) (1972). *Juvenile Delinquency, the Family and the Social Group*, Longmans, London.

Merton, R. K., and Nisbet, R. (1971). *Contemporary Social Problems*, Harcourt, Brace and Jovanovich, New York.

Mintz, N. L., and Schwarz, D. T. (1964). 'Urban psychology and psychoses'. *International Journal of Social Psychiatry*, 10, 101–117.

Morris, T. (1957). *The Criminal Area*, Routledge and Kagan Paul, London.

Pahl, R. E. (1975). 'Spatial and social constraints in the inner city', *Geographical Journal*, 141, 386–387.

Phillips, P. D. (1972). 'A prologue to the geography of crime'. *Proceedings of the Association of American Geographers*, 4, 86–91.

Phillipson, M. (1971). *Sociological Aspects of Crime and Delinquency*, Routledge and Kegan Paul, London.

Polk, K. (1967). 'Urban social areas and delinquency'. *Social Problems*, 14, 320–325.

Pyle, G. F. (1968). *Some Examples of Urban Medical Geography*. Master's Dissertation, University of Chicago, Chicago.

Pyle, G. F., and Rees, P. H. (1971). 'Modelling patterns of death and disease in Chicago'. *Economic Geography*, 47, 475–488.

Quinney, R. (1964). 'Crime, delinquency and social areas'. *Journal Research in Crime and Delinquency*, 1, 149–154.

Sainsbury, P. (1955). *Suicide in London; An Ecological Study*, Chapman and Hall, London.

Schmid, C. F. (1939). 'Suicide in Minneapolis, 1928–1932'. *American Journal of Sociology*, 39, 30–48.

Schmid, C. F. (1960). 'Urban crime areas'. *American Sociological Review*, 25, 527–542 and 655–678.

Shaw, C. R., and McKay, H. D. (1942). *Juvenile Delinquency and Urban Areas* (Revised edition 1969). University of Chicago Press, Chicago.

Smith, D. M. (1973). *The Geography of Social Well Being*, McGraw-Hill, New York,

Snow, J. (1964). Cited in L. D. Stamp, *The Geography of Life and Death*, Collins, London.

Stearns, A. W. (1921). *Mental Hygiene Concord*, 5, 752.

Taylor, S. D. (1974). *The Geography and Epidemiology of Psychiatric Disorders in Southampton*. Unpublished Ph.D. Thesis, Southampton University, Southampton.

Timms, D. W. G. (1971). *The Urban Mosaic: Towards a Theory of Residential Differentiation*, Cambridge University Press, Cambridge.

Wallis, C. P., and Maliphant, R. (1967). 'Delinquent areas in the county of London: ecological factors'. *British Journal of Criminology*, 7, 250–284.

Wilkins, L. T. (1961–62). 'Crime, cause and treatment: recent research and theory'. *Education Research*, 4, 18.

Chapter 4

Urban Education: Problems and Policies

D. T. Herbert

INTRODUCTION

Geographical studies of education in its social and environmental setting lack a strong research tradition. Despite this, the past decade has witnessed a strong movement in the United States and Britain towards recognition of the importance of those spatial qualities which underpin the system of educational provision. Some of the most critical questions which face educational policy-makers have spatial terms of reference. What is the optimal population size of a school? How should its catchment area be defined? What distance thresholds exist within the school–pupil hinterland? Are there optimal arrangements of catchment areas which satisfy social goals, such as integration and social or ethnic balance? What are the respective merits of neighbourhood schools with compact catchment areas as opposed to schools which use other criteria to select students from a variety of city neighbourhoods? The list is considerable, but there are other questions which need to be answered. Educational disadvantage has been identified as a major component within the broad spectrum of social and environmental deprivation. Characteristics such as low levels of attainment, high drop-out rates and truancy are often closely associated with other indicators of deprivation and, in common with them, are not evenly distributed over urban society as a whole (Herbert, 1975). The stereotype of the educationally disadvantaged urban child is one with parents of low occupational skills, who lives in a substandard environment, and has access in the home and neighbourhood to attitudes and values which are not conducive to schooling and achievement. In both North America and Britain, attention has become focused upon educational disadvantage, and most studies and projects have been directed at particular schools located in particular residential areas within the city.

Education and the quality of schools is an urgent and emotive issue because it concerns the young, but most attempts at educational reform have shown that schools cannot be divorced from their broader societal context. Issues such as poverty and underprivilege cannot be tackled through the educational system alone. American compensatory education programmes have accomplished a voluminous amount of activity in an attempt to answer a simple educational problem, the fact of differential educational performance among different social groups. Yet Little and Smith (1971, p. 135), in a review of the movement, concluded that the attempt to solve the problem had been forced to go further and further outside the educational system:

A purely educational response to the initial problem is unlikely to be successful. . . . Educational underachievement is seen to be merely one manifestation of a number of social and economic disparities experienced by disadvantaged groups. The long term solution must be a comprehensive range of programmes which strike at these political, social and economic inequalities.

As the education system needs to be viewed in its societal context, so schools and their pupils need to be examined in relation to the physical and social environments of which they are part.

There is strong evidence in the more recent past that the spatial implications of educational planning and the need to view school performance in its environmental contexts have not only been recognized but have also been acted upon. Recent governmental policies in Britain and America have adopted area bases and have been dealing with the neighbourhood and school as contextual frameworks. This impetus for area policies has come from a diverse research literature, which has often examined neighbourhood effects upon individual performance in an indirect way. Much of the social science literature has been explicitly concerned with societal bases for inequality; socioeconomic status of families, size of families and parental attitudes have been some of the main variables examined as hypothesized underpinnings of the educational aspirations and achievements of children. More contextual variables, such as 'community influence' and 'school effects' have often entered the investigations in indirect ways and have lacked either precision or consistency in the way in which they are defined. There are, of course, some direct studies of neighbourhood effect by sociologists (Wilson, 1959), and geographers have given it explicit emphasis (Robson, 1969). Much recent geographical research in the United States, however, has been less concerned with neighbourhood effects than with more specific spatial questions such as school location and definition of catchment areas.

On another level, American experience in the field of compensatory education has been closely linked with attempts to identify the underprivileged child and those parts of the city from which he comes. This experience is well documented and has strongly affected British studies. The Plowden Report (Central Advisory Council for Education, 1967) initiated an action research programme, with government sponsorship, in order to examine ways of identifying educanal priority areas (E.P.A.s) and of forming solutions to the problems of such areas. Reports from this project, published between 1972 and 1975 have summarized the legacy of Plowden, have outlined the conceptual bases of priority area programmes and have provided a series of detailed accounts of individual area schemes. A central problem, that of defining the educational priority area, is discussed in a paper (Halsey, 1972) which is reprinted as part of this chapter. While not explicitly discussing boundaries and territories, it examines some of the central issues underlying area policies and, in particular, the question of indices. A detailed account is given of the index developed by Little and Mabey (1971), which has proved the most widely known and accepted formulation. The area projects in Britain, which followed the Plowden recommendations, provided a range of experience and a diversity of solutions. They have also, however, evoked criticism of the overall validity of area-based solutions as opposed to those aimed at the individual child. This debate will be considered, but first some aspects of research into the contextual factors relevant to educational performance and the nature of educational disadvantage will be reviewed.

CONTEXTUAL VARIABLES AND SCHOOL PERFORMANCE: SOCIAL STRATIFICATION EFFECTS AND NEIGHBOURHOOD EFFECTS

Attempts to identify those variables which are related to a child's school performance have formed an important theme in the literature of the social sciences. Many studies have examined the roles of individual variables such as family size; others have looked at attitudinal or behavioural factors such as parental level of interest, and particularly the role of the mother; others have investigated sets of factors—including personality measures (Banks and Finlayson, 1973)—and have arrived at estimates of the relative importance of the different variables which have been considered. An important dichotomy which such studies accept is between the inate abilities of the child, on the one hand, and the derived abilities, on the other. Innate abilities, measurable through standardized intelligence tests, may indicate a child's potential; they are individual and genetic. Derived abilities are developed from the environmental contexts within which the child is placed; they may be the product of many reference groups—the family and the home, the neighbourhood and the peer groups, the school, the teachers and the fellow pupils. The sociological sciences have primarily been interested in the role of these environmental contexts, with a primary control upon level of measurable intelligence. The dilemma for educationalists occurs when known inate abilities are not developed to the full, when considerable deficiencies are identified between potentials and actual achievements, and when these deficiences recur in a consistent way among particular sections of society. The dominant theme has been that social origins, usually measured by parental socioeconomic status, affect a child's opportunities in dramatic ways. Whereas the educational chances of middle-class children are enhanced, those of working-class children are diminished. In examining this literature, the importance of such stratification variables will obviously be recognized, but evidence for neighbourhood effects will be emphasized.

British research into the relationship of contextual factors and educational performance has been voluminous, but a number of major longitudinal studies stand out in the literature. Jackson and Marsden (1962) monitored the progress of a group of children in an English industrial town. The initial discrepancy which they identified has been central to much research in this field. Whereas the social composition of their town could be dichotomized into 78 per cent. working class and 22 per cent. middle class of the pupils completing a full grammar school course and taking advanced level examinations at the age of eighteen, 36 per cent. were from working-class homes and 64 per cent. were from middle-class homes. It was further clear that, where children from working-class homes were successful in educational terms, they were drawn mainly from the more prosperous upper reaches of the working class and tended to come from small families within this group. While this evidence could be interpreted as family differences rather than a neighbourhood effect, it was further shown that very many of the successful working-class children came from districts where social classes were mixed. When the homes of successful working-class children were plotted on a map, they could be seen to cluster around the five primary schools which contained a significant minority of middle-class children (Figure 4.1). Those working-class children who were successful derived some advantage from these contacts and from shared facilities

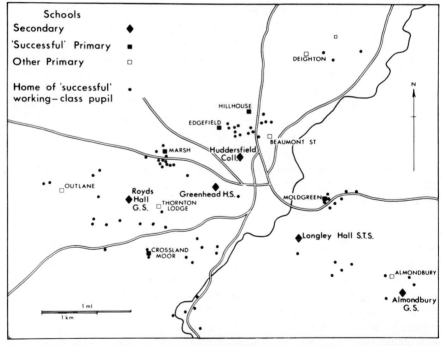

FIGURE 4.1   Homes of 'successful' working-class children and (locations of 'good' primary schools in Huddersfield. Clusters occur around those schools with a better social mix of pupils: location of Marsh Primary is estimated from the original sketch map). (Reproduced by permission of the Institute of Community Studies, from B. Jackson and D. Marsden, 1962)

and knowledge; for these children, educational success meant a sharp break with neighbourhood life while for their middle-class counterparts it was a logical extension of home and community.

The studies associated with Douglas (Douglas, 1964; Douglas, Ross and Simpson, 1968) were based upon a cohort of children born in the first week of March 1946. Of an initial sample of 5 362 children, 3 418 completed tests at the ages of eight and eleven years. One theme, strongly developed by Douglas, was that there was a considerable wastage of talent owing to the exclusion from more advanced education of children who, given different homes or different schools, would have achieved more success. A series of intelligence tests allowed children to be grouped according to ability, and it could be demonstrated that, even when this control was imposed, middle-class children consistently did better than their working-class counterparts in terms of access to grammar school places (Table 4.1). This better performance of middle-class children was attributed to parental interest and contact with the school and to good primary schools, and also reflected the high educational aspirations of neighbouring middle-class families from which they drew their friends. There was evidence here and elsewhere (Glass, 1948) that when working-class families moved to new local authority estates, there was a measurable increase in the proportion who achieved grammar school places.

An important finding from study of the cohort of children in primary schools was that performance of working-class children deteriorated between the ages of eight and eleven years. The later study (Douglas, Ross and Simpson, 1968) found that this deterioration, and hence a divergence between the social class groups, continued for reading and mathematics, but differentials were reduced in other skills between the ages of eleven and fifteen years. Whereas the

TABLE 4.1 Educational attainment and social class
(a) Social class—award of grammar school places, comparison of observed and expected

Social class	Grammar school places			Teachers' assessment	Mothers' wishes
	Awarded	Expected, if same chances as upper middle at each level of score at			
		11 years	8 years		
Percentage middle					
Upper	54.3	54.3	54.3	66.7	57.2
Lower	34.0	40.4	41.4	45.2	44.1
Percentage manual working					
Upper	18.1	25.7	31.7	27.7	29.8
Lower	11.0	18.1	25.7	16.7	22.4

Reproduced by permission of J. W. B. Douglas, 1964.

(b) Proportions staying at school and gaining certificates related to ability and social class: percentage table

Social class	Ability at 15 years				
	60 and over	55–59	50–54	45–49	44 and less
	Percentage completing session 1961–62				
Middle					
Upper	97	93	86	69	40
Lower	94	79	59	36	17
Manual					
Upper	90	67	35	22	6
Lower	80	46	27	12	3
	Percentage starting session 1962–63				
Middle					
Upper	90	82	71	42	20
Lower	78	52	37	20	8
Manual					
Upper	67	43	20	10	3
Lower	50	20	12	4	2
	Percentage gaining good certificates				
Middle					
Upper	77	33	11	4	—
Lower	60	18	6	—	—
Manual					
Upper	53	15	2	1	—
Lower	37	9	3	—	—
	Percentage gaining general certificates				
Middle					
Upper	94	79	54	27	20
Lower	87	59	38	13	1
Manual					
Upper	86	45	17	5	—
Lower	69	31	12	2	—

Reproduced by permission of J. W. B. Douglas, J. M. Ross and H. R. Simpson, 1968.

disadvantage of working-class children in terms of measurable ability tended to be reduced, other factors came into play: 50 per cent. of the lower working-class children of high ability left school at the minimum age, compared with 33 per cent. of the upper working class, 22 per cent. of the lower middle class and 10 per cent. of the upper middle class. According to Douglas, Ross and Simpson (1968), 'The social class inequalities of opportunity observed in the primary schools have increased in the secondary schools and extend to the highest levels of ability' p. 27) and 'We attribute many of the major differences in performance to environmental influences acting in the pre-school years' (p. 177). Douglas and his associates thus find substantive evidence that background circumstances have decisive influence upon educational performance (Table 4.1). Although much of their evidence centres on the home and social class, more general environmental circumstances are consistently given significant roles; the values prevalent in the neighbourhood are seen as relevant parameters.

Other major British studies, often Government-sponsored, have provided additional evidence of disadvantages affecting children in differential ways (C.A.C.E, 1954; Floud, Halsey and Martin, 1957). Occasionally the existence of a neighbourhood effect has been made very explicit (Rogoff, 1961, pp. 242–243):

> Each of the social classes will be more heavily concentrated in some kinds of community environments than in others. . . . Such structural differences may set in motion both formal arrangements—such as school, library, and general cultural facilities in the community—and informal mechanisms, such as normative climates or modal levels of social aspiration, which are likely to affect *all* members of the community to some extent—parents and children.

While this evidence for neighbourhood effects, often indirect, was emerging from research into social stratification links with schooling, one study is available for a British city which was in the mainstream of social geographical research in the 1960s. The overall emphasis in Robson's (1969) study of Sunderland was upon urban ecological structure and growth and the theme of residential differentiation. From the identified pattern of residential districts, Robson selected seven areas for detailed investigation by social survey methods. Parental attitudes towards education provided the theme of this investigation. As a methodology, the Sunderland study followed earlier approaches through social area analysis (Bell and Force, 1956) and has itself been followed by a more systematic use of area-sampling procedures (Herbert and Evans, 1974; Walker, 1975). Robson selected seven areas with social class as a main parameter; each area had distinctive features, but the clearest division was between the five low status districts, which included stable terraced row neighbourhoods, an inner-city transient district and a local authority estate, and two residential areas of middle to high socioeconomic status. A statistical analysis revealed strong links between education and social class. The correlation between social class of parent and I.Q. of child was $+0.62$, while a similar high positive association existed between parental social class and the type of school which their children attended. Questionnaire surveys were used to examine the bases for differences in attitudes towards education at a more detailed level In each of the areas, the sample was drawn only from those parents whose child was a candidate for the eleven-plus examination—a selective entrance procedure for secondary schools with very considerable implications for eventual education and attainment.

From the initial statistical analyses a set of expected attitudes towards education was hypothesized, with the general form that higher social class meant higher positive attitudes towards education. A comparison of actual to expected scores by areas showed several deviations. Three of the working-class areas (Deptford, a stable district, Upper Hendon, a central-city district with much subdivided property, and Thorney Close, a municipal estate with mainly older children) all underscored. While one of the seven areas could not be easily classified, the remaining three (Alexandra Road and Thronhill, the higher status districts, and Bishopswearmouth, a rooming house area) all had scores above the expected level. The predictions based upon social class norms did not therefore prove reliable and there was more variation within classes than existed between areas; parental attitudes towards education were strongly affected by the character of their residential district.

In his explanation of the survey findings, Robson focused upon the broader differences between classes and the differing roles of community. Working-class districts were much more strongly organized on a local community basis; the secondary modern school, which eleven-plus failures would attend, was physically part of the neighbourhood while the grammar school was not. For the working-class child, a conflict existed between community and educational roles which, in addition to crowded living conditions and the large size of families, tended to diminish individual aspirations and promote a collectivist attitude. Middle-class people, with reference groups which were national as well as local, were less locality-oriented; individualism had greater play, but the generally high priority given to education meant that high aspirations were the norm. Although this line of explanation has a strong class basis, the role of territoriality and neighbourhood was strongly emphasized. Individual attitudes and forms of behaviour were clearly affected by the local milieu: 'No matter what the area, the attitudes of individual families were more familiar to those prevailing around them than to those of the objective social class' (Robson, 1969, p. 244).

There is, in Robson's analysis, a clear and explicit suggestion that a neighbourhood effect was at work which influenced attitudes towards education and, presumably, educational attainment. Whereas his research strategy has not been replicated in an educational context in American geographical research, the sociological literature for the United States contains substantial evidence comparable to that observed for British cities. Wilson (1959) provided one of the strongest indications of a neighbourhood effect from an empirical study of an American city. Wilson's data was gathered from schools in the San Francisco–Oakland area of California, and his analysis began with the assertion that consistent and strong evidence had been accumulated in the United States to show that members of different socioeconomic strata as *groups* adhere to different values which reinforce their respective statuses. Overall, working-class people tended to devalue education in comparison with people in high social strata. Schools were classified into three main groups—upper white-collar (A), lower white-collar (B) and industrial (C)—on the basis of the socioeconomic composition of the school district populations. Each school district was ranked on selected variables and the typology was formed from the rankings, which showed a high degree of concordance. Wilson's procedure was thus analogous to a residential differentiation approach, in that he argues that school districting reflects segregation by social strata. Using information from his samples relating both to aspirations and achievement, Wilson was able to demonstrate a consistent pattern of differences among school districts which remained when the individual social origins of the children and the educational backgrounds of parents were held constant. A set of figures showing the proportion of pupils aspiring to college education by school groups and parental occupation (Wilson, 1959, p. 839) revealed that for school type A the scores for professional, white-collar, self-employed and manual worker households respectively were 93, 79, 79 and 59 (all percentages); for school type B they were 77, 59, 66 and 44; and for school type C they were 66, 46, 35 and 33. Therefore, although the aspiration level was reduced with descending socioeconomic status, it was also reduced by overall school district classification within each individual parental occupation set. Similarly, figures on actual attainment (high or median grades) by school groups and the same classification of parental occupation produced aligned evidence. For school type A the percentage attaining high or median grades by parental occupation were, respectively, 66, 50, 51 and 35; for school type B, 50, 28, 35 and 13; and for school type C, 18, 18, 11 and 11 (Wilson, 1959, p. 842). Again, attainment declines with socioeconomic status, but also with school type; whereas 50 per cent. of the children from white-collar homes in the 'best' environments achieve high grades, only 18 per cent. from closely similar homes in the 'worst' environments did so. Wilson acknowledged that some of his suggestions were based upon inference, but concluded (Wilson, 1959, p. 845):

> The *de facto* segregation brought about by concentrations of social classes in cities result in schools with unequal moral climates which likewise affect the motivation of the child, not necessarily by inculcating a sense of inferiority, but rather by providing a different ethos in which to perceive values.

Other American studies have been more specifically concerned with 'school effects', in which the school itself is regarded as the influential social environment. Michael (1971) found a relationship between pupils' aspirations for college education and the socioeconomic status of the school. Bidwell and Karaska (1975) used variables which measured school environment, organization and achievement, and concluded that the 'received wisdom', which suggested that larger schools with more resources achieved better results, was in fact correct: 'Our study provides substantial evidence of the significance of organizational structure and staffing for school district effectiveness' (Bidwell and Karaska, 1975, p. 68). The most relevant inputs, from the evidence of this study, appeared to the fiscal funds and certain postulated correlates of community and parental population characteristics. Several studies have suggested that there is a 'social origins of pupils' factor which tends to give schools a particular form of environment. Karabel and Astin (1975, p. 395) found a relationship between schools and colleges which seemed to represent their prestige rankings in their respective sectors of education: 'What seems to have developed in American higher education is a differentiated system of colleges and universities which bears a close resemblance to the tracking order of American high schools.'

It would seem common sense that schools achieve different qualities and distinctive social environments and that these have some effects upon their pupils (see Banks and Finlayson, 1973, p. 174). Recent research in the United States has, however, thrown some doubt upon the independent status of school effects. Duncan, Featherman and Duncan (1972, p. 194) concluded that within-school differences were more telling factors than between-school differences and that when other variables had been controlled the amount of influence which could be attributed directly to the school was surprisingly small: 'We are well advised to entertain modest expectations for explanations couched in terms of "schools effects" rhetoric.'

Studies in the United States which have been primarily concerned with socioeconomic background and schooling have found basic discrepancies between potential and performance. Duncan, Featherman and Duncan (1972) suggested that the British studies associated with Douglas (Douglas, 1964; Douglas, Ross and Simpson, 1968) had confirmed relationships established in the United States between educational attainment and important causal antecedents such as ability, school performance, parental encouragement, family structure and socioeconomic background, and that 'The pattern of talent loss by social origins is similar to the American case' (Duncan, Featherman and Duncan, 1972, p. 256). Karabel and Astin (1975) found that social class had a strong independent impact upon college attainment; Hauser (1968–69) also identified this link, but was concerned with the mediating influence of intelligence. Similar qualifications were made by Sewell and Shah (1968, p. 191), who suggested that 'An important and consistent finding in the area of stratification research is that the children of higher social class origins are more likely to aspire to high educational and occupational goals than are children of lower social class origins', but stressed the role of mediating factors such as parental expectations, achievements and value orientations.

American researchers into social stratification relationships to education have themselves considered the direct possibilities of neighbourhood effects. Sewell and Armer (1966) were critical of previous studies of contextual influences (Michael 1961; Turner, 1964; Wilson, 1959) in terms of the technical procedures for analysis which they had employed. Sewell and Armer used partialling procedures to test the hypothesis that the socioeconomic status of high school districts, since they presumably reflect the shared norms and aspirations of their inhabitants, would have an important effect on the educational aspirations of its youth, over and above that of family socioeconomic status or individual ability. The result of these investigations was to indicate that, by simultaneously controlling for sex, intelligence and familial socioeconomic status, the importance of the neighbourhood effect was considerably reduced. Not withstanding, Sewell and Armer (1966, pp. 167–168) were not prepared to dismiss neighbourhood effect as a factor: 'Even the small amount of variance accounted for by neighbourhood status over and above that accounted for by sex, socioeconomic status, and intelligence makes some contribution to the understanding of educational aspirations.'

A general conclusion from this review is that the main body of research literature, in both Britain and North America, leaves the concept of a neighbourhood effect intact as a contribution of some significance towards the understanding of differential educational performance. Some studies (Robson, 1969; Wilson, 1959) have given it prominence as a significant parameter; others (Sewell and Armer, 1966) accept that, even when the major mediating factors such as intelligence and family type are controlled, a residual effect remains. Probably because many statements upon neighbourhood effect have emerged as by-products of research which has its emphasis elsewhere, research strategies to examine it systematically have not been impressively developed. The 'neighbourhood' or 'community' factor itself, critical in such a strategy, has often been loosely defined. Some studies have taken school districts, which do not necessarily represent the detailed separation of residential areas, as basic units (Sewell and Armer, 1966); others have looked only at differences between 'communities' of different population sizes. Sewell and Orenstein (1965) used a classification of farm, village, small city, medium city and large city, based upon arbitrary population limits. Most writers have labelled neighbourhoods by one or two easily accessible measures, usually socioeconomic status (Wilson, 1959), but have then proceeded to characterize such qualities of neighbourhood (such as ethos, climate of opinions or consensus of values), which are not measurable in such adept ways. Where labels of high or low socioeconomic status are allocated, this is again often arbitrary (Sewell and Armer, 1966). Levels of uniformity within units strongly affect the justification of partialling by individual socioeconomic status; comparing uniform areas on the one hand and comparing mixed areas on the other are different strategies. If only because of the insufficiency of attempts to define the neighbourhood factor, research into its significance in the context of education must be regarded as incomplete. A much more systematic amount of control needs to be imposed upon the area-sampling procedure from which territorial units are selected for sample surveys; alternative statistical procedures are available for isolating neighbourhood effects from aggregate data (Johnston, 1974).

EDUDATIONAL DISADVANTAGE AND SCHOOL ORGANIZATION IN THE UNITED STATES

More recent American research into the geography of education has not contained any study in depth of the neighbourhood effect; the type of study completed by Robson (1969) for a British city has not been replicated. American geographers have become closely concerned with the social conditions which inspired compensatory education in the United States. Underprivilege exists and is manifest in the educational system. Although underprivilege affects more than one section of American society, it has proved impossible to avoid an emphasis upon contrasts between ethnic groups. Educational disadvantage is heavily concentrated in American's black urban communities.

Rose (1971) identified two aspects of black education in the United States which were the bases of its problems. Firstly, inner-city schools had a long record of limited success in the preparation of black children for useful roles in American society and, secondly, there was strong evidence that black parents placed greater confidence in education than in any other social process. Continued failure in education was thus most likely to produce frustration, despair and its repercussions in the black community. Basic facts about the conditions which militate against black children are very well known, and legislation to overcome the adverse conditions for schooling has been in existence for more than two decades. The hard fact is that progress towards enacting the legislation and solving the problems has been painfully slow.

Lowry (1973) has provided a closely argued account of the changing geography of schools and education over a thirty-year period in Mississippi. His account clearly demonstrates the slowness of response to reformist legislation and shows the strong inertia factors, both societal and geographical, which were at work. Lowry distinguished four phases. During the early 1940s the doctrine of 'separate but equal' education for black and white children had *de jure* standing and meant a legal system of school segregation. A good deal of school consolidation took place during this phase but only affected white children; large modern schools served the white population, but black children still attended dozens of one- or two-classroomed schools scattered over a wide area (Figure 4.2). A second phase dates from the Supreme Court ruling of 1954 which was against the doctrine of 'separate but equal' and therefore antisegregationist. Mississippi responded, but not in line with the Supreme Court ruling; it put much more money into Negro schools but kept segregation. The third phase begins in 1968, when Congress moved against laggards. Mississippi introduced a 'freedom of choice' plan and completed consolidation of Negro schools; in Hinds County, for example, nine large schools replaced 109 small schools. But 'freedom of choice' did not break down segregation because races would not mix. A pattern of *de facto* school segregation emerged which mirrored residential separation of ethnic groups. In the fourth phase, the Supreme Court ruled against the sufficiency of 'freedom of choice' and advocated more direct means, such as zoning, pairing of schools and bussing, of integrating schools. These measures, and attempts to implement them, established a conflict situation between black and white sections of the population. The percentage of Negroes in predominantly white schools rose from just over 5 to around 25 per cent; but opposition from the white population and from school administrators was strong. There was a dramatic scale of withdrawal of white pupils from public schools into the private sector; the higher the proportion of Negroes in the population, the higher the scale of

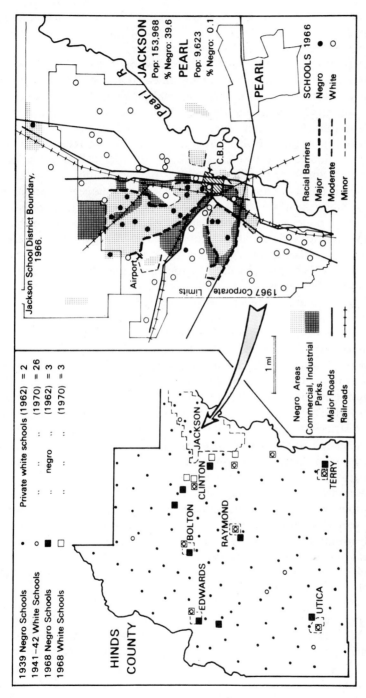

FIGURE 4.2 Ethnic differences in school provision, Hinds County, Mississippi. Hinds County Schools are shown by race for 1940 and 1968; Jackson Public Schools by race are shown for 1966 with major Negro residential areas in 1971. (Reproduced by permission of *Annals* of the association of American Geographers, Vol. **63** (1973), from M. Lowry, Figure I, p. 169 and Figure 5, p. 172)

white withdrawal. Repercussions such as these, which benefit no section of American society, have led to a re-examination of the whole integrationist policy. Integration in schools was not realistic as long as segregation existed in other facets of life, particularly in residential areas.

National policies for education, concerned with themes such as under-privilege and desegregation, have to be implemented at a local level. It is here that the school administrators and educational policy-makers face decisions which contain strong spatial implications. Many decisions have been made, but it is doubtful if many of these have been prefaced by any kind of careful research aimed at evaluating the spatial alternatives. Two recent studies by geographers exemplify the possibilities of this type of detailed investigation.

Jenkins and Shepherd (1972) examined the alternative strategies for decentralizing high school administration in Detroit. State legislation in 1969 required the subdivision of Detroit into decentralized regional school boards, between seven and eleven in number, each of which would be responsible for between twenty-five and fifty thousand students. This particular piece of research had the objective of identifying the range of possible solutions to this adjustment, which was basically a regionalization problem, and assessing the implications. Given an initial set of twenty-one districts which had to be grouped from a smaller number, there were 7 330 possible amalgamations with constraints of contiguity and enrolment size and 158 possibilities with all constraints set by the legislature. The relative advantages of various solutions were examined, with limited available background data, in the context of four alternative desiderata, Black community control was a solution in which black parents were able to control the education of their own children; white community control produced a parallel situation for white parents. A 'homo-geneous' solution gave control to both sections of the community within particular districts of Detroit, while an integrative solution provided the kind of mix desired by Supreme Court guidelines.

The results of grouping procedures showed that while white community control was easily attainable, and was in fact difficult to avoid, a very selective grouping was needed to even approach the black control solution. Several amalgamations would produce 'homogeneous' solutions which—the authors suggested—could work with goodwill on both sides and a genuine desire for the fair distribution of resources. The integrative solution was difficult to achieve and the research results showed how far short of desegregration the high schools were in Detroit. Jenkins and Shepherd (1972) concluded that the demographic and geographical disadvantages of black communities were virtually insurmountable for the task of integration, but that 'homogeneity' or community control of neighbourhood schools could be a viable strategy.

Maxfield (1972) produced a more technical study on the spatial planning of school districts, using the Athens school district in Georgia as a case study. Maxfield posed the spatial problems in a systematic way; those which he identified included the location of boundaries for catchments and the optimal positions of new schools. He demonstrated the possible uses of linear programming procedures, specified the data input needs for this type of research and concluded that the formulation and analysis of several comprehensive and alternative plans provided a better basis for decision-making. The main spatial implications of educational planning were, in the short term, the allocation of students to schools and, in the long term, designation of sites for new buildings.

A final example of geographical research in this context is provided by Hall (1973), who developed a programming model for the location of high schools. The terms of reference for this model were to find location for new schools and to allocate students in such a way that the cost of transporting all students to schools was minimized. A number of constraints were accepted. Each school was allocated a maximum capacity, with strict upper and lower limits of black and white students, and a specified number of new schools were to be constructed. When the model was applied to one Chicago district, it was found, to a large extent, to confirm commonsense expectations; all spatial solutions placed the new schools in the eastern half of the district and gave at least one school a dispersed catchment area. No single location criterion could be singled out as being particularly diagnostic, but a set of criteria should be incorporated into the decision-making process.

Although projects of the type described above clearly have applied potential, there is little evidence, as yet, that the research is influencing the policy-makers. Some of the research has been conducted after the decisions have been made, and in some cases (Jenkins and Shepherd, 1972) derived solutions are simply compared with those arrived at by policy-makers and differences are noted. Much of this technique-orientated research into the spatial implications of educational policy is clearly still in a stage of comparative infancy. It is likely that more highly sophisticated models will be formed which attempt to incorporate a wide range of variables; the problem then will be to translate these into meaningful terms to both policy-makers and public. A further, less tangible problem is the fact that many of the issues involved in educational planning are highly subjective. The correct size of schools, the correct mix of schools and the upper limits of catchment areas constitute value-judgements, yet these are variables to which some measurement must be attached. These are questions to be answered and problems which require a longer established research tradition; more immediately, however, there are themes which have already received a great deal of research attention and of government funds; compensatory education is one such theme.

THE COMPENSATORY EDUCATION MOVEMENT IN THE UNITED STATES

Compensatory education in the United States developed rapidly in the 1960s and was strongly linked with a general federal reaction against poverty and its associated qualities. As part of the Civil Rights Act of 1964, Congress commissioned a survey concerning the lack of equal educational opportunity for individuals by reason of race, colour, religion or national origin in public educational institutions at all levels in the United States. The resulting Coleman Report in 1966 (Coleman and coauthors, 1966) contained striking evidence of the extent of school segregation by ethnic groups in all parts of the country. While the South was more segregated than the North, it was still a fact that fully 72 per cent. of black first grades in the urban north attended predominantly black schools. A federal commission report in 1967 (United States Commission on Civil Rights, 1967) suggested that Negro children suffered serious harm when they were educated in racially segregated schools. Many studies examined the level of underachievement in depressed areas and the evidence for cumulative deficit (that pupils from depressed areas fall further behind normal as they grow older) is conclusive (Little and Smith, 1971, p. 27).

Compensatory education has become identified with an approach which attributes problems to the intellectual deficits of the learner and seeks to develop school-based programmes to improve the skill areas in question (Little and Smith, 1971, p. 41). In their review of American experience, Little and Smith (1971) grouped projects on a threefold basis. There were those projects which sought to bring about changes within the schools, often linked with curricula; those projects which attempted to forge closer relationships between schools and communities; and those projects which aimed at integration. The number of individual projects linked with one or more of these desired changes has been considerable. A very large number of pre-schooling experiments have been initiated, which Weikart (1967) classified as traditional, structured or task-oriented, according to their methodology. The 'Head Start' programme, set up in 1964–65, reflected a contemporarily high level of faith in the efficacy of early intervention in the educational process. In 1965, child development centres were set up in poverty areas to provide eight weeks of summer pre-schooling for four to five-year-olds. In the first summer, over a half-million children enrolled in 2 400 communities and this level of attendance has since been maintained. Subsequent surveys, however, have suggested that summer programmes have had little sustained effect and that little detectable difference could be measured between 'head start' and 'non-head start' children. The 'More Effective School Programme' initiated in ten New York schools in 1964 had a wider frame of reference. Attempts were made to improve the quality of schooling through measures such as the reduction of class sizes and provision of more specialists, but it is now clear that a dramatic increase in resources has not brought about a clear-cut improvement in performance. The 'Follow Thru' programme, 1967–68, emphasized the need for an adequate level of provision of a wide range of services, such as health and nutrition, facilities for parental and community participation, in addition to instructional content. The need for parental involvement has almost become an orthodoxy of compensatory education; Gray and Klaus (1965) noted a diffusion effect where parents were involved, which was transmitted to younger children. Many projects included home visits, and forms of community school were often proposed, sometimes involving staffing of schools on a rota basis from morning to late evening. Compensatory education in the United States has great diversity and range; Little and Smith (1971) found great difficulty in forming some overall assessment of its achievements. They suggested that much of the early optimism had not been fulfilled; where rigorous evaluation had taken place, results have often been disappointing or, where significant, have not been maintained for any length of time. Pre-schooling had not been as effective as thought, but there were signs that the best programmes produced a general intellectual advance. 'Although there have been some "paper programmes" it would be wrong to use this description to cover compensatory education in general ... a range of positive findings can be listed.' (Little and Smith, 1971, p. 134).

It is with the integrationist projects that the real conflicts of interest have arisen. In order to meet the integration levels stated in federal legislation. community schools are not sufficient; a school needed to set its quotas and to draw different types of children from different parts of the city. Although integrated residential areas were rare, the ideal mix had to be reproduced in school populations. Possible vehicles for integration are well known: some areas adjusted the zoning of catchments to provide a mix of black inner city and white suburb; pairing of black and white schools was a possibility; a plan for Pittsburgh envisaged increasing school size to serve large mixed catchments; while bussing has received most publicity. All these measures and others have been tried, but their success has clear limitations. Rose (1971) viewed the spending of educational funds as a window-dressing exercise; Pettigrew (1970) argued that separation in schooling was increasing. He described the case of Cincinnatti, where in 1950 seven out of ten Negro children attended predominanatly black schools but by 1965 nine out of ten did so. Pettigrew ascribed reasons for this trend to the fragmented nature of school district organization, local authority practice and the effects of private school enrolment. 'This pattern of growing separation is typical of American central cities, the very cities where Negro Americans are concentrated in greatest numbers' (Pettigrew, 1970, p. 191).

Of all the specific measures to bring about integrated schools, bussing has raised the most emotive issues. Armor (1973) reported a study in Boston which tried, over a short time period, to assess the achievements of a bussing policy. Among the bussed black students there was no gain in literacy or numeracy, no increase in aspirations, a decline in self-esteem, a heightening of racial identity and a progressive move towards being in favour of attending nonwhite schools. Between 1968 and 1970, the number of pupils of favour of integration declined, although there remained a majority in favour; there was a rise in college entry from black students but there was also a very high drop-out rate. Among the white children, there was a large decline in the level of support for bussing and little sense of social togetherness emerged in the schools. This particular study cannot be taken as conclusive, but the slow pace of change, the conflicts and the generally negative findings on American compensatory education have led to increased questionning of its principles. Jensen (1969) was stimulated to reopen the debate on the relative importance of genetic and environmental factors; Negro writers such as Rose (1971) saw little hope of positive change. *De facto* residential segregation remains a huge impediment in the way of school integration and black leaders have tended to de-emphasize integration as a goal. Community control over the local school system would not mean integration, but would transfer power to leaders of the black community.

Some of the evidence on integrationist policies is conclusive; the progress towards integration has been minimal (Farley and Taueber, 1974) and opposition from the white population has been considerable. On other aspects, the picture is blurred. Some writers argue that urban blacks prefer integrated schools (Hermalin and Farley, 1973), others that their feelings are moving against them (Armor, 1973). Even when integrated schools exist, the actual amount of 'real' integration within them may be small. The peer groups remain ethnically segregated and the potential effects of integration are thus restricted (Duncan, Haller and Portes, 1968–69); Armor's (1973) study reported a decrease of inter-racial experiences, the longer contact at school existed. This separation within schools would support the idea that an overall 'school effect' has little meaning and that the primary community of identification remains the segregated residential neighbourhood.

EDUCATIONAL PRIORITY IN BRITAIN

American research and activity, both on the broad front of the fight against poverty and on the narrower issue of educational disadvantage, had strong repercussions in Britain. A whole series of projects sponsored by the Schools Council have examined compensatory education (Schools Council, 1968a, 1968b, 1970), but the Plowden Report (Central Advisory Council for Education, 1967), perhaps more than any other single document, provided a landmark in the study of educational underprivilege and was a major impetus towards the adoption of area-based policies. Plowden identified the same basic problem which had prompted compensatory education in the United States—low achievement levels of particular groups—but was not faced with an ethnic problem of comparable dimensions. Factors other than race dominated Plowden thinking. In terms of relative chances of income, status and welfare at birth, the impact of the educational system on the lives of children remained heavily determined by family and class origins. Advocacy of a close relationship of social deprivation in neighbourhood and home with educational deprivation, was well founded in research; the real test of an educational system should be equality of achievement rather than equality of opportunity. Plowden shifted the emphasis from secondary and further education to the primary school; the perspective was straightforward—what deprived areas needed were good, normal, primary schools. The gap had to be narrowed between the fortunate and unfortunate in terms of educational advantage, research was recommended and the two innovative recommendations were a policy of 'positive discrimination' towards priority areas and a programme of 'action research' for such areas.

When the programme of educational priority, in response to the Plowden Report, was set up in Britain, a primary task was that of area definition. In the policy statement on educational priority (Halsey, 1972), the problem of defining areas and of developing indices is discussed.

The Definition of Educational Priority Areas*

In this discussion, we pose the problem of definition as it has been inherited from Plowden and we report on the London study in search of an adequate formula.

Both theoretically and administratively, the definitions we inherited from Plowden were not in terms of individual childern, nor classes, nor streams, nor even primarily schools, but areas. From the theoretical side, this definition has been challenged as a false conception of the problem of inequality in education. We have referred to Bernstein's criticism of compensatory education—that it distracts attention from educational to cultural deprivation. The point was well taken. There is no doubt that the danger exists, but at the same time it is important not to misrepresent Plowden. They certainly speak of a 'vicious circle', which has all the echoes of the theory of a cultural cycle of poverty. Nevertheless, their emphasis is on the schools.

Thus the vicious circle may turn from generation to generation and the schools play a central part in the process, both causing and suffering cumulative deprivation (Central Advisory Council for Education, 1967, p. 50).

We have ourselves seen schools caught in such vicious circles and read accounts of many more. They are quite untypical of schools in the rest of the country . . . tiny playgrounds; gaunt looking buildings; often poor decorative conditions inside; narrow passages; dark rooms; unheated and cramped cloakrooms; unroofed outside lavatories; tiny staff rooms; inadequate storage space with consequent restriction on teaching materials and therefore methods; inadequate space for movement and PE; meals in classrooms; art on desks; music only to the discomfort of others in an echoing building; non-soundproof partitions between classes; lack of smaller rooms for group work; lack of spare room for tuition of small groups; insufficient display space; attractive books kept unseen in cupboards for lack of space to lay them out; no privacy for parents waiting to see the head; sometimes the head and his secretary sharing the same room; and, sometimes all around, the ingrained grime of generations . . . (Central Advisory Council for Education, 1967, pp. 50–51).

What these deprived areas need most are perfectly normal, good primary schools alive with experience from which children of all kinds can benefit. What we say elsewhere about primary school work generally applies equally to these difficult areas. The best schools already there show that it is absurd to say,

---

*Reprinted from A. H. Halsey (Ed.) *Educational Priority*, vol. I (1972), H.M.S.O., pp. 43–53. With permission of A. H. Halsey and the Controller of Her Majesty's Stationery Office.

as one used to hear, 'it may be all very well in a nice suburb, but it won't work here'. But, of course, there are special and additional demands on teachers who work in deprived areas with deprived children. They meet special challenges. Teachers must be constantly aware that ideas, values and relationships within the school may conflict with those of the home, and that the world assumed by teachers and school books may be unreal to the children. There will have to be constant communication between parents and the schools if the aims of the schools are to be fully understood (Central Advisory Council for Education, 1967, p. 51).

But even if the emphasis is on schools, it can still be argued that it is fundamentally misconceived in that the appropriate 'unit' is the individual child. An example of this criticism, which in one form or another usually comes from those who are pessimistic about the Plowden approach and suspicious of its origins in American thinking on compensatory education, comes from Henry Acland. His major point is that not all low academic achievement is concentrated in E.P.A. schools. He then goes on to scorn the vague generality of Plowden conceptions of what schooling is about and to recommend concentrating on the narrow issue of school achievement' (Acland, 1971a, p. 451). He warns us that 'imprecisely defined programmes tend to evaporate leaving little behind' and that 'teaching an E.P.A. child about the way his local government works may put him even further behind in the conventional scholastic race' (Acland, 1971a, p. 451).

Again these points are well taken insofar as they refer directly either to the vagueness of the aims set by Plowden for E.P.A.s or to the danger of preparing children for a world which will not exist unless radical reforms are also carried through to ensure that after his education the child will be confronted by adequate opportunities for work and for the exercise of power and influence over his environment. But whether these criticisms have any relevance to what Acland (1971b, p. 508) calls the 'E.P.A. demonstration projects', he could not know in advance of the publication of our results. Two points can, however, be made about his essay before we come to the description and findings of our projects. Firstly, Acland's conception of the aims of schooling in E.P.A.s is narrow and contentious, and we do not accept it. Nevertheless, even if we did, it should certainly not be assumed, nor can it be inferred from any research evidence, that changes in curriculum, better and more stable teaching staffs, parental involvement or pre-schooling will be necessarily ineffective in relation to achievement standards. Secondly, Acland's argument about the distribution of low achievers is not confirmed by our own evidence. He reanalysed national survey data collected on behalf of the Plowden Committee, defining E.P.A. schools as those schools in the sample which had scores in the lowest 10 per cent. on two out of five indicators (social class, family size, incomplete families, parents from abroad, too few bedrooms), and defining underachievement as a score in the lowest 10 per cent. of the test score range. On the basis of this analysis, he concluded that 'for the special E.P.A. pupils only one fifth or less were under-achievers, compared with one tenth for the whole sample. . . . In other words, there is some concentration of "slower" children in the E.P.A. schools. But the difference is not educationally exceptional' (Acland, 1971a, p. 451). Using the same definition of underachievement, we found that Acland had grossly underestimated the proportion of underachievers in the E.P.A. project schools. Although only 16 per cent. of children were underachievers in the junior departments of the West Riding E.P.A. schools, there were 23 per cent. in Deptford, 33 per cent. in Liverpool, and 49 per cent. in Birmingham. These proportions are undoubtedly inflated by the large numbers of immigrants with language problems in many of the schools, but they nevertheless represent a problem for the E.P.A. teacher which is, on any terms, 'educationally exceptional'.

The difference between Acland's estimate and our own is not surprising when we consider how they were reached. He defined as E.P.A. those schools falling in the bottom 10 per cent. on certain social criteria of a national sample of 173 schools. However, in England and Wales as a whole, only 570, or 2.5 per cent., of maintained primary schools were recognized as schools of exceptional difficulty in 1968, and it was from among these that the E.P.A. project schools were largely selected. It follows that those which Acland took to represent E.P.A. schools must have been, on the whole, considerably better off than the schools which are officially regarded as E.P.A.

However, whatever the distribution of low achievers may be, the point is that programmes directed at individual needs are not in conflict with the area approach; indeed the two are complementary. The area approach is based on recognizing the complex forces in school and community which determine the meaning and effectiveness of educational experience including attainment. It also recognizes that schooling is more than the transmission and competitive testing of academic skills. To take the wider approach is admittedly more difficult, especially for 'hard-nosed' evaluation. Nothing less than a generation would be necessary to test some of the Plowden hypotheses, however refined by research designs. But, as we shall see, some elements in the actual designs of the four projects made precise testing of achievement hypotheses possible, and our conclusions do not support Acland's pessimism.

Returning now to the Plowden conceptions, we may note that the Newsom Report, published in 1963, had already hinted at the idea of E.P.A.s (Central Advisory Council for Education, 1963). Newsom and his colleagues wrote about education in the slums, though with care to write of 'schools in slums' and not of 'slum schools', and they added 'there is no satisfactory objective criterion of a slum' (Central Advisory Council for Education, 1963). With the advent of Plowden there was an attempt at closer definition. The key word is deprivation and the plea was for 'objective criteria for the selection of educational priority schools and areas' (Central Advisory Council for Education, 1967). Plowden was quite categorical in demanding that the 'criteria required must identify those places where educational handicaps are reinforced by social handicaps' (Central Advisory Council for Education, 1967, p. 57), and suggested eight characteristics (occupation, family size, receipt of state benefits, housing, poor school attendance, proportion of handicapped children, incomplete families and children unable to speak English). They were aware that 'an infallible formula cannot be devised' and called for 'wise judgement and careful interpretation' (Central Advisory Council for Education, 1967, pp. 57–59).

Most Local Education Authorities (L.E.A.s) would claim that they could pick out schools in an E.P.A. category without a complicated analysis based on specific indices, and there is some truth in this claim. For example, the Birmingham L.E.A., faced in 1967 with a possible E.P.A. experiment backed by the Advisory Centre for Education and the Ford Foundation, named a number of schools in Balsall Heath and Sparkbrook which might be included. Eventually, these became the schools suggested for experiment and evaluation in the Birmingham project. One of them failed to qualify as a school of exceptional difficulty by a substantial margin and one (an infant school) failed by a small margin, but the others were very near to the top of the list of deprived schools. We shall argue below that local diagnosis and flexible formulae are essential, but the desirability of seeking more precise and widely acceptable criteria is also obvious.

The reference in the Plowden definition to both schools and areas indicates a muddle which still remains and which was not disentangled by the Department of Education and Science (D.E.S.) Circular 11/67 dealing with a supplementary building programme for E.P.A.s. It was recognized in this circular that there must be an identification first of districts which would satisfy the Plowden criteria and second of schools within these districts to be replaced or improved. However, the Secretary of State went on to say that he 'does not intend to designate or define educational priority areas . . . (and) that the authorities themselves are well placed to judge to what extent their areas contain districts which suffer from the social and physical deficiencies which the Plowden Council had in mind'.

In many ways, the response to Circular 11/67 was a familiar exercise for L.E.A.s in submitting building programmes, though in this case the criteria were not, as in the past, a matter of the need for new schools on new housing estates, nor of additional accommodation required because of an increase in the birth rate. The claims had to be based on an assessment of the degree of deprivation in different districts.

It was the second part of the Plowden exercise which identified schools (i.e. schools of exceptional difficulty) in which there should be additional allowances for the staffs (£75 for qualified teachers). The amending order to The Remuneration of Teachers (Primary and Secondary Schools) 1968 gave statutory authority to these payments and Section R of the Burnham Report 1969 set out the criteria for recognizing these schools:

1. The social and economic status of parents of children at the school.
2. The absence of amenities in the homes of children attending the school.
3. The proportion of children in the school receiving free meals or belonging to families in receipt of supplementary benefits under the Ministry of Social Security Act 1966.

4. The proportion of children in the school with serious linguistic difficulties. The standard of school building was not, in this case, a primary factor.

Local authorities tended to name all schools in the areas identified in accordance with Circular 11/67, and, in order to ensure that none which might conceivably have a claim was excluded, a number of borderline cases was usually added.

Certain criteria were applied to all the schools and points awarded. Thus, in Birmingham, the L.E.A. and the teachers thought 191 schools deserved to be considered by the Secretary of State and fifty were approved as schools of exceptional difficulty for the purpose of additional allowances for teachers. Clearly recognition by the D.E.S. was bound to be somewhat limited because, in the first instance, the cost of the £75 allowances for the country as a whole was to be restricted to £400 000 per annum. If all the schools named by Birmingham had been recognized, the additional cost in teachers' salaries in a full year would have been around £177 000. In fact, the fifty approved cost the authority about £46 000.

This serious gap between schools where deprivation was substantial and those recognized officially as schools of exceptional difficulty was certainly not peculiar to Birmingham. A survey of the five county boroughs adjacent to Birmingham to the North-West, and collectively described as the Black Country, showed that the variations between expectancy and reality were broadly similar. These six large urban authorities (including Birmingham) with a total population of over 2 million, submitted 278 schools out of a total of 976 for recognition as schools of exceptional difficulty, but only 78 were accepted by the D.E.S. Put another way, the L.E.A.s in this vast conurbation considered that over 25 per cent. of their schools were of E.P.A. type, but only 8 per cent. were so recognized. Allowing for overstatement by L.E.A.s and the national limitation placed on allowances for schools of exceptional difficulty, it would be reasonable to suggest that at least 15 per cent. of the schools in these urban areas would have satisfied the Plowden criteria for positive discrimination.

Limited resources combined with the administrative procedures involved in the local application of multiple criteria and the vetting of L.E.A. submissions by the D.E.S. inevitably resulted in the creation of local anomalies. For instance, ten schools in Birmingham were one point only (maximum 100) below the last school admitted for recognition by the D.E.S.; and one case is known of an infant school on the same site as a junior school failing to get recognition, while the junior school was approved. On the criteria used, the most likely source of this anomaly was the percentage of children with serious language difficulties. But, in any case, there ought to be some common criteria other than the broad headings indicated by the D.E.S.

The D.E.S. recognized the problems involved in attempting to identify schools which were to be recognized as of exceptional difficulty, and attempted to ensure some standardization in interpretations of the Burnham criteria; the details were set out in the D.E.S. letter to local authorities dated 28th March 1968. They were asked for information under four broad headings, two of which related to the socioeconomic status of the child's home and parents, one to the incidence of free school meals (and therefore an extension of the socioeconomic factor) and the other to linguistic difficulties but not necessarily to immigrants. Sources of data were indicated. The age and/or condition of school buildings were not relevant in this context.

Our study of five attempts by L.E.A.s to define E.P.A. schools showed a relatively common pattern of criteria, though there were some interesting differences in detail, including quite substantial difference in the 'weighting' given to various indices in order to arrive at a 'points' total capable of being set in an order of priority.

In several cases, it was made clear that catchment areas were not easily defined and the use of statistics based on enumeration districts of the 1966 Census were sometimes seriously out of date, as in areas of recent development or distorted by overlap. Free choice of school was another hazard, as it was possible for various children living in the same road to attend a number of different primary schools, sometimes on religious grounds. Truancy is difficult to define and to quantify, and attendance figures may fluctuate widely for other than socioeconomic reasons. Staff turnover can be suspect unless carefully adjusted to reflect a genuine flight of teachers from repellent areas. However, such factors as standards of housing, large families, unemployment, social class, living density, immigrants and free meals were common to most lists of criteria.

It is widely acknowledged that the Inner London Education Authority (I.L.E.A.) index was the most sophisticated of those used by L.E.A.s, and we look at this in detail below. Some other authorities arranged their indices to total to ten, with each index scoring ten points, while one authority scored twenty-five points for free school meals and dropped social class to five points. In many ways, the non-takeup of statutory benefits like free school meals is a sound indicator of deprivation, as it can cover such factors as large families, broken families and unemployment, and, to this degree, to weight it heavily merely reinforces other factors already taken into account. But such variations in weighting, from as low as ten points to as high as twenty-five points out of a hundred for free school meals, suggest a need for the development of agreed national criteria.

The I.L.E.A. index

Alan Little and his colleagues in London began work on the construction of an index in the spring of 1967, after the appearance of the Plowden Report, conducting a pilot enquiry with a view to measuring and weighting the eight Plowden criteria, to which were added two others—pupil turnover and teacher turnover. The index was intended to relate to schools rather than to areas (Little and Mabey, 1971).

On the basis of the pilot study, a general study was begun later in 1967, collecting data from all I.L.E.A. primary schools but limiting it to those criteria which were felt to be both satisfactory and readily measurable. This meant that the criteria of truancy and inability to speak English were rejected as unsatisfactory and that those relating to size of family, incomplete families and proportion of disturbed or physically handicapped children were eliminated as not readily and adequately measurable.

At this point, Circular 11/67 (August 1967) intervened. Consequently, the criteria mentioned in the circular were added and considerations of national comparability were also brought into the problem. Thus, for the general study, the following criteria were used: (a) occupation, (b) supplements in cash from the state, (c) overcrowding of houses, (d) lack of basic housing amenities, (e) poor attendance, (f) proportion of handicapped pupils, (g) immigrant children, (h) teacher turnover and (i) pupil turnover. Poor attendance was included because specifically asked for in the circular, although the research group had originally thought it not a meaningful index. The measures and sources of information which were used in respect of each of these criteria were as follows.

(a) *Occupation.* The measure taken was the proportion of occupied males in unskilled or semi-skilled jobs (Registrar General's socioeconomic groups 7, 10, 11, 15, 16, 17). The 1961 Census was used as the source because the 1966 data were not available at that time.

(b) *Supplements in cash from the state.* The measure taken was the percentage of children in the school receiving free meals, as recorded on the annual return in September 1966. This return is the basis of information supplied by L.E.A.s each year to the Department of Education and Science, so that this measure provides national comparability.

(c) *Overcrowding of houses.* The measure was the percentage of households living at a density of more than $1\frac{1}{2}$ persons per room. Once again the source was the 1961 Census, so that, although outdated, standard national comparisons could be made.

(d) *Lack of basic housing amenities.* The measure was the percentage of households lacking one or more of the four basic amenities. The source was the 1961 Census.

(e) *Poor attendance.* This was measured as the average absence during a sample week and was taken from the annual return in May 1967. On this measure, there was no comparable data from other authorities.

(f) *Proportion of handicapped pupils.* The measure here was the percentage of children of low ability at the eleven-plus transfer stage in 1967. Low ability was defined as those placed in the bottom two of seven groups, which contained 25 per cent. of the children. The National Foundation for Educational Research had standardized the test for the authority on a national sample and therefore national comparability was assured.

(g) *Immigrant children.* This was measured as the proportion of immigrant children, as recorded on the annual D.E.S. return in January 1967.

(h) *Teacher turnover.* The measure adopted was the proportion of full-time teachers in school in July 1967 who had taught there for less than three academic years. It provided national comparability. In the national survey reported in Volume II of the Plowden Report, figures were given of staff movement over a three-year period.

(i) *Pupil turnover*. The measure here was the percentage of pupils in the school who spent an incomplete year there. Unfortunately, the 1965–66 records had to be used and no national comparisons could be made, apart from a crude approximation using the 1961 Census mobility tables.

Given the assembling of these measures, the next problem to be tackled was that of combining them into a single index for each school. The Plowden Report itself had evaded this question. The basic problem, of course, concerns what weight should be given to each factor, since almost certainly they are not all equal. And a further complication is the possibility that important criteria have been omitted (e.g. parental attitudes and family composition). In fact, the London team, in the limited time available, decided to give each measure equal weight in the index. The final scores, Y, were obtained in the following way:

$$Y = \begin{cases} \dfrac{X - (\overline{X} - 2s)}{4s} \times 100 \text{ if } \overline{X} - 2s < X < \overline{X} + 2s \\ 0 \text{ if } X < \overline{X} - 2s \\ 100 \text{ if } X < \overline{X} + 2s \end{cases}$$

where
$x = $ the original score for a school
$x = $ the mean for all I.L.E.A. schools
$s = $ the standard deviation of the original scores

After the general study had been completed, and apart from decisions to improve the data where appropriate on the basis of the 1966 Census and to explore further the problem of weighting, progress was once again overtaken by events. This time it was the D.E.S. memorandum on increments for teachers in schools of exceptional difficulty which, as we have seen, specified the criteria to be used. The I.L.E.A. team accordingly recalculated the index, which was the same as the one we have just described, except for the following modifications. Firstly, the 1966 data were available and used. Secondly, a single measure (that of the percentage of households without an inside lavatory) was used instead of a composite measure of housing stress. Thirdly, from the 1966 data it was possible to obtain a crude index of large families. The measure used was the percentage of children living in households containing six or more people. Fourthly, information on pupil turnover was updated and improved as schools were asked to record the number of pupils who spent an incomplete year in their school in 1966–67. This revised index, then, was made up of ten items, each given equal weighting in the way that we have described.

The picture which emerged is shown in Table 4.2. This table records the percentage observations for the first, fiftieth, hundredth and 150th schools in order of degree of disadvantage as measured by the index. The final index consisted of approximately 600 schools, infant and junior schools on the same

TABLE 4.2 Index for E.P.A.: percentages for each criterion

School	(a)	(b)	(c)	(d)	Criteria* (e)	(f)	(g)	(h)	(i)	(j)
1st	47.8	43.4	15.9	35.6	29.5	14.7	68.1	75.0	83.3	55.5
50th	42.1	39.1	10.7	30.4	34.3	12.3	53.0	65.0	71.4	39.1
100th	39.3	36.6	9.1	26.2	13.5	10.8	35.0	49.4	66.7	28.5
150th	32.7	33.2	5.4	22.2	11.4	9.5	21.8	28.9	57.1	23.5
E + W Average	31.9[a]	26.7[a]	1.2	19.8	5.1	N.A.[b]	2.5	25.0	35.6[c]	9.5[a]

Notes
[a] National figures abstracted from 1961 Census as 1966 figures not available.
[b] National data not available.
[c] Not strictly comparable; figures used for E + W abstracted from Plowden Report.

*Criteria
(a) Social class composition
(b) Family size
(c) Overcrowding
(d) Housing stress
(e) Cash supplements.
(f) Absenteeism
(g) Immigrants
(h) Retarded/handicapped pupils
(i) Teacher turnover
(j) Pupil turnover

site being treated as one unit. Average percentages for England and Wales also provide the national norms on the same basis in the table.

In the school figuring first on the index, nearly half of the employed men in the immediate area were in semi-skilled or unskilled jobs, half of the children in the area were in large families, one-eighth of the households in the area were technically overcrowded and over one-third of them were without inside lavatories. Nearly one-third of the children received free school dinners, an average of one-seventh of the children were absent in a selected week, two-thirds of' the children were immigrants, three-quarters of them were placed in the lowest quartile on an ability test, over half of them had an incomplete year in the school and four out of five teachers in the school had been there for less than three years. Looking at the 150th school and comparing it with the 'national average', there are only small differences in social class, family size and housing stress. However, more than twice the national average receive free dinners; instead, of one immigrant pupil for every forty children it is one for every five. The incidence of teacher turnover is 50 per cent. above the national average and pupil turnover more than twice the national average. Whereas nationally a school class is defined as having ten out of forty pupils of low ability and performance, this school has sixteen. For schools like this one, the problem is not so much the area (housing stress, overcrowding, class composition) but much more the social pathologies which are reflected within the school (high rates of teacher turnover, large numbers of backward pupils).

Attempts were made to refine the index further by a weighting of the measure of each criterion. First correlation coefficients between the criteria measures were worked out for the authority as a whole, for country and voluntary schools separately, and for each of the ten administrative divisions. The ten measures used were:

(1) Occupation	(6) Immigrants
(2) Lack of inside lavatory	(7) Teacher turnover
(3) Overcrowding	(8) Pupil turnover
(4) Free meals	(9) Absenteeism
(5) Handicapped children	(10) Large families

The correlations were in general rather low and therefore when, as a second step, component analysis was carried out it was not possible to extract principal components accounting for a large proportion of the total variance. It was found that the first component accounted for 25.2 per cent. of the variance over all the I.L.E.A. schools, with a range of 23.2 per cent. to 38.4 per cent. between divisions. The first four components accounted for 61.8 per cent. of the variance over the authority as a whole, with a range between divisions of 60.9 per cent. to 71.6 per cent. Across the divisions, there was marked similarity in the weighting of the principal components. In nearly all cases, variables 1, 3, 4, 5 and 6 had heavy weightings.

As a means of ranking schools this principal components analysis was unsatisfactory. It would, of course, have been possible to rank on the first component about which there was much similarity across divisions, but this method would have been unsatisfactory given that the first component accounted for only 25 per cent. of the total variance. There are several possible reasons for the unsatisfactory result, but at all events it was decided that the analysis did not warrant weighting and ranking according to loadings of the principal component and, for the time being therefore, equal weighting of all ten items constitutes the index.

Little and Mabey (1971) drew the following conclusions from their work on an E.P.A. index: 'It is the logic of this index that is important, not its detail; in other words attempting to designate areas of special concern by objective, reproduceable criteria and measures which are agreed prior to the designation. In addition, the reason for giving equal weighting to these factors was not because we thought that a weighted index would not be more useful, it was simply because there is not theoretical or empirical justification for a differential weighting scheme. A further issue is whether any system of weighting (either intuitively defended or empirically evolved) would be satisfactory either for one local area or for the whole country. Put another way, are the same criteria satisfactory for the variety of local conditions that add up to the United Kingdom? We cannot give a definite answer to these questions: the only assertion we would make is that the attempt to obtain general agreement is worthwhile, and initially this should concentrate upon outlining relevant criteria, and after that developing adequate measures. The index described above is an example of what might be done; it is the first step in rational resource allocation but not a final answer.

Essentially the index was an attempt to create an instrument that turned a policy objective into administrative practice. Its main limitations stem from the following:—

1. Lack of either clarity or specificity in the policy objective(s).
2. Lack of empirical-theoretical support for the policy objectives.
3. Lack of precision in criteria for determining policy.
4. Lack of adequate measures of agreed criteria.

In a sense they are limitations that stem from ignorance about the meaning and cause of multiple deprivation and lack of available data about the distribution of deprived areas. A final point is worth making about the index as an administrative tool; it was designed to help with determining both the volume of 'need' in a large authority and the distribution of extra resources designed to help educational priority areas. It was not designed as a means of evaluating the effectiveness of any help that was to be given. Possibly it might enable a comparison to be made between degree of deprivation and amount of resources mobilised, but its very nature does not permit any measurement of the impact of resources allocated. To do this another, and different, index would be necessary (although some of the criteria might be common). The reason for this is that the Plowden Report recommended the use of the education system as a means of funnelling resources to disadvantaged areas to compensate children for these disadvantages. The Plowden strategy did not recommended operation on the socio-economic causes of deprivation, merely using the school as a means of compensating for these deprivations.'

Research into educational priority area policies

Since the publication of this paper (Halsey, 1972), the concept of educational priority has received detailed examination. Five areas were selected for designation as E.P.A.s. Three of the areas, in London, Birmingham and Liverpool, were located within the central parts of large cities, a fourth comprised two small, isolated and economically depressed mining towns in the West Riding and the fifth was at Dundee in Scotland. Although all of these areas clearly warranted the description of being deprived, there was diversity among them and the notion of a unique kind of deprived area has little value. There was a communality of problems among the schools in inner-city areas; they were strongly developed by urban development schemes, by transient populations, by ethnic diversity and by instability of staff and student tenure. While the areas in London and Liverpool were comparatively stable working-class districts, the Birmingham area was strongly affected by recent immigration. The West Riding did not resemble the inner-city areas in many ways, its misfortunes were primarily economic and there was a good sense of community and a relatively stable population.

All the initial E.P.A. projects have now been completed and reports have been published (H.M.S.O., 1972–75); in addition, there have been independent publications such as that on community schools (Midwinter, 1972, 1973). In a review of the impact of the E.P.A. projects, Little (1975) identified some of the differences among them. The notion of deprivation was clearly varied and occurred in different kinds of circumstances in different kinds of areas. An acknowledgement of this diversity militated against global solutions to the problem of educational disadvantage. The Liverpool project was always more action-based with an emphasis upon localized remedies; its faith in community schools, a policy by which schools could be used to regenerate the community and the community to revitalize the school, questioned the Plowden belief that the good primary school was in itself enough. West Riding was the exceptional area and there the remedies, pre-schooling, home visiting and the Red House centre, involved the practitioners in the educational system (Smith, 1975). London's targets were the indirect decision-makers, the politicians and the administrators (Barnes, 1975) Little suggested that of the many activities attempted, those closest to the problems of the classroom received most acceptance, but by practitioners rather than a professional research audience. On the other hand, the projects did contain carefully designed studies which were in the mainstream of educational research. Although the projects have been completed, research along E.P.A. lines continues and E.P.A. schools have been defined on a national basis. The Department of Education and Science has an Educational Disadvantage Unit as an established part of its structure. As Little argues, a function of this unit now should be to ensure that funds are channelled into the right schools and the right places in order that both experimentation and active policies can be maintained.

Within each of the designated E.P.A.s, project teams had faced the tasks of understanding the bases of disadvantage and of prescribing solutions. Elsewhere, however, there remained doubts on the efficacy of the area-based approach; reference to the discussion by Acland (1971a) in the reprinted paper has raised some of the relevant issues. In a study based upon the inner areas of a large West Midlands city, Wilson and Herbert (1974) considered the problem of identifying deprived children on an individual rather than on an aggregate basis. A social handicap measure, based upon social class, family size, school attendance, child's clothing and parental contact with schools, was used to classify 'focus boys', aged 6 and 10 years, from the main sample of fifty-six families and 'control boys' from the same neighbourhoods and schools. The 'focus boys' generally had high scores and were severely socially handicapped, while the 'control boys' had lower scores. A series of tests demonstrated the all-embracing nature of deficit in the abilities of boys with severe social handicaps; the 'focus boys' consistently scored well below the 'control boys' over the range of abilities. Cognitive problems of inner-city children appeared to be considerable and, in the basic skill of reading, even the less handicapped boys failed to meet their potential. Wilson and Herbert attributed the extent of problems to the particular features of their study area which had high rates of immigration and of pupil turnover, and a preponderance of large families. Some studies (Entwisle, 1968–69) have argued that inner-city children are more advanced in linguistic ability than their suburban counterparts at the time of school entrance. Wilson and Herbert (1974, p. 68) concluded that there was a considerable range of ability within the inner city, some of which was unrealized: 'Remedies for these difficulties can hardly be sought within the school, both because the school's problems are great and multiple and because the roots of these difficulties are in the family and in the structure of society.'

The study by Wilson and Herbert confirms some of the inequities of the social system and demonstrates the extent of educational disadvantage and the ways in which it operates within the inner city. The types of neighbourhoods and schools with which they were concerned would fall within the classification of E.P.A.s; what they have shown is that social handicaps can vary considerably within such areas. Although their evidence supports the need for more discerning and individual definitions of disadvantaged children, there is also information to suggest that there are general problems which face children in these kinds of areas and that there are general difficulties with which schools have to cope.

Barnes and Lucas (1974) were critical of the concepts and guidelines which emanated from the Plowden Report. Their analysis was based upon data collected for schools in the I.L.E.A. area for 1968 and 1971. An index of relative school deprivation, based upon measures close to those recommended by Plowden, was used to rank schools; literacy surveys were used as a basis for child-based data sets. For each of the school criteria on which individualized data were available, children were assigned an 'at risk' or 'not at risk' score; from the cumulative index a dichotomy of disadvantaged and non-disadvantaged children was formed. From a comparison of individual items, the proportions of at-risk children are consistently higher in E.P.A. schools (Table 4.3); the range is from 14.1 to 50.1 in E.P.A. schools, compared with 13.1 to 40.0 in non-E.P.A. schools. While acknowledging these differences, Barnes and Lucas (1974, p. 56) argued that they were not substantial and that the total number of disadvantaged children was greater outside the E.P.A.s: 'It seems likely that the majority of disadvantaged children are not in disadvantaged areas and the majority of children in disadvantaged areas are not disadvantaged.' When disadvantaged children attended better schools, their improvement was marginal; in virtually every case, reading ability was low and resembled that of children in E.P.A. schools rather than the standard in their own school group. Barnes and Lucas, while acknowledging the deficiencies of their own project, argued that there was only a loose correlation between the distributions of disadvantaged schools and disadvantaged children. School and area-based policies could not adequately deal with the heterogeneous concept of educational disadvantage.

The study by Barnes and Lucas was limited to an inner-city area which inevitably lacks the range of environments which comprise the urban area as a whole. Some of their statements, 'Most poor families do not live in poor areas' (Barnes and Lucas, 1974, p. 51), make little sense in a perspective of the wider urban system and suggest that relative differences within their limited study area do not provide adequate absolute standards for comparison. Again, they criticize extreme points of view which were not advocated by Plowden or by the

TABLE 4.3 Proportion of children at risk and not at risk on the single items of risk (percentages)

	Immigrant children	High pupil mobility	High teacher mobility	High absenteeism	Large families	Free meals	Low verbal reasoning scores	Low social class
Least privileged group of schools (E.P.A. schools) N = 4,158								
Not at risk	67.75	81.48	70.66	73.71	57.96	68.22	49.86	37.45
At risk	30.57 }32.25	14.14 }18.52	23.74 }29.34	17.27 }26.29	34.53 }42.03	29.56 }31.76	30.47 }50.14	50.07 }62.55
Don't know	1.68	4.38	5.60	9.02	7.5	2.2	19.67	12.48
All other schools N = 26,338								
Not at risk	83.55	84.20	81.65	75.67	67.46	82.79	64.09	52.11
At risk	16.45 }16.45	13.03 }15.80	15.15 }18.34	17.59 }24.33	27.59 }32.53	16.57 }17.21	17.80 }35.91	38.40 }47.89
Don't know	—	2.77	3.19	6.74	4.94	0.64	18.11	9.49
Total N = 30,496								
Not at risk	81.56	83.99	79.97	75.48	65.90	80.73	62.19	49.98
At risk	18.22 }18.44	13.05 }16.00	16.53 }20.03	17.52 }24.52	28.55 }34.10	18.42 }19.27	19.52 }37.81	39.96 }50.02
Don't know	0.22	2.95	3.50	7.00	5.55	0.85	18.29	10.06
Number of cases of risk in the least privileged schools : Number of cases of risk in all other schools	1:3.2	1:5.4	1:4.0	1:5.9	1:4.9	1:3.4	1:4.5	1:4.9

Source. Barnes and Lucas, 1974, pp. 43–108. Reproduced by permission of J. H. Barnes and H. Lucas and Sage Publications Ltd., London.

E.P.A. researchers. Area-based policies have reflected an acceptance of some of the basic facts of the social geography of educational disadvantage, but they do not claim to be the only relevant approaches. Halsey (1972, p. 181) has argued that although the E.P.A. is a viable administrative unit for positive discrimination, the ultimate unit has to be the individual child and his family:

> The district as a means of identifying problems and allocating resources is held by us to be no more than a convenient framework within which closer and more detailed work has to be done with schools, school classes, individuals and families in order to realise a fully effective policy of positive discrimination.

Neither was it suggested that the educationally deprived area was a stereotype to which one kind of response could be made; there is 'No unique description of either E.P.A. or E.P.A. school . . . diagnosis of its ills and the prescription for its amelioration must always be based on detailed local study' (Halsey, 1972, pp. 78–79).

While cognisance of the demonstrable facts of a spatial clustering of educational disadvantage and its links with other forms of deprivation has clearly affected official policies, it is acknowledged that area-based approaches form one of several complementary alternatives. Area and school are aggregate units within which individual variations will occur. In most situations, however, particular areas and particular schools will contain disproportionate numbers of disadvantaged children. Use of detailed individual social handicap measures as a main policy in identifying deprived children is time-consuming, expensive and often not practical. Much social planning has perforce to use aggregate approaches with which its research resources can cope as a basic framework. Some attention needs to be focused upon the 'worst' schools and the environments, both physical and social, within which they are placed. At successive stages of a strategy for improvement, more detailed attention can be given to particular classes and particular children. Taken together, these various scales and stages of a policy of positive discrimination towards educationally disadvantaged children are not incompatible.

CONCLUSIONS

The school years form a major element in people's lives and have strong formative effects. School itself houses at least one reference group of crucial importance and provides a distinctive social environment. Outside school, there are other environments of at least equal importance—home, neighbourhood and peer groups are the main elements of these. From a very diverse research literature, it can be demonstrated that each of these has *some* effect and makes some contribution towards a comprehension of educational attitudes and performance. The emphasis here has been upon environmental contextual factors, particularly neighbourhood; clearly, however, each factor is partial and cannot be seen in isolation. The links between home and school and between communi-

156

ty and school are important, and, as a recent British study has concluded, 'What this study has demonstrated, more than anything else, is the necessity for focusing research attention on the interaction effects between pupils, the homes they live in and the schools which they attend' (Banks and Finlayson, 1973, p. 192).

Many qualities of the school environment and its setting have spatial implications. Although examples of these implications have been identified and discussed, few of them have been adequately researched. Decisions affecting school catchments, for example, which affect a range of matters from school composition to local house prices, are habitually made on an *ad hoc* basis, with political expediency as a main consideration. Educational planners cannot but benefit from the development of more systematic procedures from which alternatives can be identified and decisions made. The literature of E.P.A.s in Britain contains detailed work on indices, but the spatial definition of areas and schools is weakly exemplified; the application of indices to identify stress schools on a national basis could have benefited considerably from expertise in spatial analysis. As with so many aspects of societal behaviour, educational performance and practice can only be adequately comprehended with a multi-faceted approach, of which the spatial perspective forms an essential part.

REFERENCES

Acland, H. (1971a). 'What is a "bad" school?'. *New Society*, **9**, 450–452.
Acland, H. (1971b). 'Does parental involvement matter?'. *New Society*, **16**, 507–510.
Armor, D. J. (1973). 'Has bussing succeeded?'. *New Society*, **23**, 120–122.
Banks, O., and Finlayson, D. (1973). *Success and Failure in the Secondary School: An Interdisciplinary Approach to School Achievement*, Methuen, London.
Barnes, J. H. (Ed.) (1975). *Educational Priority: Curriculum Innovation in London's E.P.A.s*, H.M.S.O., London.
Barnes, J. H., and Lucas, H. (1974). 'Positive discrimination in education, individuals, groups, and institutions. In T. Leggatt (Ed.), *Social Theory and Survey Research*, Sage, London.
Bell, W., and Force, M. T. (1956). 'Urban neighborhood types and participation in formal associations'. *American Sociological Review*, **21**, 25–34.
Bidwell, C. E., and Karaska, J. D. (1975). 'School district organization and student achievement'. *American Sociological Review*, **40**, 55–70.
Central Advisory Council for Education (1954). *Early Leaving*, H.M.S.O., London.
Central Advisory Council for Education (England) (1963). *Half our Future* (The Newsom Report), H.M.S.O., London.
Central Advisory Council for Education (England) (1967). *Children and Their Primary Schools* (The Plowden Report), H.M.S.O., London.
Coleman, J. S., Campbell, E. Q., Hobson, C. J., Mc Pantland, J., Mood, A., Weinfeld, F. D., and York, R. L. (1966). *Equality of Educational Opportunity*, United States Government Printing Office, Washington, D.C.
Douglas, J. W. B. (1964). *The Home and the School*, MacGibbon and Kee, London.
Douglas, J. W. B., Ross, J. M., and Simpson, H. R. (1968). *All Our Future*, Peter Davies, London.
Duncan, O. D., Featherman, D. L., and Duncan, B. (1972). *Socio-economic Background and Achievement*, Seminar Press, New York.

Duncan, O. D., Haller, A. O., and Portes, A. (1968–69). 'Peer influences on aspirations: a reinterpretation'. *American Journal of Sociology*, **74**, 119–137.

Entwisle, D. R. (1968–69). 'Developmental linguistics: inner city children'. *American Journal of Sociology*, **74**, 37–49.

Farley, R., and Taueber, A. F. (1974). 'Racial segregation in the public schools'. *American Journal of Sociology*, **79**, 888–905.

Floud, J., Halsey, A. H., and Martin, F. M. (1957). *Social Class and Educational Opportunity*, Heinemann, London.

Glass, R. (1948). *The Social Background of a Plan: a Study of Middlesborough*, Routledge and Kegan Paul, London.

Gray, S. W., and Klaus, R. A. (1965). 'An experimental pre-school program for culturally deprived children'. *Child Development*, **36**, 887–898.

Hall, F. L. (1973). *Location Criteria for High Schools*, Research Paper No. 150, Department of Geography, University of Chicago, Chicago.

Halsey, A. H. (Ed.) (1972). *Educational Priority: E.P.A. Problems and Policies*, Vol. 1. H.M.S.O., London.

Hauser, R. M. (1968–69). 'Schools and stratification process'. *American Journal of Sociology*, **74**, 587–611.

Herbert, D. T. (1975). 'Urban deprivation: definition, measurement and spatial qualities'. *Geographical Journal*, **141**, 362–372.

Herbert, D. T., and Evans, D. J. (1974). 'Urban sub-areas as sampling frameworks for social survey'. *Town Planning Review*, **45**, 171–188.

Hermalin, A. I., and Farley, R. (1973). 'The potential for residential integration in cities and suburbs: implications for the bussing controversy'. *American Sociological Review*, **38**, 595–610.

Jackson, B., and Marsden, D. (1962). *Education and the Working Class*, Routledge and Kegan Paul, London.

Jenkins, M. A., and Shepherd, J. W. (1972). 'Decentralising high school administration in Detroit; an evaluation of alternative strategies of political control'. *Economic Geography*, **48**, 95–106.

Jensen, A. R. (1969). 'How much can we boost I.Q. and scholastic achievement?'. *Harvard Educational Review*, **39**, 1–123.

Johnston, R. J. (1974). 'Local effects in voting at a local election'. *Annals of the Association of American Geographers*, **64**, 418–429.

Karabel, J., and Astin, A. W. (1975). 'Social class, academic ability, and college quality'. *Social Forces*, **53**, 381–398.

Little, A. (1975). 'Where are the priorities now?'. *Times Educational Supplement*, **3117**, 17.

Little, A., and Mabey, C. (1971). *An Index for Designation of Education Priority Areas*, Inner London Education Authority Working paper.

Little, A., and Smith, G. (1971). *Strategies of Compensation: a Review of Educational Projects for the Disadvantaged in the United States*, O.E.C.D., Paris.

Lowry, M. (1973). 'Schools in transition'. *Annals of the Association of American Geographers*, **63**, 167–180.

Maxfield, D. W. (1972). 'Spatial planning of school districts'. *Annals of the Association of American Geographers*, **62**, 582–590.

Michael, J. A. (1961). 'High school climates and plans for entering college'. *Public Opinion Quarterly*, **24**, 585–595.

Midwinter, E. (1972). *Social Environment and the Urban School*, Ward Lock, London.

Midwinter, E. (1973). *Patterns of Community Education*, Ward Lock, London.

Payne, J. (Ed.) (1974). *Educational Priority: E.P.A. Surveys and Statistics*, H.M.S.O., London.

Pettigrew, T. F. (1970). 'Racial segregation and Negro education'. In D. Moynihan (Ed.), *Urban America*, Voice of America, Forum Lectures, Washington, D.C. pp. 187–197.

158

Robson, B. T. (1969). *Urban Analysis: A Study of City Structure with Special Reference to Sunderland,* Cambridge University Press, London.

Rogoff, N. (1961). 'Local social structure and educational selection'. In A. H. Halsey, J. Floud and C. A. Anderson (Eds.), *Education, Economy, and Society,* The Free Press, Glencoe, Illinois. pp. 242–243.

Rose, H. M. (1971). *The Black Ghetto: A Spatial Behavioural Perspective,* McGraw-Hill, New York.

Schools Council (1968a). *Enquiry 1: Young School Leavers,* H.M.S.O., London.

Schools Council Project in Compensatory Education (1968b). *Compensatory Education— An Introduction,* University College of Swansea.

Schools Council (1970). *Cross'd with Adversity: the Education of Socially Disadvantaged Children in Secondary Schools,* Methuen, London.

Sewell, W. H., and Armer, J. M. (1966). 'Neighbourhood context and college plans'. *American Sociological Review,* **31,** 159–178.

Sewell, W. H., and Orenstein, A. M. (1965). 'Community of residence and occupational choice'. *American Journal of Sociology,* **70,** 551–563.

Sewell, W. H., and Shah, V. P. (1968). 'Parents' education and children's educational aspirations and achievements'. *American Sociological Review,* **33,** 191–204.

Smith, G. (Ed.) (1975). *Educational Priority: the West Riding Project,* H.M.S.O., London.

Turner, R. H. (1964). *The Social Context of Ambition,* Chandler, San Francisco.

United States Commission on Civil Rights (1967). *Racial Isolation in the Public Schools,* Government Printing Office, Washington.

Walker, R. L. (1975). 'Urban subareas as sampling frameworks: a further development', *Town Planning Review,* **46,** 201–212.

Weikart, D. P. (1967). *Results of Pre-school Intervention Programs.* Ypsilanti, Michigan (mimeo).

Wilson, A. B. (1959). 'Residential segregation of social classes and aspirations of high school boys'. *American Sociological Review,* **24,** 836–845.

Wilson, H., and Herbert, G. W. (1974). 'Social deprivation and performance at school'. *Policy and Politics,* **3,** 55–69.

Chapter 5

Cities in the Mind

T. R. Lee

Whereas traditional approaches to the analysis of city structure have been almost exclusively concerned with the description, measurement and classification of objective qualities, a newer approach has emerged over the past two decades which is not merely different but in direct contrast. It is subjective rather than objective. Its emphasis is on studying the world not as it is but as it seems to be; not as physical reality but as perceived experience; not as a thing but as a 'seeming'.

New methods are frequently proclaimed by their enthusiastic proponents as superior to the old ones, but such claims usually need to be qualified—new methods are often better only *for certain purposes* and this one is no exception. The subjective approach to the study of cities is not intended to supersede the objective; it is supplementary and may hopefully become complementary. It opens up new ways of conceptualizing urban phenomena and gives a more complete way of distilling out and expressing some of the complex social patterns that exist, but it leaves large areas of understanding to be accessed more effectively by other means.

The approach is at the early stages, where it is given a variety of names. To some extent, these express different nuances and it is perhaps premature to tie on a label until we are fully satisfied that it will encapsulate the true essence. For example, 'mental mapping' and 'cognitive mapping' imply that the inner representation in the central nervous system is somehow isomorphic with the physical environment, whereas it is at least partially coded in verbal form and not wholly, if at all, in pictorial terms.

The use of the word 'image' is similarly thought by some to beg the question because it is generally taken to imply a pictorial representation, although this need not necessarily be so. Cognitive psychologists have usually preferred the word 'trace', precisely because it does not convey any implications of form; but for our present needs this seems a little craven, just because it is form that actually concerns us. The same could be said for 'inner representation'. In not presuming too much, it says too little. In both cases, we are aware that psychologists have been cautious not to imply anything about the neurological mechanisms involved, about which we know very little at present. 'Perception geography' is a name that emphasizes the immediate response to the environment and neglects the long-term cognitive structures on which this response is founded. 'Environmental psychology' encompasses a wider range of methods than the particular one we are considering. Also, many of its studies lie within the objective tradition.

However, the purpose in conducting this survey is not a quest for the semantic grail—it doesn't exist. The need is to parade the various links and associations which may add together to form a composite picture of this new approach. Perhaps, for me, it is enough for the time being to rely on the word 'subjective' in the sense of ' . . . having its source in the mind' (O.E.D.) to capture the essence. After all, the most important difference from other approaches is the orientation to individual minds, one at a time, before the data are aggregated. Its task is to externalize in order to observe what individuals have in their minds to correspond with the built environment. What form does it take'. How is this form related to the individual's past experiences and current needs? What is its life-cycle? How is it constructed and how is it used in everyday perception, navigation and mobility? Later, I shall propose the concept of '*schema*', because although it carries no specifically neurological overtones it has implications of morphology and, more, of dynamic function. But this is a case that must follow and not precede the more detailed evidence.

The aims of the new approach are simply to improve our understanding of human behaviour in cities. As with other forms of urban analysis, there is an implicit assumption that environment and behaviour are connected in a cause-effect relationship and that if cities could be designed or organized more effectively it would be beneficial to society. When made explicit, this may have, for some, the distasteful flavour of environmental determinism. It should therefore be said at once that environmental psychologists see human beings as interacting with the environment, influenced by it but not controlled exclusively by it, selective in their use of it and, indeed, able to divert it to their own purposes.

Nonetheless, we need to understand this interaction if we are to engage in the massive reshaping of the urban environment made possible by modern technology and planning. For this purpose, the environment–human response side of the interaction is the most important focus. Simple, mechanistic stimulus–response approaches have been found to be extremely limited. There are too many important mediating variables in the human being himself, and attention has therefore switched to the ways in which the environment is perceived and 'known' by people—in short, to what the environment *means* to them.

The main theme of this chapter will consist of a description of the various attempts that have now been made to look at the city through the eyes of those who live in it—as reflected in the minds of its inhabitants. First though, we shall briefly review the efforts of psychologists, mainly in the laboratory, to understand how the immediate spatial environment is perceived and given enduring representation in the mind.

IMAGERY IN PSYCHOLOGY

Fechner (1860) carried out observations on imagery which were later developed by Galton (1880), who asked his subjects to call up a picture of their breakfast table and then to answer questions on the degree of clarity, colour and brightness they observed. This work led to the conclusion (which is still with us) that there are very large differences between individuals in their capacity to image. But the problem is fraught with the difficulty of conveying comparable standards of vividness when the experience is only accessible to private introspection. Also, it would seem that the very process of externalization and self-examination would be even more destructive of pictorial images than of other 'traces'. Drawing is notoriously difficult for most people, resulting in a product that the majority plainly acknowledge to be quite different from what is 'in their mind's eye'. The other main method of access requires an even more drastic recoding into verbal terms.

A number of scales of the vividness of imagery have been developed over the years and have been quite widely employed in studies of imagery and learning, but not, so far as is known, to the cognition of the built environment. There are some studies of human maze learning in the classical experimental psychology literature that are quite revealing. Twitmyer (1931) compared performance with and without prior visual experience of the stylus maze. This was achieved by using as 'experimentors' people who had no anticipation that half of them would be asked to serve as subjects on the following day. It was found that these subjects showed an initial advantage in performance, but they had to learn the 'feel' of the maze and of its parts. A maze does not feel the same as it looks! The person who expects to find his way by reading a map in advance is well aware of this. However, it does seem that cognitive knowledge can be acquired by observation as well as by direct experience.

Perrin (1914) compared human performance on a full-size maze in an amusement park with a laboratory stylus maze of the same pattern which resembled the famous Hampton Court maze. In both cases, the learning processes were gradual, with the first and early gain being *a general orientation to the place*—a rough knowledge of the position of the exit in relation to the starting point. The subjects reported their attempts to build up a visual imagery of the pattern, a verbal description of the place or just a direct feeling of how to move.

The most intriguing group of laboratory animal behaviour studies that are relevant to our interests were carried out as part of the controversy between the theories of learning proposed by Hull and by Tolman (Hilgard and Bower, 1966). The most elegant (if not the most impartial!) summary of the work is contained in the well-known article by Tolman (1948). Until fairly recently, maze learning has not been seen primarily as an illustration of spatial learning, for this would after all have pre-empted the argument in Tolman's favour. Rather, it was seen at the time by psychologists as a standard laboratory task requiring behaviour to be emitted, with the emphasis only on mobility in the sense that this requires the sequential emission in the correct order of a number of actions. It was not seen as distinctively different (and, indeed, the difference is not large) from the performance of any motor skill. Psychologists were simultaneously studying how people could learn a sequence of switches to display different lights or sequences of nonsense syllables to form a list.

Perhaps the main point is that their search, led by 'connectionist' theorists like Thorndike (1911) and Hull (1943), was upon the mechanism that connected stimuli with responses. Hull saw the rat in the maze as an organism containing an incredibly sensitive set of receptors that could pick up the faintest clues from the maze environment and form a neural connection between these impressions and the movements that he subsequently found to be successful in moving through the maze. Reward, or 'reinforcement' as psychologists call it, was and still remains the crucial element. Actions which pay off are retained and those that lead nowhere tend to die away. It is hardly necessary to say that, although this concept continues to have a profound explanatory power, its operation is far from simple. Anyway, Hull's theory suggested the gradual joining of a series of stimulus–response links which in turn were more strongly associated with the next appropriate link in the chain than with subsequent or preceding ones. It implied a mechanistic explanation in the behaviourist tradition and was greatly respected at the time because of the apparent readiness with which the results of experiments could be quantified.

Tolman's approach was characterized as 'molar' as distinct from 'molecular'. He argued that the behaviour of the rat indicated that he 'knew' where he was in the maze! He learned by constructing a map in his head, which Tolman called a *cognitive map*, and in some way this could be consulted when necessary. Tolman's theory included intervening variables like 'expectations', which seemed highly plausible but which were intangible and contested. The whole notion of imagery was one of the red rags that inflamed the bull of behaviourism —if this partisan metaphor may be allowed. Neither images nor cognitive maps could ever be more than hypothetical constructs and the behaviourists were pledged to distrust everything except movements and verbalizations, of which all scientific observers could give accurately corresponding reports. We cannot discuss in detail the intriguing experiments that were carried out to illuminate this controversy, but a brief description is relevant to our interest, providing we bear in mind the similarity between a maze and a city.

Hull's theory implied that one learns which way to turn from the experience of either ending up in a blind alley or making progress towards the goal. The latter experience was rewarding in the same way as finally arriving at the food-box goal gave a larger satisfaction which spread backwards to strengthen the preceding responses. However, in a series of experiments called the 'latent learning' experiments, rats were left in mazes to wander about all night without any evident goal box being present. They could not form stimulus response links because there was no reward located anywhere. They had nowhere to go. However, when a goal box full of delicious bran mash (or whatever rats had a taste for in those days) was added to the maze, they quickly revealed that a great deal had been learned about its design. Another experiment involved a simple cross-maze, in which rats were taught to start at the end of one arm and to find a reward only if they turned right at the cross-roads. The straight-ahead and left-hand turn would be predicted to be eliminated by a lack of satisfaction under Hull's theory. A Hullian rat would have learned, quite simply, a right-hand *movement* and this would have been strongly implanted. However, when rats in the cross-maze were put in at the opposite end after this intensive learning, they did *not* reproduce a right-hand movement—but the left-hand turn which now took them to the goal. It appeared that they 'knew' where the goal was—or they had a cognitive map or image.

More complex experiments devised situations in which the shortest path to the goal was blocked, leaving open a number of alternative paths which had been observed but never experienced by the rat. The doughty animal chose the shortest route as if he knew the entire pattern in spite of his lack of direct reinforcement. The famous 'sunflower' maze was a device which forced the animal to take a roundabout route to reach the goal and, when this had been learned, it was substituted by a series of straight-line radiating paths. Instead of choosing the highly reinforced initial left-hand turn which it had apparently acquired in previous experience, it tended to choose the straight path which led over towards the right but directly towards the goal.

It would be too simple to report that Tolman won the day. In the event, in spite of prodigious expenditure of effort, the controversy turned out to be only a semi-event. Perhaps the most crucial experiments were the ones done when most people had lost interest, but which showed that a rat behaved like a Hullian rat in the very early stages of learning and when it had only a very restricted view of the situation. Later on, and in situations where it had a wider conspectus of the environment, it seemed to behave like a Tolman rat.

Few would dispute now that learning a complex city seems to depend upon an inner representation like a cognitive map, although the nature of this model is less sure. Also, the initial or highly over-learned strip maps that we acquire in driving repeatedly from home to work on the same route often appear to be run off almost automatically as a series of stimulus–response links. We become conditioned to make certain turnings, and most people have had the experience of finding themselves well along the usual but incorrect route on those rare occasions when they had intended to take an unusual turn to a new destination.

In recent years, there has been burgeoning interest in imagery in connection with verbal learning, and it must be sufficient to say that the experiments in this area are variations on the theme that subjects are asked to connect two totally disparate words either in the normal way, by thinking of their sounds, or by actively attempting to form pictorial images of the objects which the words symbolize. For example, if one is asked to form the improbable paired associate theatre–zebra, one can think of that distinctive animal sitting on his haunches in the back stalls and holding a pair of opera glasses to his eyes. In both children and adults, but particularly in the former, this strategy leads to faster learning.

The ultimate and definitive test for the existence of imagery must be that experimental subjects should show evidence that they are consulting an inner representation and acquiring information by this means *which could only be stored in pictorial form*. Needless to say, these conditions are almost impossible to meet with certainty. However, a most ingenuous strategy has been developed recently by Shepard and Feng (1958). They give their subjects a manual problem-solving task to perform, such as folding up a three-dimensional paper cube from a two-dimensional flat outline of squares. They ask the question whether two widely disparate marks on the flat version would finish up next to each other or still disparate on the ultimate cube. The basically identical task can be replicated with widely differing degrees of complexity. Sometimes the answer is immediately apparent; in other cases the form is so complex that the answer takes a while to perceive. The point, however, is that Shepard and Feng find a high correlation between the speed with which the person can arrive at the decision by manually folding the forms and his speed when attempting to image the necessary folding actions. The implication is that when the task has to be performed in the head, the same series of operations must be followed through as when using the hands.

This and many other experiments suggest that the long period of obscurity and even disgrace that characterized the concept of imagery is drawing to an end. It is to be hoped that the next and intriguing stage will be an attempt to distinguish those cognitive operations which are best performed by imagery and which by the use of language. Imagery enables us to store a lot of information about a single object but language is greatly superior for storing concepts which distil an essential quality from many objects. It is difficult to form an image of 'up', or 'long'. Only the images of individual objects or situations come to mind and these are poor tools of thought compared to words. On the other hand, much of the information we need to store about space and the environment, in particular, is unique to us—and imagery seems to serve us well.

THE PHENOMENAL APPROACH TO URBAN STRUCTURE

Some early presentiments of a subjective approach appeared towards the end of the nineteenth century, when there was a prevalent view that humans had an innate sense of spatial orientation, comparable to their senses of smell and taste. The extraordinary homing and migratory abilities of birds and fishes gave credence to this idea, but a number of studies failed to provide any confirmation. The importance of the research, however, is that it invoked the concepts of ego-centrism and domi-centrism, two inner representations which, however acquired, could be consulted in the mind and which gave man a framework for navigation in space.

One early writer (Trowbridge, 1913) even used the expression 'imaginary map' in the title of a paper in *Science*. He also described a test in which his subjects were required to mark the directions of cities on a circular sheet of paper. Other early studies in the same tradition rotated blindfolded subjects and then asked for the city directions or presented circular maps of well-known places with instructions to put them in the 'most natural' position. Lord (1941) asked subjects to represent the spatial geography of an area by placing dots and numbers representing 16 cities in Michigan on a test paper in relation to a central mark showing a city familiar to them all. In psychology, the most ardent early advocate of the phenomenal approach was undoubtedly Kurt

Lewin (1938, 1951). His principal concept was the 'life space', which can contain, of course, either social or physical objects, and the intriguing diagrams he made to illustrate it are still the epitome of phenomenalism for psychologists. He used topological concepts such as vector, valence, boundary, etc., to model the life space, together with formulae using mathematical notation, but most of his research could have been, and seems to have been, done without the benefit of both these appurtenances.

Lewin also used the concept of *social* space, but hardly developed it, and it is not clear from his writing whether the concept was intended to aggregate the life spaces of a number of individuals or to represent the existence of other people in one individual's life space. His life spaces were linked to the physical environment, but only in a symbolic way; for example, a barrier preventing access to a goal could be represented as a partition wall or as a forbidding parent. Some authors have failed to synchronize geographical and social space, others have ignored one or the other, but Lewin treated them as the same thing and this created difficulty in using his theory to guide research.

The French sociologist Chombart de Lauwe (1952, 1960) adopted a distinction between objective and subjective social space and in his study of each of the arrondissements, quartiers and secteurs of the city of Paris he gathered empirical data at both levels. Subjective social space was simply defined as a space perceived by members of particular human groups, and he was able to demonstrate its difference from the objective concept originally advocated by his mentor, the geographer Sorre (1955), whose notion of objective social space was of a physical area containing a social group sharing norms of perception and behaviour engaged in interaction structured by focal buildings ('points privilégé', or what Lynch, 1960, later called 'monuments') such as churches, schools, theatres, and so on. The definition of social space used by de Lauwe was as follows: 'the spatial framework within which groups live; groups whose social structure and organisation have been conditioned by ecological and cultural factors'.

The major theoretical importance of de Lauwe's work lies in the synthesis it proposes of social and physical space:' . . . its primary value perhaps is in the connection postulated between the internal subjective order (attitudes, traditions, and aspirations) and the external spatial order, within an urban milieu' (Buttimer, 1969).

A comprehensive subjective approach to the city itself did not emerge until the 1960's, the earlier work was concerned with its subdivisions, mainly with the urban neighbourhood. It is convenient, however, to depart from the chronological development of ideas and to look first at those studies which have been conducted at the larger scale.

Some examples of urban imagery

The work of Lynch (1960) is certainly the best-known study of urban imagery, probably because it excited the interest of planners and translated the issues from the academic arena into the realm where decisions are made. Residents of Boston and New Jersey were given lengthy interviews in which they were asked to describe the city, to indicate locations and to make outline sketches. The operation was partly facilitated by making both real and imaginary journeys. This method has all the advantages—and disadvantages—of the clinical approach in psychology. The maps are gently persuaded out of the subject's consciousness and not given a presumptive form by a rigid framework .of imposed instructions. The maps which emerged are excellent exemplars of the schematic nature of imagery—of the abstraction, distortion and regularization that takes place in the dynamic processes of perception and memory.

An ingenious method is employed to illustrate on the maps the perceived 'strength' of different elements in the city. Paths and edges, for example, are marked in with lines whose thickness indicate the approximate percentage of respondents who mentioned them. (Figure 5.1 provides an example of a map derived by the Lynch method). An interesting feature is the presentation of different maps for several alternative modes of elicitation. On the other hand, only rather small numbers of subjects appear to have been used, and there is no indication of how the *forms* of their separate and individual images have been synthesized into the collective representations which Lynch presents. This must necessarily rely on his own intuitive judgement. Also, the study does not include a breakdown into people with different histories or with different functional relationships to the city—so the antecedents of imagery do not emerge.

An emphasis is usefully put upon the 'legibility' or 'imageability' of city plans and Lynch draws attention to the importance of five kinds of element: paths, landmarks, edges and districts. These are obviously crucial to 'knowing' a city, which in turn is indispensable to existence within it. It does also raise, however, some very important questions about the relationship between the simplicity or clarity of layout and its interest or aesthetic appeal. Is there some optimum point on a dimension of simplicity/complexity or are some townscape forms intrinsically more satisfying than others?

De Jonge (1962) took some of these points further in a comparison of images of Rotterdam, Amsterdam and The Hague, using small goups of about two dozen residents from each. Amsterdam emerges as the most legible city because of its unique spider-web pattern, formed by concentric canals related to a very strong linear core consisting of the Central Station, the Mint Square and a traditional meeting place and site of the Royal Palace, the great square known as The Dam.

De Jonge presents quantitative evidence that where the ground plan is salient people's maps give priority to roads and nodes, but where this is not so they resort much more to landmark buildings. He specifically attributes the strong affection which people have for Amsterdam to its imageability. This gains further support from a comparison of two residential districts in Delft, one with a grid-iron layout and great uniformity in architecture and the other with more variety of form and a rememberable ground plan. However, the

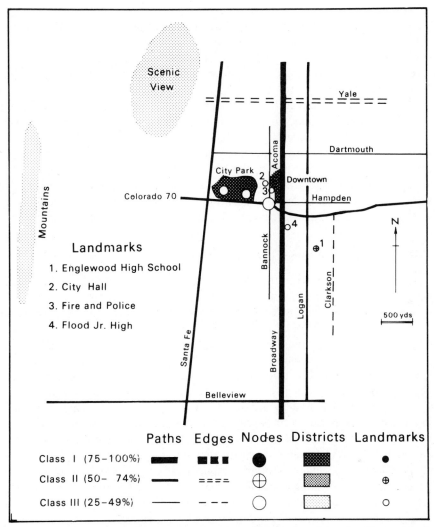

FIGURE 5.1 A Citizens' Image map of Englewood, Denver, Colorado. (Reproduced by permission of J. D. Harrison and W. A. Howard and Sage Publications Ltd., London. From *Environment and Behaviour*, vol. **4** (1972), p. 396)

difficulties of the problem are highlighted by reference to yet another district in The Hague, where the geographic complexities baffle long-term residents as well as visitors. De Jonge is forced to conclude that 'an area where visitors have trouble orienting themselves may be popular ... on account of its quaint and exclusive character or because of other attractive qualities'.

We must certainly be cautious in drawing conclusions from these studies to avoid the danger that cities will be planned 'from the air'—as buildings have too often been planned as monuments for external spectators. However, the important thing to bear in mind is that although the elements of the city are functional and not graphic and the attention of planners should be on the behaviour which is both the cause and the result of the perceptions of the city— it is precisely this behaviour which is reflected (in a manageable form) in the image of the city. We must learn how to read the image. Francescato and Mebane (1973) investigated the composite images of two great cities, Milan and Rome. They found both to be highly legible cities but in very different ways; the Milanese laid emphasis on work, activity, dynamism and active recreation and sport, while the Romans saw their city in terms of its art, culture, and history and mentioned the monuments, buildings and museums most frequently. As to the question of the applicability of map-sketching as a tool, a very clear pattern emerged from the people who refused to draw a map. Older and lower class respondents refused far more frequently even though they were quite willing to answer all the other questions (see also Appleyard, 1970).

The representation of named parts of the city

There is a very important but often neglected distinction in imagery studies between a strictly personal area (a 'beat', or a 'turf', territory, district, etc.) which may have no acknowledged correspondence with anyone else's area and the personal perception of an area that has a common frame of reference given to it by a name, even if the name is as vague as the 'West End' or the 'Town Centre'.

A good example of the latter is a study of the inhabitants' images of Highgate Village (Eyles, 1968). It is ironic that Eyles began his study by searching for an objective base from which to proceed. If one is to measure the inhabitants' perceptions, one has first to decide who are the inhabitants. However, there is no formal delimitation of Highgate Village in a political or administrative boundary. The officials of two distinguished local societies were asked, but although they were extremely helpful they could only give their own mental maps of Highgate Village. Similarly, estate agents were thought to be prone to stretch the area to its absolute limits because the attribution of the name is inclined to enhance the value of their properties. Inevitably, Eyles had to make an arbitrary delimitation of his population to be sampled.

The questions he asked were 'Have you heard of Highgate Village?' and 'Would you mind drawing what you think the Village is on this map?'. He then went on to point and name each of the residential roads in the selected areas. It is again significant that about 80 per cent. of his sample of one hundred were able to draw maps and there were apparently systematic differences with length of residence, social class and residential location within the area. The subjects showed high agreement on a 'core' area, but less correspondence over a second peripheral area; they tended to 'pull' the Village towards themselves.

An interesting methodological feature of Eyles' approach is that he at least looked at the possibilities of expressing differences in shape by their approximation to mathematical formulae. This was not a successful exercise and one would suppose that the influence of variations in the physical environment is likely to remain the major determinant of shape. However, it is entirely possible that there is, for example, an elliptoid form with the longer axis stretching in the direction of the city centre. This applies more to personal neighbourhoods and would require very large samples for its elucidation.

This study might also be used to highlight a theoretical point of which researchers need to be keenly aware. It is probable that the residents in the locality studied by Eyles have cognitive structures *both* of their personal neighbourhoods and of the 'acknowledged district' of Highgate Village. The latter is an essential frame of reference for answering questions such as 'Where do you live?' and 'In which cinema did you see that film?'—in fact, for a great deal of sociospatial orientation at a given scale. The crucial requirement is that people living outside the area should also have Highgate Village in their cognitive structures, otherwise, communication fails. Hence (and to illustrate the point about scale), if one were answering such questions for a Scot or a New Yorker, one might get a blank stare unless one substituted something like 'North West London'. It follows that there is a methodological trap to be avoided here. The respondents must all be brought to focus in on the equivalent structure— and it should be the one intended.

Another study of the images of an 'acknowledged district' was a large-scale study of the images formed of the *city centre* by over 1 000 citizens of Karlsruhe, carried out by Klein (1967). His method was to present a total of twenty-four cards bearing the names of well-known streets and landmarks, with a request to pick out those which '. . . in your opinion are part of the town centre'. The use of this method emphasizes that imagery may be accessed by means other than mapping. Like all methods, however, this verbal one has its imperfections: it is entirely probable, for example, that comparisons across social classes or sex are partially confounded because many people have constructed for themselves a *pictorial* image of the city centre and hence, although they might respond to a particular place when presented visually, they do not recognize its name.

A good deal of useful information was nonetheless derived in this study, using the simple technique of recording the percentages of people who included each of its streets or landmarks within their image of the city centre. There is high agreement on some boundaries, less on others. Klein says that in the east and south-east there is no clear border, but 'the decline is continuous'. This raises an important but so far unresolved problem. Does a lack of correspondence between people's judgements necessarily imply a vaguely perceived boundary? It is a tempting conclusion, but there is normally no way of distinguishing it from the alternative (i.e. that there is simply a high variance of nonetheless clear individual boundaries).

A comparison between men and women in the sample gives very good support for the functional origin of differences in city perception. Women had a wider-ranging area, and preferred to include an elegant shopping precinct and the cultural centre. People who live nearer to the centre and who have been resident for longer nominate a smaller area—probably an example of increasing differentiation. Social class differences are shown which appear to be functionally related to occupation and, hence, activity. Perhaps the clearest and most interesting finding from this study is the clear shift of the perceived centre towards the home. Those living on the east shift their town centre eastward and vice versa, resulting in a relatively small overlapping area of unanimity.

Urban neighbourhoods and the subjective approach

The evolution of the subjective approach to urban residential structure has been a gradual one but found its earliest expression in neighbourhood studies. It can be said, for example, that although the Chicago School were highly objective in their approach, working mainly from the map base, they recognized what McKenzie (1921) called a 'rudimentary sense of selfconsciousness' by the citizen of his 'natural area'. Another early writer, McClenahan (1929), had interviewed 649 families in a residential area of Los Angeles, and impressed by the range of associations they had formed in all parts of the city proposed the new concept of the 'communality'—an urban social structure which ' . . . has no attachment through its membership to a definite locality' and ' . . . whose members are drawn together on a basis of the common interest or interests sub-served'.

An important but little known contribution was made by Sweetser (1941, 1942). His analysis was at the person-to-person level. Interviews were held with the fifty-four residents of a city block in Bloomington, Indiana, who were asked to specify individually with which of each other and of the eighty-five persons in the facing streets of the surrounding blocks they had neighbourly relations. The latter were defined in two ways—'associational' and 'acquaintanceship'—and separate *personal* neighbourhoods were charted and reproduced. The effects of variables such as age, sex, length of residence and occupation upon the size and composition of the neighbourhoods were examined.

If there are shortcomings of this pioneering study, they are to be found in the very limited sample and in the arbitrary prior restriction imposed by the investigator on the area from which friends could be nominated. Sweetser's main conclusions were that each person's urban neighbourhood is 'compositionally unique' and 'spatially discontinuous'. The former of these descriptions anticipates a number of subsequent studies. The latter is clearly a function of the operational definition which governed the method of data collection, which has affinities to 'social space' (de Lauwe, 1960) and to 'social networks' (Bott, 1955). If neighbourhood is defined in terms of a perceived set of social relationships, the less conscious mutual awarenesses that characterize neighbouring below these threshold, but which are nonetheless important in providing sociospatial *continuity*, will not become manifest. However, Sweetser was well ahead of his time and, instead of fruitlessly searching for the 'true' concept of neighbourhood, he recognized that different definitions and approaches suited different purposes of enquiry and application.

Another glimmer in the emergence of a subjective approach was a paper by

Riemer (1951) entitled 'villagers in metropolis'. This title was clearly intended to be ironical. Riemer was sceptical of the planning strategy of the neighbourhood unit which was enjoying an official vogue at the time. However, he did clearly state that 'the empirical approach to our problem may concern itself either with (a) neighbourhood *consciousness* or (b) neighbourhood behaviour.' In pursuit of (a), he put the question 'what do you consider your neighbourhood?' to a sample of 197 people. Their answers were apparently 'vague', but he does report that 181 of them gave an answer in terms of contiguous housing blocks. Perhaps because he was unsure what conclusion to draw from his subjects' lack of agreement, but certainly because he felt that the proximity-relations, primary-group type of neighbourhood was rapidly declining in importance, he did not take the matter further. His notions of individual and family 'contact clusters' in different parts of the city, developed tentatively in the paper under discussion and demonstrated empirically in a latter paper, align him more closely with the 'social space' theoreticians. However, the social relationships that comprise the data are, in a sense, perceived ones. The empirical study of contact patterns (Riemer and McNamara, 1956) was carried out by asking respondents to give the number and location of all their trips over the past month and to divide them into personal and commercial. The results show a J-curve distribution against distance from the home, but are not too easily interpreted. Riemer took them to confirm the view that 'friendship patterns are no longer restricted to within a neighbourhood setting'.

It is, in fact, difficult to see how they ever could have been, or the commercial life and communication system of cities would never have developed. The question that has to be asked is whether a sufficiently high proportion of such contacts are local, to imply the continued viability of the neighbourhood concept and its encouragement by planning. The size of this proportion must be largely a matter of judgement, but first the statistics must be appropriately interpreted. The distribution of each subjects' trips was represented by a *mean* score, and for a highly skewed J-curve distribution this is a most unsuitable measure of central tendency. Furthermore, the mean of the individual means was then employed—further compounding the distortion. The first of these cannot be converted back from the data given, but if we take the second mean it is evident that the mode of the distribution is at 1.5 miles and the median at about 1.7 miles—already very different from the *mean* figure quoted of 2.84 miles.

When we add to this the facts that the city concerned is Los Angeles—one of the most mobile cities in the world—and that the sample was drawn from the telephone directory, then we could surely argue (as Foley, 1950, had argued a year earlier on finding that 47 per cent. of trips were within a mile and 37 per cent. had been made on foot) that 'our large cities, for all their urbanity, seem to contain an impressive degree of local community life . . .'.

One most appropriate way of looking at this question of local concentration has emerged from the study of the microecology of friendships (Schachter and Back, 1950; Merton, 1947, 1957; Smith, J., Form, W. H., and Stone, G. P.,

1954). For example, Merton (1947), reporting some details of the Columbia Lavanburg project, writes: '... close personal relations in Craft town it was soon evident, were largely a product of residential propinquity. The residents had 54 per cent. of their friends within the same, adjacent, or cross street units, *although these contained only 2.5 per cent. of the population*' (my italics).

Imagery and neighbourhood planning

A study by Lee (1954, 1968) was carried out in Cambridge in the context of the immediate post-war years, when Britain was going through a 'phoenix from the ashes' upsurge of post-war planning and rebuilding. Part of this was the vast and intrepid social experiment of the New Towns. Both for these and other residential development, planners and architects had become fully committed to the notion of the neighbourhood unit. This had originated with a book by Clarence Perry in 1929, but had remained during the inter-war years little more than an exciting ideology with a few scattered projects throughout the world. Now, in reaction against the drab uniformity of pre-war 'housing estates' and ribbon development, the Government in various forms had come out in firm support of neighbourhood units.

These were to house 10 000–15 000 people in such a way that a section of the city would be made distinct by accentuating its boundaries with major roads and open spaces and restricting the internal roads to a small radiating network oriented to the centre of the unit, which would contain a community centre, the primary school and a range of shops. Apart from its rational objectives for distributing goods and services, the cherished aim was to create a sense of identity, a feeling of belonging—in fact, a community. Needless to say, it has, and still has, its critics. Their principal argument is that the modern city dweller is highly mobile and prefers a relative anonymity from his close neighbours, choosing instead to seek out those who share his special interests in all parts of the city. A good deal of emphasis is put upon the effects of car ownership. In the early critical assaults, they described the neighbourhood unit as 'village green planning', 'whimsical' and 'bucolic nostalgia'.

Lee's objective was to evaluate the planning construct for contemporary conditions. With a sample which was drawn to be representative of the residential areas of the city, he developed a technique in which the respondents were asked to 'please draw a line round the part which you consider acts as your neighbourhood or district'. It can be argued that these instructions predispose the obliging subject to construe her world in a way that may be unnatural to her. However, it should be emphasized that it was used only after a large number of pilot interviews had suggested that some kind of neighbourhood structuring of the city was widespread and salient, and that people described their area mainly by delineating its *boundaries* in a variety of ways. That is, they would describe the physical changes or the social differences that led them into accepting one part as 'theirs' and another part as 'someone else's'. Those who had difficulty in orienting themselves to a map could nonetheless give quite full verbal accounts both of their feelings and behaviour in the local area.

The superimposition of the maps drawn by the sample presented a picture which resembles a plate of spaghetti (Figure 5.2A); that is, although it was estimated that about 80 per cent. of the people could delineate a neighbourhood, these turned out to be highly personal and idiosyncratic. A comparison between results from Lee's method (Figure 5.2A), which was concerned with size, contouring and population variation of the environmental image, and those from Lynch's method, which was concerned with form and content, is provided by the simulated maps of Cambridge, Figures 5.2B and 5.2C. The images on Lee's map were measured in a variety of ways. Firstly, their area was found to form a skewed distribution with a mode at about 75 acres and a mean at 110 acres. This was substantially less than the 350–400 acres which had been necessitated by the requirement to house 10 000–15 000 people at the prevailing density standards (30–35 persons per acre) in the early New Towns. However, perhaps one of the most pedestrian, but nonetheless important, findings was that the average area was quite unrelated to very large changes in population density. Other things being equal, the average area of neighbourhoods in the outer suburbs was similar to that in the inner core. The reason is presumably that we are dealing with a spatial territory governed by the means of mobility, i.e. walking, and the number of people is not a dimension that becomes evident to the resident; nor is she, within the normal limits of city population density, restricted in the number of friendships she can make by the sheer availability of people.

Fortunately, contemporary planners look favourably on substantially higher population densities for housing development, and it is therefore possible to conceive of achieving the necessary number of consumers to support the services and facilities within the kind of spatial area that appears to correspond with people's perceptions.

Further measurement of the neighbourhood maps was achieved by counting their content of houses, shops and amenity buildings. Because of the stability of area under different densities, it was possible to express these scores as a ratio by using a standard 'imposed environment' score. This was derived by similarly counting the content of the *locality* of each of the respondents—a half-mile radius drawn round their home at the centre. The ratio scores are therefore an expression of the *proportion* of the environment imposed upon the subject which she 'takes unto herself' and could be expected to reflect her particular mode of functioning in the urban environment. A single weighted score called the 'neighbourhood quotient' was derived to express the size and complexity of neighbourhoods while holding constant the physical area in which they were drawn. This was found to be related to social class, to age, to length of residence and to whether the husband worked in the locality or elsewhere. The concept used to explain these findings was the 'socio-spatial schema', and a discussion of this has been reserved for a later section of this chapter.

174

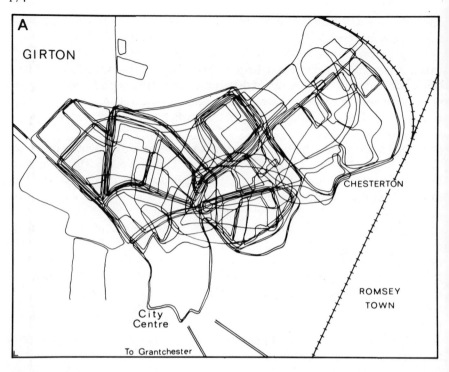

A

GIRTON

CHESTERTON

ROMSEY TOWN

City Centre

To Grantchester

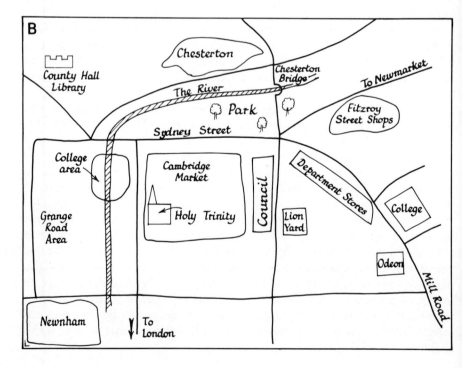

B

County Hall Library

Chesterton

Chesterton Bridge

To Newmarket

The River

Park

Fitzroy Street Shops

Sydney Street

College area

Cambridge Market

Council

Department Stores

College

Grange Road Area

Holy Trinity

Lion Yard

Odeon

Newnham

To London

Mill Road

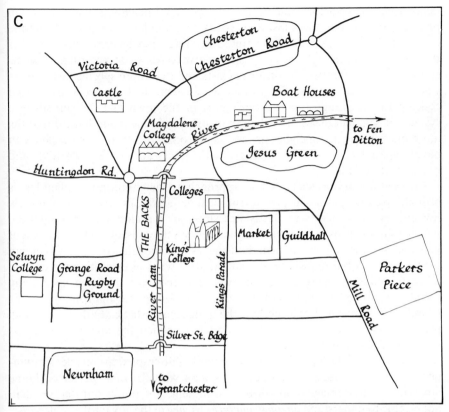

FIGURE 5.2 Approaches to mental mapping. A. Superimposed neighbourhood maps for Cambridge. B and C. Simulated maps as they might be drawn by Cambridge residents

A perception study of The Murray, a planned neighbourhood unit forming part of East Kilbride, a Scottish New Town, (Henry and Cox, 1970) could be regarded as a follow-up application of Lee's earlier, more general study of neighbourhood. The Murray appeared to have all the faults predicted from the earlier study; that is, in spite of the repetition of its name under every street sign, the residents failed to see it as a significant area for them. This was almost certainly due to the large area (300 acres) required for the low density housing of 10 000 people. A questionnaire confirmed that more housewives used the shops in the town centre than in their own neighbourhood and 63 per cent. had a 'local pub' outside The Murray. The respondents were asked to draw the boundary of that area which they thought to be The Murray on a piece of tracing paper over their street map of the whole of East Kilbride. It is again significant that 90 per cent. of the sample were able to do this, but superimposition of their efforts showed the same profusion as in earlier studies. An interesting distinction could be drawn between 'planners neighbourhoods' and 'personal neighbourhoods'. The former seem to have a formal origin and to be an attempt by the respondents to reproduce what the planners intended—with major roads as principal boundaries. The personal neighbourhoods are often precisely drawn but use subsidiary roads as boundaries or general sectors, both containing 'a selection of their most meaningful social provisions as well as their friends'. Although these are alternative types of structuring, it seems entirely likely that a two-tier strategy exists and that more specific instructions would elicit both images. The former would seem to be a necessary spatial concept for directing others to one's part of the town and for perceiving a systematic segmentalization of the urban structure. One might hazard that the more one's home area neighbourhood is personal, the more it is necessary to have a spatial reference for discourse with others about the town itself and one's position in it.

Application of the social space approach to neighbourhood planning is brought to a high point of expression in Buttimer's (1972) study of four Glasgow housing estates. This is modestly described as a preliminary investigation, which is fair in terms of the small sample sizes and the consequent tenuousness of conclusions about how to plan housing estates in Glasgow (an Olympian goal!), but as a bid to develop the quantitative ways of extracting the essence of each estate by aggregating the lives of individuals (i.e by a specifically social–psychological approach) it seems more successful than many. If this sounds laudatory, it should perhaps be added parenthetically that the actual presentation of the methods and statistics on which the approach depends leaves something to be desired.

The most important point is that Buttimer has attempted to consider simultaneously (a) individuals' social activity spaces with (b) their perceived home area and (c) their image of an ideal environment. She points out that we shall not be able to understand *ongoing human existence* in the city until a coalescence of these can somehow be converted into research data. There is obviously a long way to go. The advance in the Glasgow study lies mainly in relation to social activity spaces (a) where she employs the centrographic technique known as the standard deviation ellipse (Caprio, 1970; Hyland, 1970).

First the activities are determined by direct questioning; then they are divided into three separate orbits.
1. Local trips to shops, schools, play areas, etc., and casual frequent neighbourly contacts.
2. An intermediate zone of trips to church, the doctor, friends, etc.
3. A more diffuse zone, mainly distant social visiting.

An aggregation of each of these zones for the forty-odd subjects in a given estate is derived by the standard deviation ellipse method, yielding two orthogonal coordinates and an ellipse which indicates the volume of interaction, degree of spatial concentration and directional bias of the activity in relation to the city centre, and the general shape of the distribution.

When the three ellipse/coordinate models for each activity zone are superimposed for a given estate, it becomes possible to characterize it by the extent of overlap and to ask questions such as: 'Do the residents tend to gravitate in the same direction for their social contacts as they do for their shopping?' and

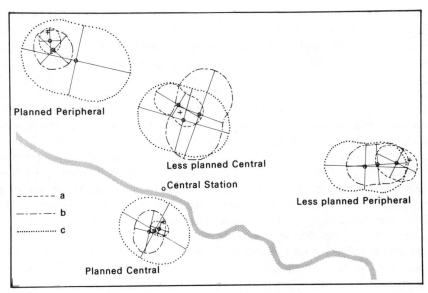

FIGURE 5.3 Standard deviational ellipses for samples drawn from four Glasgow housing estates. a. The micro service space ellipse covers very local trips to shops, bus stops, play areas, etc; b. The macro service space ellipse covers longer trips to city centre, main school, etc.; c. The participation spaces ellipse includes visits to friends and to voluntary associations. (Reproduced by permission of A. Buttimer and Sage Publications Ltd., London. From *Environment and Behaviour*, Vol. **4** (1972), p. 294)

'What is the relevant dispersion of each of these activity zones in different estates?'. (See Figure 5.3).

The difficulty still to be overcome is familiar to psychologists in other settings. If we derive three different measures of central tendency to express what happens to a sample of people, we are likely to emerge with a different picture than if we take an average measure for each individual first. In effect, this is an important difference between the approach of Lee (1954) and that of Buttimer (1972). The sociospatial schema is a *fusion* of activity zones for a single individual, but it creates a problem in proceeding from here to the group. If one aggregates the separate activity zones first, as Buttimer has done. one may produce a picture that does not represent the situation of any single one of the individuals.

The concept of 'home range' is defined as 'that series of linkages and settings traversed and occupied by the individual in his normal activities' (Gelwicks, 1968; Stea, 1968). In effect, this is similar to social space, but the concept seems to have been attractive to those whose emphasis is upon the widening home range that occurs in the course of child development, particularly in ethnological studies where it has considerable potential. In addition to the use of free-hand sketch maps, a method has been developed in which children of about 8 to 10 years old were given large-scale photographs of their neighbourhood covered with a semi-transparent overlay (Anderson and Tindall, 1972). Initially, they were oriented by asking them to locate their house, school and the homes of their best friends, and the procedure then developed into a close examination of the paths they used and the various 'activity nodes' which they frequented.

The assessment of the size and articulation of the home range can be measured in two ways. Firstly, by taking the length of non-redundant pathing and, secondly, by counting the number of activity nodes under a set of headings such as recreational, commercial (stores, cinemas, bowling alleys, etc.) and friendships. Some interesting results have emerged. For example, boys employed much more area than girls, but the difference between urban and suburban areas was relatively small. There is a hint of confirmation here of the finding by Lee (1954) that neighbourhoods do not vary consistently by density. It appears to be the geographical span that is important and not the content. Activity node data have shown that similar differences between the sexes appear to exist in the central city, but that in suburban areas both sex and age differences are very small. The fact that suburban children use a smaller number of activity nodes may be due to their access to more 'backyard' meeting places, but it is interesting to note that this may, in turn, be a consequence of the relatively lower provision of recreation nodes within what is regarded as the appropriate home range.

It is notorious that policy-makers consider research findings to be generally irrelevant or too late. The converse charge is that major decisions are made on inadequate information with intemperate haste leading to mistakes which slow rather than quicken progress. There is no hope of closing this gap, it is intrinsic to the respective roles, but there are signs of a narrowing. The absorption rate of research in the behavioural sciences is increasing rapidly, probably because the generation now assuming high executive positions in government have included at least some training in these areas during their University careers by contrast with the strongly classical backgrounds of the previous generation. Also, the accumulated stock of knowledge is increasing and what may be too late for one decision may still have some relevance for the next.

This appears to be the case with residential, New Town and neighbourhood planning where, for example, the authors own research is being consulted if not directly applied after two decades. In this and other aspects of urban planning we should not underestimate the pervasive influence of even 'ivory tower' research. Administrators always keep an eye on ivory towers, even if only to rail at them, and in the present case there are signs that the general orientation of architects and planners is changing towards a more 'person centred' approach.

There are two recent examples of research commissioned specifically to enlighten policy which can be described briefly. The first is concerned with political representation areas and the second with the planning of urban motorways.

The Royal Commission on Local Government in England (1969) was set up to consider the redefinition of electoral boundaries. It contracted Research

Services Ltd. to carry out a survey of over 2,000 people carefully chosen to represent the electors of the whole country. This is a welcome feature in an area of investigation where samples have often been blatantly unrepresentative or the investigator has failed to give sufficient indication of his sampling methods for any safe generalization to be made.

The question asked in this study was as follows: 'Is there an area around here, where you are now living, which you would say you belonged to, and where you feel "at home"?'. This was followed by a '. . . comprehensive and sometimes lengthy probing of the informant's verbal description of the area, using place and street names for identification as they were volunteered by the elector'. Detailed maps were then employed by the interviewer—or in cases of doubt, by office-based staff—to ascertain the most appropriate size of local government unit which would be equivalent to the area described.

It is this last feature which makes it difficult to draw comparisons between the results and those of other studies, since local government units themselves show considerable variation in size. It is strongly implied, but not stated explicitly, that the 'home area' is a bounded whole. Once its approximation to the nearest size of the local government unit had been determined, it appears that the probing ended and the more detailed dimensional data are not reported.

Nonetheless, a great deal of useful findings emerged from this study. Once again, the number of refusals shows an uncanny similarity to other studies. Approximately 80 per cent. of electors claimed to possess some feelings of attachment to a 'home' community area. The propensity increases with length of residence. In the majority of cases, the area is found to be considerably smaller than the smallest local government unit in which the elector resides, and this reinforces the dubiety of using these units as the scale of reference.

A recent study by Lee, Tagg, and Abbott (1975) has been concerned with the barrier effects of major urban roads and motorways upon residential communities. There have been widespread objections by the public for some years over the unpleasant effects of noise, fumes and visual degradation of the environment created by major roads, but these have recently been exacerbated by modern motorway designs which make movement across the road line virtually impossible except at widely separated underpasses or bridges. It is feared that social life will be hampered and established communities may break up or be amputated if, for example, a proposed inner motorway ring were to be built in London. The intrusion of the M4-motorway through Chiswick and many other cases have already given rise to considerable public opposition.

The phenomenon has been termed 'social severance'. It is obviously an extremely pervasive effect, arising from a variety of physical characteristics of the road environment and influencing many aspects of people's everyday lives. It seemed a clear case where much of the relevant human response might be measured in the synthesized form of cognitive maps of the neighbourhood. In addition, the opportunity was taken to cross-validate the method against some similar techniques, and a good deal of behavioural data on mobility for different 'trip' purposes were also gathered.

The study was carried out in seven widely scattered parts of London. Three working-class areas were compared with three middle-class areas. In each case, one was a 'control site' and the other two varied in the length of time for which a major road had supposedly created 'severance'. The seventh was included as an example of a particularly long established barrier road.

The total sample comprised almost 1 000 people and each was asked to draw a neighbourhood map. They were also given a set of twenty-four cards bearing the names of landmarks and asked to sort these into two piles—those which they considered to be within and outside their neighbourhood. A subset of ten of the same landmarks were used in a distance-estimation task, the respondent being asked to place them in rank order by distance from the home. A blank street map on which the interviewee was asked to name the streets pointed to by the interviewer was also employed in part of the survey, but was found to be too time-consuming. It should nonetheless provide valuable comparative data on an adequate sample.

Trips to friends, shops, work, school, clubs, churches, pubs, libraries and doctors were measured by identifying the actual addresses on a map, and these were subsequently given precise grid references so that distances from the home could be derived by computer. A variety of indices of severance were obtained by these methods and it is helpful to consider them grouped under three main headings: size adjustment, bridging and shifting.

Size adjustment includes indices such as the total area of the neighbourhood, the number of included landmarks, the number of landmarks known to the respondent, etc. Bridging includes whether the neighbourhood boundaries cross the motorway line, what proportion of trips are made across the line, what proportion of landmarks are included from the other side of the motorway, etc. Shifting includes only two indices, the extent to which the perceived distances of destinations from the other side of the motorway are overestimated by comparison with those on the same side and the extent to which the spatial centre of gravity of the neighbourhood is displaced from the home in the direction away from the motorway.

Sampling was carried out so that comparisons could be made not only between sites but in sites. A major parameter was the distance a person lived away from the road line and a system of area sampling was therefore employed by taking three axes at right angles to the road line (i.e. 0 m, 400 m and 800 m from a major crossing) and then drawing clusters of people on both sides of the line at 0 m, 200 m, 400 m, 600 m and 800 m back. (See Figure 5.4).

The advantage of this approach is that one is not limited to an inevitably crude comparison of the means of index measurements between, say, the control sites and motorway sites (crude, because they are likely to differ in many ways other than the presence of the motorway), but it becomes possible to compare the *slopes* of measurements with distance back. Differences in these slopes can be much more confidently attributed to the effect of the road.

The initial hypothesis of this study was that in the motorway sites, and particularly for people living near to the road line, neighbourhoods would be small

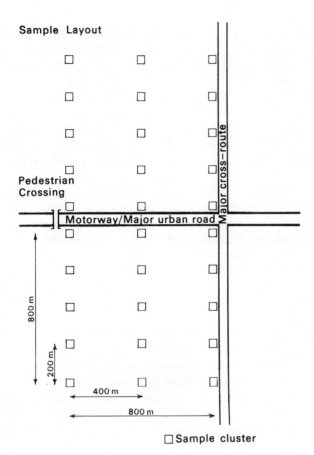

Sample Layout

Pedestrian
Crossing

Motorway/Major urban road

Major cross-route

800 m

200 m

400 m

800 m

☐ Sample cluster

FIGURE 5.4   Area   sampling   framework   for   social
severance study

and bridging would be substantially reduced. In the event, the second part of this prediction was confirmed, but not the first. People appear to make reasonable adjustments, even to some extent *enlarging* their neighbourhoods and shifting them back to compensate for the loss of facilities on the other side. The absolute level of their social activity remains much the same.

It must be noted, however, that some people who would have found the adjustment difficult may have removed themselves from the area or chosen not to live in it in the first place. Also, the apparent accommodation that we observed in this study was at least *possible*, because the sites were chosen to have reasonably homogeneous and adequate facilities on both sides of the road line. Where this is not the case, then the severance response could be much less benign.

SOME CONCLUSIONS: SOCIOSPATIAL SCHEMATA

Enough has probably been reported of the main research studies on urban imagery to indicate clearly that people must form 'inner representations' of the external environment. We must not presume that these are pictorial in form and it is clear that there are large individual differences in the clarity of the images as well as in the particular ways in which people structure their environment. The use of the expressions 'visual' or 'pictorial' is particularly liable to mislead us. They are the most convenient semantic terms available to imply something that is not verbally coded or expressed in translated symbols, and it is, of course, a commonly reported experience that we 'see things in the head', although what we see is highly ephemeral and of varying degrees of vividness.

A helpful amendment to the layman's conception of 'photographs in the mind' is to say that imagery is a process and not a product. (Bycroft, 1974). An image is what we experience when we introspect or scan in the act of retrieval; a process not dissimilar from that which occurs when we seek meaning through perception of the external world. Images are no more photos in the mind than percepts are photos on the retina. The analogy still holds when the scanning is not deliberate; the image can be triggered involuntarily by associations in the stream of consciousness just as percepts can be cued by external stimuli.

Regrettably, the unevenness of the inner representation is unlikely to be accurately portrayed by the graphical reproduction efforts of our subjects and these are an unavoidable source of distortion.

It is significant that such images do not fade like old photographs, but patchily, and with complete blanks in places. There are whole chunks of information that we cannot supply when we introspect upon our images. This does not destroy their 'wholeness' quality and there is plenty of evidence from caricature type reproductions to suggest that 'wholeness' can be achieved without detailed infilling.

Representations of this kind have been given the name of schema, particularly by Bartlett (1932) who took the expression from Sir Henry Head, a distinguished neurologist, who in turn had developed it to describe sensory-motor brain mechanisms and particularly the vivid 'phantom limb' phenomenon that frequently follows amputation. Bartlett used the term quite widely, although mainly in relation to remembered material and the inner templates that appeared to form as a result of the development of a skilled activity; for example, a stroke at cricket or golf. Piaget and Inhelder (1956) have also developed the concept in a similar way and have made more explicit the means by which new experiences are incorporated into the schema either by the process known as assimilation (which is a kind of growth by accretion) or by accommodation, which is a modification in the schema to incorporate the new input.

Although the notion of the schema is only a loose interpretive model, it does have distinctive properties that are not found in other psychological models of perception, memory and the programming of behaviour. For example, Bartlett (1932) makes it clear that stimulus inputs do not exist in their own right once they have been experienced; they are incorporated into the schema in one way or another and once this has occurred there is an inevitable modification of the schema but the original stimulus is finished and dead. Such a process can account for the quite dramatic restructuring of spatial images that sometimes occurs when new environmental experiences are aided. It is not uncommon, for example, to acquire two sequential strip images of different routes and then to discover the interconnections between them on a later occasion. This can lead to a complete restructuring of the angles and general orientations of the original strip maps. This process of movement from sequential learning into total learning, giving the experience of a whole, bounded section of the environment which, to use the gestaltist expressions, appears to stand out as a 'figure' from the undifferentiated 'ground', is very characteristic. If we add to this the fact that such structurings are frequently nested, one within the other, we are at the beginning of seeing the way in which our total cognitive spaces become articulated into the vast detailed cognitive mappings of the world that are essential for our mobility.

At the centre is the body image which we must learn in order to find our way to the toes or the mouth, for example, in our earliest days. Then we have a room schema, a house schema, an institutional building schema, road, precinct, neighbourhood, 'this side of town', our town, our region, country, continent, etc., etc., with an ultimate feeling for 'outer space'. Perhaps the latter is the clearest indication of the enormous disparity that can sometimes exist between objective measures of physical space and the schematic structures which we form in our own minds. It is easy and indeed customary to think of this as distorted or erroneous perception, but it is more profitable to think of it as a comparatively more accurate basis for the prediction of behaviour.

The structuring of space is a highly complex matter which for us is comparable to language. It has its own grammar consisting of basic coordinates like 'up–down', 'in–out', 'over–under', 'near–far', and so on. Part of these basic rules are given to us by the nature of our senses (e.g. we have an innate sense of the upright), in conjunction with the consistent signalling system of the outside world (e.g. the lightness and darkness of the ground and the sky and the existence of a horizon; the fact that distant objects project only small images on the retina and the sun casts shadows).

The large majority of our schematic spatial material is, however, acquired slowly and laboriously, but in enormous quantity, by our direct learning experiences. It is self-evident that the young child has to learn the meaning of the objects he encounters in terms of their 'whatness'. He must discriminate between objects for the consequences they have for him. For example, he must learn that certain objects are edible and give a satisfying feeling if introduced into the digestive system. Other objects, such as pebbles and tin-tacks will be less satisfying. However, the child must also learn simultaneously in what positions this multitude of objects is normally located. For each and every physical and social object, he must acquire and store a 'whereness'. This is an aspect of learning and socialization which has been almost totally neglected by psychologists. It is obvious that there is no value in learning that confectionery is good to eat unless one knows where confectionery is likely to be located.

Having learned what is good, one must be able to move towards it, and the opposite also applies. The required degree of mobility varies, from reaching and grasping out to space travel; and different cultural groups have very different scales of mobility, depending upon the range of environment within which their survival needs can be fulfilled. However, mobility is virtually a *sine qua non* for all human beings.

To acquire this mobility, the child must store information in cognitive structures, for it is inconceivable that there should be anything that is not somewhere. If this is questioned, then one has only to ask oneself what objects have absolutely no locational association or to challenge oneself with familiar objects in the 'wrong' places. Imagine, for example, a Freisian cow sitting in a crystal chandelier or a small plantation of dandelions sprouting downwards from the ceiling.

If such cognitive, schematic spatial structures exist for the real world, they must exist also for social objects which are similarly disposed about in space or, to put it another way, separated by gaps. People are more complicated to enregister because they certainly move their positions, though not without consistency. A large proportion of the social groupings with which we are familiar both create and inhabit the particular built environments such as schools, neighbourhoods and court rooms in our perceived physical world, and this makes it inevitable that we should conceptualize their activities in sociospatial schemata.

Although it has been possible to refer in this chapter to some studies which have examined the application of the concept of urban imagery to problems of the real world and to the needs of planners and decision-makers, the 'applied' qualities of these approaches are not yet strongly developed. Where researchers have probed in these directions (Buttimer, 1972), they have produced encouraging results, but the methodologies are still at early stages of development. Attempts to operationalize specific concepts have also been limited, though Lee (1968) formed some positive conclusions from his use of 'socio-spatial schemata'. Having established that a typology of neighbourhoods did exist, he examined the concept of consentaneity—'agreement and interdependence but not necessarily in reciprocal systems' (Lee 1968, p. 244). From his survey and subsequent analysis in Cambridge, Lee (1968, p. 263) suggested that 'Consentaneity of schemata occur in varying degrees and its measurement provides a means of predicting behaviour for a given aggregate of people with a territorial base'. This evidence suggested that planning should be directed towards heterogeneous physical and social layouts which deliberately emphasized local satisfaction of needs. Studies in urban imagery of this kind can lead to specific and firm recommendations relevant to the information bases from which planning decisions are made. On a broader front, however, the whole question of public participation and ways in which decision-makers in more recent years have been constrained to confer with the people whom they represent—or by whom they are employed—bears testimony of the acceptance that the 'subjective' views of ordinary inhabitants of the city need to be heard and heeded. Most of the individual members of an urban population group will have no particular expertise on urban problems; they will view their urban environment in imprecise and imperfect ways. But in the last resort, they are people who have to occupy the urban environments which the planners attempt to modify and form, and their views and the images from which those views emanate should form a strong point of reference. Although images may be diverse and individual at the most detailed level of generalization, at higher level consensus will begin to emerge. It must be the task of the decision-makers to comprehend the images and to narrow the gap between their objective blueprints and the subjective needs of the urban prople they seek to serve.

As to areas of research, there is a need for work on the synchrony between verbal report and sketching. Most investigators and supplemented cognitive mapping with some kind of interview of their subjects, but this has generally been unstructured and intuitive. As pointed out earlier, this has some advantages, but they pertain mainly to the early hypothesis stages of investigation and should be replaced with methods that allow of repeatable data and such lends itself to quantification. The possibilities of co-ordinating sketch mapping with repertory grids or Q sorts need to explored.

Another question that needs to be answered is whether the presence, the latency, the size or the detail of an element depicted in a map signify merely its visual impressiveness or do they indicate a functional significance for the subject; if so, to what degree in each case.

Perhaps the major problem, for purposes both theoretical and applied, is how to aggregate individual 'inner representations' of the urban environment into collective ones. Research in the Lynch tradition has normally relied on some cartographical methods of accentuating the importance of elements in proportion to the number of people who have included them, but accuracy and objectivity have been difficult to control. Finally, if urban living is to be fully comprehended, it will not be by measurement of the environment itself, or of peoples perceptions, cognitions or behaviour, but by understanding the connections between these. Many years of frustrated effort by psychologists have taught that behaviour cannot be directly predicated from environmental stimuli except in the simplest cases. Behavioural responses are mediated through perceptions and cognitions. Furthermore, it is not only perceptions and cognitions of the physical environment that are implicated. Any environmental behaviour that takes place in a social context has to reckon with the ways in which each person expects other people to behave (normative expectations) and the extent to which he normally complies with these tendencies. We have a long way to go.

REFERENCES

Anderson, J., and Tindall, M. (1972). 'The concept of home range: new data for the study of territorial behaviour'. In W. J. Mitchell (Ed.), *Environmental Design: Research and Practice*, Proceedings of the EDRA 3 Conference, Los Angeles, University of California.

Appleyard, D. (1970). 'Styles and methods of structuring a city'. *Environment and Behaviour*, **2**, 100–117.
Bartlett, F. C. (1932). *Remembering*, Cambridge University Press, Cambridge.
Bott, E. (1955). 'Urban families: conjugal roles and social networks'. *Human Relations*, **8**, 45–84.
Buttimer, Anne (1969). 'Social space in interdisciplinary perspective'. *Geographical Review*. **59**, 417–426.
Buttimer, Anne (1972). 'Social space and the planning of residential areas'. *Environment and Behaviour*, **4**, 279–318.
Bycroft, P. (1974). *Environmental Representation and Cognitive Spatial Ability*. M.Sc. Dissertation, University of Surrey.
Caprio, R. J. (1970). 'Centrography and geostatistics'. *Professional Geographer*, **22**, 15–19.
Eyles, J. D. (1968). '*The Inhabitants' Images of Highgate Village*, Discussion Paper No. 15, Department of Geography, London School of Economics, London.
Fechner, G. (1860). *Elements der Psychophysik*, Breitkopf, Leipzig.
Festinger, L., Schachter, S., and Back, K. (1950). *Social Pressures in Informal Groups*, Stanford University Press, California.
Foley, D. (1950). 'The use of local facilities in a metropolis'. *American Journal of Sociology*, **56**, 238–246.
Francescato, D., and Mebane, W. (1973). 'How citizens view two great cities: Milan and Rome'. In R. M. Downs and D. Stea (Eds.), *Image and Environment* (Chapter 8), Aldine, Chicago. pp. 131–147.
Galton, F. (1880). 'Psychometric experiments'. *Brain*, **2**, 149–162.
Gelwicks, L. E. C. (1968). *Home Range and the Use of Space*. Paper presented to the Institute of Gerontology, University of Michigan, Ann Arbor.
Henry, L., and Cox, P. A. (1970). 'The neighbourhood concept in New Town planning. A perception study in E. Kilbride'. *Horizon*, **19**, 37–45.
Hilgard, E. R., and Bower, G. H. (1966). *Theories of Learning*, Appleton-Century-Crofts, New York.
Hull, C. L. (1943). *Principles of Behaviour*, Appleton-Century-Crofts, New York.
Hyland, G. A. (1970). 'Social interaction and urban opportunity: the Appalachian inmigrant in the Cincinnati central city'. *Antipode*, **2**, 68–83. Reprinted in E. Jones (Ed.) (1970), *Readings in Social Geography*, Oxford University Press, Oxford. pp. 250–263.
de Jonge, D. (1962). 'Images of urban areas: their structure of psychological foundations'. *Journal of the American Institute of Planners*, **28**, 266–276.
Klein, H. J. (1967). 'The delimitation of the town centre in the image of its citizens'. In W. F. Heinemeijer, M. Van Hulten and H. D. de Vreis Reilingh (Eds.), *Urban Core and Inner City*, E. J. Brill, Leiden. pp. 286–306.
de Lauwe, P. H. C. (1952). *Paris et l'Agglomeration Parisienne*, Paris.
de Lauwe, P. H. C. (1960). L'Evolution des Besoins et la Conception Dynamique de la Famille'. *Rev. Francaise de Sociologie*, **1**, 403–425.
Lee, T. R. (1954). *A Study of Urban Neighbourhood*. Unpublished Ph.D. Dissertation, University of Cambridge, Cambridge.
Lee, T. R. (1968). 'Urban neighbourhood as a socio-spatial schema'. *Human Relations*, **21**, 241–268.
Lee, T. R., Tagg, S. K., and Abbott (1975). 'Social Severance by Urban Roads and Motorways'. Unpublished paper presented at a Symposium on Environmental Evaluation, Canterbury.
Lewin, K. (1938). *The Conceptual Representation and the Measurement of Psychological Forces*, Duke University Press, Durham. North Carolina.
Lewin, K. (1951). *Topological Field Theory in the Social Sciences*, Harper, New York.
Lord, F. E. (1941). 'A study of spatial orientation of children'. *Journal of Educational Research*, **34**, 481–505.

Lynch, K. (1960). *The Image of the City*, Harvard University Press, Cambridge, Massachusetts.

McClenahan, B. A. (1929). *The Changing Urban Neighbourhood*, University of South California, Los Angeles.

McKenzie, R. D. (1921). 'The neighbourhood: a study of local life in the city of Columbus, Ohio'. *American Journal of Sociology*, 27, 145–168.

Merton, R. K. (1947). 'The social psychology of housing'. In W. Dennis, (Ed.), *Current Trends in Social Psychology*, University of Pittsburgh, Pittsburgh.

Merton, R. K. (1957). *Social Theory and Social Structure*, The Free Press, Glencoe, Illinois.

Perrin, F. A. C. (1914). An Experimental and Introspective Study of the Human Learning Process in the Maze. Psychological Monograph 16, 70.

Perry, C. (1929). 'The neighbourhood unit: a scheme of arrangement for the family life community'. *A Regional Plan for New York and its Environs*, 7, 22–140.

Piaget, J., and Inhelder, B. (1956). *The Child's Conception of Space*, Routledge and Kegan Paul, London.

Riemer, S. (1951). 'Villagers in metropolis'. *British Journal of Sociology*, 2, 31–43.

Riemer, S., and McNamara, J. (1957). 'Contact patterns in the City'. *Social Forces*, 36, 137–141.

Royal Commission on Local Government in England (1969). 'Research Studies 9'. *Community Attitudes Survey*, H.M.S.O., London.

Shepard, R. N., and Feng, C. (1972). 'A chronometric study of mental paper folding. *Cognitive Psychology*, 3, 228–243.

Smith, J., Form, W. H., and Stone, G. P. (1954). 'Local intimacy in a middle-sized city'. *American Journal of Sociology*, 60, 276–284.

Sorre, M. (1955). 'Geographie psychologique, traite de psychologie appliquee, livre 6'. *Conditions et Regles de Vie*, Presses Universitaires de France, Paris.

Stea, D. (1968). *Home Range and Use of Space*. Paper presented at the Conference on Explorations of Spatial-Behavioural Relationships as Related to Older People, Institute of Gerontology, University of Michigan, Ann Arbor.

Sweetser, F. L. (1941). *Neighbourhood Acquaintance and Association: A Study of Personal Neighbourhoods*. Unpublished Ph.D. Dissertation, Columbia University, New York.

Sweetser, F. L. (1942). 'A new emphasis for neighbourhood research'. *American Sociological Review*, 7, 525–533.

Thorndike, E. L. (1911). *Animal Intelligence*, Macmillan, New York.

Tolman, E. C. (1948). 'Cognitive maps in mice and men'. *Psychological Review* 55, 189–208.

Trowbridge, C. C. (1913). Fundamental methods of orientation and imaginary maps. *Science*, 38, 888–897.

Twitmyer, E. M. (1931). 'Visual guidance in motor learning'. *American Journal of Psychology*, 45, 165–187.

Chapter 6

Community, Communion, Class and Community Action: The Social Sources of the New Urban Politics

Colin Bell and Howard Newby

As a poet of the historic consciousness I suppose I am bound to see landscape as a field dominated by the human wish—tortured into farms and hamlets, ploughed into cities. A landscape scribbled with the signatures of men and epochs. Now, however, I am beginning to believe that the wish is inherited from the site; that man depends for the furniture of the will upon his location in place, tenant of fruitful acres or a perverted wood. It is not the impact of his free will upon nature which I see (as I thought) but the irresistible growth, through him, of nature's own fluid unspecified doctrines of variation and torment.

Laurence Durrell
Justine, p. 112

What cities, towns, neighbourhoods and villages do to their inhabitants has long interested social scientists. The precise significance of *place* for social activity of all kinds has been the subject of lively debate. This debate, though long, has not been conclusive; for instance, a recent comprehensive survey of the 'urbanism as a way of life' controversy concluded that despite literally hundreds of studies since Wirth's famous article the data 'are often inadequate and when adequate are often contradictory' (Fischer, 1972, p. 227). Much, however, has been learned about urban neighbourhoods, even if few precise and positive statements can be made about the effects of living in this locale rather than that one. And what has been learned and where much of the argument has centred has been about *community*. What community means has been disputed for even longer than the effects of place (for a summary see Bell and Newby, 1971), but there are now some distinctions that can be made with some confidence.

These theoretical and conceptual distinctions are both important and necessary, for without them much of the debate has in the past been confused. We are confident that the distinctions and the approaches made in this chapter will

189

allow a securer advance to be made in the study of urban social structure. The theoretical distinctions we make pivot on the necessary analytical separateness of *place, community* and *communion*. Having introduced these concepts, we will proceed to discuss some further tools of objective theoretical analysis—specifically, the interpersonal social network and the idea of housing class. Finally, we shall examine the promise held out by spatially generated social inequalities for local political action.

LOCALISM AS AN IDEOLOGY

The growth of urban industrial capitalism since the end of the eighteenth century has brought about the steady dilution of localism as a structural principle of contemporary society and yet the same period has witnessed, parallel to this trend, the growth of a consciously articulated ideology of 'community', which had previously remained unarticulated and taken-for-granted (see Bell and Newby, 1971, chapter 2; Williams, 1961; and Wolin, 1961, chapter 10). It is within this apparent paradox that an analysis of localism must begin, for perceptions about the *actual* local basis of social activity have become so intertwined with the *desire* to promote such a basis that it is important to insist upon a clear separation of the two.

In many traditional societies, such as pre-industrial England, localism had a particular economic basis in the system of agricultural and craft-manufacturing production. In particular, where the ownership and/or control of land was the crucial resource in the possession of power, then the hierarchical nature of society was always likely to be reflected in *local* terms through the ownership of land over a finite geographical area. Landowning élites therefore maintained their own local spheres of influence by their control of the most important means of production and created out of this a national society that consisted of little more than a federation of local 'little kingdoms'. What this meant in terms of social relationships has been perceptively summarized by Raymond Williams. For as Williams (1973, p. 166) points out:

> Neighbours in Jane Austen are not the people actually living nearby; they are the people living little less nearby who, in social recognition, can be visited. What she sees across the land is a *network* of propertied houses and families, and through the holes of this tightly drawn mesh most actual people are simply not seen (our emphasis).

In this context, power was inextricably linked to the characteristically local form of territoriality (see Dumont, 1972, chapter 7; Perkin, 1968, p. 94). This was reflected in the conditions of those at the base of the social hierarchy; where, as in many traditional societies, economic activity was based upon a struggle for subsistence, then individuals were tied to the locality by economic interdependence and cooperation (and often legal constraints, too). The 'community' therefore becomes, under these conditions, what Williams (1973, p. 104) has called 'the mutuality of the oppressed'—the product of a series of often draconian constraints upon social and geographical mobility which constitute an almost total powerlessness within the local social system. These constraints form the institutional framework of traditional societies, and, tenuous though the connection may at first appear, localism is connected to the establishment of a stable and orderly social hierarchy which will guarantee the long-term maintenance to traditional élite power and privileges. Traditional élites have long recognized that social stability can only arise within the context of an inegalitarian and hierarchical social structure if those in subordinate positions can be persuaded to subscribe to the system which endorses their own inferiority (i.e. to regard the hierarchy as *legitimate*). Thus legitimation, as Weber (1964) recognized, represents the process whereby the system of social stratification moves away from being based upon potentially unstable coercive relationships to those of stability, order and harmony. Moreover, legitimation by tradition is the most stable form of legitimation, because not only is the tradition itself regarded as the legitimate source of authority but also the *person* holding the authority position. This makes the exercise of power extraordinarily flexible; those in traditional authority positions are deferred to across *all* their roles and an individual invested with traditional authority can even act in radically untraditional ways by virtue of his *personal* possession of authority (Weber, 1964, pp. 341–342).

Because traditional authority requires this personal exercise of power, it is typically based upon personal, particularistic, diffuse, face-to-face forms of interaction rather than the impersonal and the contractual. This places a premium upon certain kinds of social organization. In particular, a degree of self-containment or totality is necessary, so that as far as possible an élite hegemony over the subordinates' definitions of their own situation may be created. The corollary is a strong emphasis on a specifically *local* form of territoriality, so that the locality forms the spatial framework within which the sum total of social relationships are played out and within which the traditional authority of elite individuals or groups holds sway. It also limits the access of subordinate individuals to alternative definitions of their situation which are potentially disruptive, conflictual or are in any way subversive to the criteria of legitimacy which authenticate the individuals' memberships of élite authority positions. Thus, where their 'horizons' are sufficiently limited in this way, the subordinates share elite evaluations and moral judgements as the 'correct' evaluations and will regard their leadership as 'natural' and immutable since, in the limiting case, no other alternatives can be conceived or desired (Newby, 1975; Parkin, 1971).

We may observe the ideological alchemy which such a situation promotes over and over again in the study of 'community'. Undoubtedly, 'community' has a real social basis in the essentially localized structure of traditional, pre-industrial England. And yet we can also observe how 'community' *as an ideology* has been used to interpret the *nature* of relationships *within* this local social system. For example, one may observe how a rigid and arbitrary exercise of power has been converted into an ethic of 'service' to those over whom the local élite rule (Williams, 1961, pp. 314–318) and how an exploitative system has been converted into an 'organic' society of 'mutual dependency' (Guttsman, 1963, chapter 3). This ideological usage of 'community' has emphasized a *common* adherence to territory, a solidarity of place, to both élites and subordinates alike. It has derived the existence of any conflict of interest, but has instead interpreted relationships as being characterized by harmony, reciprocity, stability and affection. In this way, the traditional landowning élite has placed an ideological gloss on its monopoly of power within the locality.

The growth of urban industrial capitalism marked the end of a society based upon a federation of local social systems, but also, through the combined pauperization and conglomeration of workers in towns and factories, it signalled the breakdown of the personalized modes of control afforded by the structure of traditional society. Virtually the whole spectrum of the nineteenth century propertied classes feared the consequences of the loss of 'community' for the stability of society, since the growth in scale of both industry and settlement broke the 'vertical ties' of localism and enabled access to definitions of the situation less conducive to social harmony. Indeed, 'community' with its implications of harmony, stability, integration and consensus are to be viewed increasingly as a rural phenomenon, while the industrial city was defined as non-community—conflict, disorder, isolation and, above all, *class* (Davidoff, L'Esperance and Newby, 1975; Glass, 1968). A frantic search was made for a method of renewing the relationships of 'community' in the new urban industrial setting as a social sedative that would promote new forms of integration and stability. These explorations took a number of forms. One was charity (Harrison, 1965–66; Newby, 1975; Stedman-Jones, 1971, part III); another, following the experiences of Robert Owen, was a paternalistic form of managerial style (Birch, 1959; Martin and Fryer, 1973; Stacey, 1960). In this paper, however, we are concerned with a third method of recreating 'community'—the neighbourhood.

At the beginning of the nineteenth century, the typical reaction to the growth of urban industrialism was voiced by Southey: 'A manufacturing poor is more easily instigated to revolt. They have no local attachments; ... A manufacturing populace is always rife for rioting. ... Governments who found their prosperity upon manufacturers sleep upon gunpowder' (Coleman, 1973, pp. 34–35). The way to counteract this threat, according to Thomas Chalmers, was 'the principle of locality', by which the 'vast overgrown city' could be broken down into small parochial units where 'the two extreme orders of society' could be brought 'into that sort of relationship, which is highly favourable to the general blandness and tranquility of the whole population' (Coleman, 1973, pp. 42–46; Glass, 1968, pp. 71–72). This was a theme much repeated during the nineteenth century; Cooke Taylor, for example, wished to turn Manchester into a loosely-knit series of industrial villages or suburbs 'affording employees opportunities of coming frequently into personal communication with their workpeople, and exercising a healthy control over their domestic habits and private morals' (Coleman, 1973, pp. 84–85). The city, therefore, represented the breakdown of community as it had been traditionally regarded, yet it led to redoubled attempts to assert the ideology of 'community' as a guide to social control. In so doing, 'community' had to be adapted to the new urban setting as a palliative to the threats of chaos and anarchy presented by the ecological separation of the working class from their 'betters'.

These sentiments, as both Ruth Glass (1968) and Norman Dennis (1968) have shown, have remained extraordinarily strong among urban planners through the inception of the 'neighbourhood unit', inspired by the writings of Ebenezer Howard (1965) and first explicitly proposed by the American city planner Clarence Perry in the 1920s (Perry, 1939). Specifically, the neighbourhood unit was to do the following (Keller, 1968, p. 126; Mann, 1965, p. 17ff):

1. Introduce a principle of physical order into the chaotic, amorphous and fragmented world of urban living.
2. Reintroduce local, face-to-face, personal forms of interaction and thereby invest the anonymous and isolated urban world with a renewed sense of community.
3. Encourage the formation of local loyalties and attachments among an often recently arrived and residentially mobile urban population.
4. Stimulate feelings of identity, security, stability and continuity in an environment which appeared to threaten such feeling and promote alienation, conflict and disorder.
5. Provide a local training ground for the development of larger loyalties to city and nation.

From the beginning, therefore, the neighbourhood unit was, for their planners, a social as well as a mere physical planning concept, an attempt to re-establish the social controls of localism which the expanding towns and cities had largely outgrown. The personal, face-to-face relationships of traditional authority, unlike the impersonal solidarities of class, could only exist in a society distributed in small units in which everyone (virtually) knew everyone else. On the basis of some rudimentary social engineering, it was therefore believed that the threats to social order implied by urbanization could be subverted by the creation of 'urban villages', 'garden cities' or some other such return to the 'wholesome straitjacket of provincial conformity' (Riemer, 1951) which had characterized the essentially local social structures of traditional society.

The neighbourhood unit idea undoubtedly had some basis in social fact, just as in traditional society 'community' as an ideology often corresponded to some actual local social system which bounded the everyday social relationships of its inhabitants. A series of studies—most famously those of Bethnal Green (Townsend, 1957; Young and Willmott, 1957)—have demonstrated that the urban neighbourhood possesses a very definite reality in the 'mutuality of the oppressed', in many ways similar to that of traditional village society (Gans, 1962). Life in, or on, the verge of poverty ties an individual to his immediate neighbours through a reliance on mutual cooperation and dependency equally in an urban as a rural setting. The local social system of the neighbourhood is, therefore, a product of extra-local economic constraints, made manifest through the housing market, for instance, rather than the careful nurturing of any 'spirit of community'. In this sense, as Dennis (1968, p. 84) remarks:

> There who live in the pious hope that it is only a matter of time before housing estates settle down and take on the appearance of the Bethnal Green stereotype are therefore probably mistaken. It would be more realistic to predict that in so far as housing estates represent that exaggerated result of processes which are common to our society, it is only a matter of time before our Bethnal Greens become socially indistinguishable from housing estates.

The problem with the neighbourhood unit idea is not, therefore, that it cannot be shown to coincide with the existence of a local social system, but that it misinterprets the nature of this system. Certain value-judgements have been superimposed upon the existence and desirability of the urban neighbourhood, which have elevated the *local* basis of social structure above all others. These value-judgements, which, as we have indicated, have a long historical pedigree, have brought about the taken-for-granted assumption that the desired content of human relationships (affection, integration, identity, etc.) can only be promoted through the creation of *local* forms of territoriality and *local* social systems. *Prima facie*, there is no logical reason why this should be the case. Why then has such an idea proved to be so astonishingly prevalent among those prepared to diagnose the alleged pathology of urban society?

COMMUNITY AND COMMUNING

Sociologists have hardly been immune to these value-judgements concerning the affects of urbanization and industrialization on the social fabric of local social systems. These judgements have entered sociological theory through the writing of Ferdinand Tonnies and the strong impetus given to his approach through Wirth and Redfield (see Bell and Newby, 1971, chapter 2; and Kasarda and Janowitz, 1974). Tonnies, in particular, has been enormously influential, and his concepts of *gemeinschaft* and *gesellschaft* have been represented by Nisbet as one of the 'unit ideas' of the sociological tradition (Nisbet, 1968, chapter 3). It is most important to emphasize, however, that Tonnies' concepts originally referred to forms of human association, not types of settlement. *Gemeinschaft* extended beyond the purely *local* community to include any set of relationships characterized by emotional cohesion, depth, continuity and fulfilment; *gesellschaft*, on the other hand, referred to the impersonal, contractual and rational aspects of social relationships. What in retrospect can be seen as Tonnies' most mischievous legacy was to ground these types of relationship in particular patterns of settlement and in particular geographical locales. Accordingly, urbanization and industrialization wrought, through the associated increases in population size and density, a transformation in the essential character of their social relationships, from the primary relationships of the *gemeinschaftlich* local community to the secondary associational contacts of urban *gesellschaft*. Subsequently, *gemeinschaft* and *gesellschaft* were abandoned as concepts and became reified into actual human settlements which could be observed and investigated (Discher, 1972; Redfield, 1947; Wirth, 1938). From being a typology of social relationships, Tonnies concepts became a taxonomy of settlement patterns (Bell and Newby, 1971, chapter 2); Tonnies, 1957) through their incorporation into a rural-urban or folk–urban continuum.

The survival of this perspective on urban society was undoubtedly due to a much wider anti-urban characteristic of Anglo-Saxon culture, to what Ruth Glass (1968, p. 142) has called 'a lengthy, thorough course of indoctrination, to which all of us, everywhere, have at some time or other been subjected'. More recently, however, it is a perspective that has fallen into disrepute. A large number of locality studies have established the presence of *gemeinschaftlich* social systems in the centre of large urban conglomerations, while a number of rural studies, from Lewis' on the original 'folk society', Tepotzlan, to the work of Bailey and his students, have indicated 'the underlying individualism, ... the lack of co-operation, the tensions ... the schisms ... the pervading quality of fear, envy, and distrust in interpersonal relations' in many rural villages (Bailey, 1970, 1971; Lewis, 1951, p. 123). From an examination of mostly American studies of urban and suburban communities, Gans has argued that 'ways of life do not coincide with settlement patterns' (Gans, 1968); and, further, Pahl (1968, p. 293) has stated categorically that 'Any attempt to tie patterns of social relationships to specific geographical milieux is a singularly fruitless exercise'. Detailed community studies have therefore demonstrated that, far from there being a linear continuum from *gemeinschaft* to *gesellschaft* superimposed upon the size and density of human settlement, relationships of *both* types are found in the *same* community (Bell and Newby, 1971, p. 51). We are being asked to consider, in other words, whether 'community' is a sociological variable at all or merely a 'geographical expression'.

This leads us into the most delicate and confusing area of all. What exactly do sociologists mean by 'community'? As we have noted elsewhere, the definition of 'community' has been a thriving sociological pastime and we have no intention of repeating here a detailed analysis of the multitude of approaches to the concept (see Bell and Newby, 1971, Chapter 2; and Hillery, 1955). Nevertheless, the question posed at the end of the previous section leads us to examine once again this vexed issue, since it is apparent from the analysis outlined there that there has been a largely unexamined assumption of the coincidence of a local social system with a particular kind of social relationship. What an examination of 'community' therefore forces us to confront is the connection (if any) between three broad perspectives on 'community': community as a 'geographical expression', i.e. a finite and bounded physical location; community as a 'sociological expression', i.e. a local social system (see Stacey, 1969); and community as a particular kind of *human association* irrespective of its local focus. Tonnies, it should be noted, was concerned with the third of these in his concept of *gemeinschaft*. Subsequent sociologists elided all three, and current urban and rural sociologists have concentrated on the second. What, however, the devotees of 'community' have prescribed is the *third* of these—a particular kind of relationship—to which its spatial grounding (in the neighbourhood, village or whatever) has only been a subsidiary consideration. Thus, what so concerned nineteenth-century observers was not urbanization and industrialization *per se* but the effect of these processes on the breakdown of traditional forms of authority and the threat they posed to disorder. Localism was elevated as a structural principle only because it was perceived to be conducive to maintaining an identification with traditional social relationships. Tonnies understood the contingent nature of localism; for him *gemeinschaftlich* relationships were linked to the 'community of place' only insofar as those who affirmed a 'community of blood' (kinship) and a 'community of mind' (friendship) wished to live in reasonable proximity (Tonnies, 1957, p. 55). What has been consistently confusing, however, has been Tonnies' use of the same term—*gemeinschaft*—to describe the *affective* quality of this relationship and its rootedness in *traditional* ties of communality. As Schmalenbach (1961, p. 335), in a seminal paper, has pointed out:

> Tonnies emphasized community so much that he must bear the responsibility for the confusion. Tonnies (and everyone else) knows that rural neighbours may become mortal enemies when, for example, a boundary is disputed, just as brothers may become enemies when an inheritance is challenged. Despite this, neighbours and brothers always remain neighbours and brothers. Neighbourliness and brotherhood persist psychically. There is probably no better example anywhere to demonstrate how minor a role 'feelings' play as a basis of community.

It is apparent that what most people mean when they articulate their desire for community is precisely these 'feelings' of community—what Schmalenbach prefers to call 'communion' (Bund). Community he reserves for the form of human association which refers to traditional bonds (Schmalenbach, 1961, pp. 331–332):

> Community, then, can be characterized as that order of social coherence which develops on the basis of natural interdependence .... The natural ... includes all those attributes that one has inherited collectively, into which one has grown and been born ... a matter of custom and of shared modes of thought or expression, all of which have no other sanction than tradition.

As Schmalenbach points out, community implies the recognition of something taken for granted and the assertion of the self-evident—they are 'given'; they simply exist. For this reason, our membership of communities is largely unconscious unless it is threatened; otherwise one just belongs, and generally irrevocably so.

Communion, however, is radically different. Emotional experiences are the very stuff of this relationship. Communion is the form of human association which refers to affective bonds and is therefore related to the Weberian concept of charisma and charismatic authority. 'It is indeed the case,' writes Schmalenbach (1961, pp. 332, 335), 'that communions are borne along by waves of emotion, reaching ecstatic heights of collective enthusiasm, rising from the depths of love or hate .... They are bound together by the feeling actually experienced. Indeed, each one is *en rapport*.' Communion is, then, a precarious and unstable structure by its very nature, requiring intense mutual involvement which is difficult to sustain. Communions thus try to overcome their inherent precariousness through the development of an ethos of loyalty, by which it is hoped that some degree of permanent organization will be obtained. This, however, merely converts communion into a communal (*gemeinschaftlich*) or societal (*gesellschaftlich*) association by attempting to create an enduring arrangement through a set of rules. (There are obvious parallels here with the routinization of charisma). Communion can therefore be a product of community, but community itself does not consist of feelings or emotions, for community precedes emotional recognition by its members. Communion is simply the subsequent form of community experience at the level of consciousness.

Breaking down Tonnies' original concept of *gemeinschaft* in this way enables the connections between local forms of territoriality, the composition of local social systems and forms of human association to be examined much more clearly. There has been a common belief among the more sentimentally oriented community sociologists that community coincides with communion. Often feelings are construed as the basis of community relations because they are erroneously thought to be deeper or more 'meaningful' than rational thought—a product of the Romantic tradition. The contemporary yearning for 'community' is, however, an expression of a desire for communion (for an example of confusion between the two, see Scherer, 1973). It seems likely that the extension of rational, *gesellschaftlich* forms of association will periodically provoke reactions of this kind involving the promotion of new forms of intimate human communion, which may in turn provide the basis of various kinds of political mobilization. We shall return to these points below.

SOCIOLOGICAL APPROACHES TO THE URBAN COMMUNITY

We need now to proceed to look at two different ways that allow the 'community' to be analysed both as a sociological expression and as a particular kind of human association. For all the sentiment that communion no doubt expresses, that is no reason to cease objective analysis. We wish to argue here that, firstly, at the interpersonal level, or communion, social network analysis can be used and that, secondly, conflict over a key and scarce-valued resource, housing, provides an approach to the community at the institutional level.

Social networks

Since Wirth (1938), and before him Simmel (see Levine, 1971), it has been continually argued that urban man was isolated, anomic, acted out segmented roles, and so on—all in contrast to some arcadian rural past. This position has always left it open for each new generation of sociologists to rediscover 'community' in the city: Little Sicilies in the 1920s, Young and Willmott (1957) in Bethnal Green in the 1950s and Gans (1962) discovering the aptly named urban villagers. What is clear is that we need objective ways of getting at individual's and families' local social situations, their social milieux, in some better way than the overly contrasted blanket terms of 'isolation and anomie' versus 'community'.

In fact, this has now been available to us for twenty years. Bott, when she took up Barnes' (1954) notion of social network, wrote in a classic statement that 'the immediate social environment of urban families is best considered not as the local area in which they live, but rather as the network of actual social relationships they maintain, regardless of whether these are confined to the local area or run beyond its boundaries' (Bott, 1957, p. 99). We would change the word 'urban' to 'all'. However, there is a major confusion in Bott's original formulation of types of social network. She ranged the networks of the families that she studied from looseknit to closeknit; this may most simply be understood as the proportion of connections within the network, or, in everyday terms, the number of people one knows who know each other independently of oneself (in the looseknit case few would, in the closeknit most would). There are serious difficulties in precisely operationalizing 'know'. Is it friendship, acquaintance, kinship, or what? And, similarly, what are the nodes of the network—individuals, families, groups? All these matters have been fully debated (Boissevain, 1974; Mitchell, 1969; Mitchell and Boissevain, 1972). Further, as one of us has argued elsewhere (Bell and Healey, 1973), the absolutely looseknit network appears to be an empirical absurdity, for what has frequently been described as looseknit on closer inspection turns out to be a series of closeknit networks only linked by one person.

In order to resolve the most fundamental confusion in the notions of the social network and to relate it to more traditional notions of the community, it is necessary to distinguish between *structure* (which is what 'close' and 'loose' usually are taken to describe) and what we will here call *plexity*. Plexity may be simply understood as the degree of complexity of the connection. A full elaboration of our understanding of complexity would involve a discussion of at least the normative, exchange and communication content of the social relationship. If we combine these two, we arrive at a simple typology of the range of social milieux, of local social situations in which individuals and families find themselves. (See Figure 6.1)

Space prevents us from fully explicating each configuration of this typology. For the sake of our argument, we will merely take boxes A and B which represent the extreme and limiting cases and may be treated as ideal types. A is the traditional community as normally understood: social relationships are multiplex in that, for example, neighbours are workmates are kinsmen are leisure-time companions, and the social network has a dense structure in that everyone

Plexity	Structure		
	Dense	Looseknit	Single
Multiplex	A		
Simplex			
Uniplex			B

FIGURE 6.1   A typology of range of social milieux

knows everyone else. B is the situation of idealized urban anonymous anomie: social relationships are uniplex (the taxidriver and his fare), fleeting, impersonal and anonymous, and the social network structure is single-stranded in that only one person knows the others. Both of these are extreme, and with time there is always a tendency for drift in the direction of A away from B. In A informal social control is strong and in B weak or absent; there will be localized social support in A, none in B. Interestingly, Abu-Lughod (1961) has suggested that the Wirthian experience of urban anonymity represents the experience of moving out of the social situation represented by A into B and back into A in the evening. We would further suggest that there are long-term changes of this nature with changes in the family cycle: born into A, leave for B in late 'teens and return to a form of A once married with young children. *And* this is associated with movement through the urban structure.

This interpersonal analysis can, of course, be related to the institutional level of community for local 'sub-communities', or natural areas (in the Chicago terminology) can be characterized in the terms of our network typology and are given limit by the operation of socioeconomic processes such as the housing market. It is to this that we now turn.

Housing classes

Much recent analysis of the spatial distribution of the inhabitants of British towns starts with the acceptance in varying degrees of the notion of housing class (Davies and Taylor, 1970; Haddon, 1970; Rex and Moore, 1967). In the decade or so since it was originally propounded by John Rex, this approach has cut a wide swathe through urban sociology. Somewhat schematically, what was originally suggested was that an individual's position in the stratification system was not entirely determined by relationships to the means of production, ownership of capital, nor in the alternative formulation, position in some functional division of labour, nor even by situation in the labour market. In order to understand the social situation that had developed in Birmingham in the 1960s, it was necessary to introduce the concept of *housing class*. An individual's or group's specific housing class is, according to Rex and Moore, determined by *degrees of access* to housing, 'and it is this which immediately determines the class conflicts of the city as distinct from the workplace' (Rex and Moore, 1967, p. 274).

There is a variety of accesses: in Britain principally between the public sector of municipally owned *council housing* and the private *owner-occupier*, so called. There is a third and dwindling, but nevertheless locally vital, sector of privately *rented* accommodation. As access to these three sectors varies, there are at least three major housing classes. There are significant variations and distinctions within these housing classes—by price, for instance, within the owner-occupied sector—all spatially varied too. Within the council house sector there are enormous variations; many large local authorities will own much 'patched and propped' nearly moribund housing stock as well as spick and span new estates, and access to them varies as Rex and Moore showed. Whether these variations within the major housing classes should also be called classes or perhaps should be viewed as status groups whose limits are set by the housing class could be disputed.

Indeed, Rex and Moore's original formulation has been much criticized, yet the basic idea stands. It has focused attention on the housing market as the crucial allocative mechanism of life chances in British cities. In Rex's own words: 'the basic process underlying urban social interaction is competition for scarce and desired types of housing. In this process people are distinguished from one another by their strength in the housing market or more generally in the system of housing allocation' (Rex, 1968, p. 215). This has had particular consequences for the sociology of urban race relations, which cannot be elaborated here. There do appear to be systems of distribution and allocation that are both social and spatial and that operate independently to those created by both the labour market and the economy, as conventionally understood. Further, in the words of Pahl (1974b, p. 2) this time, Rex and Moore 'suggested that the formal bureaucratic rules and procedures operated by local authorities had systematic and punitive effects and they argued that this *could* give rise to common feelings of actual and potential deprivation which would generate conflict' (our emphasis). And we should all note that these ideas are closely related to the spatial structure of the city.

Here, then, is a powerful analytical instrument for approaching the underlying institutional mechanisms of the urban social system. It focuses attention on how people got where they are in the city and onto systematic spatial inequalities. It is a dynamic approach; as the housing market changes so too does the urban social structure. Further, people move through the housing market, with changes in the family cycle for example. Indeed, a combination of these two factors, position in the housing market and stage in the family cycle, is the best, but still crude, predictor we have of the spatial location of an individual family in the urban structure.

HOUSING CLASS CONSCIOUSNESS

What we wish to examine in the rest of this chapter is how far these objective distinctions lead toward, or determine, certain subjective feelings; or in Schmalenbach's terminology discussed above, Can one say 'from community to communion' and, more importantly, in what circumstances does this lead to action, political or otherwise? If the existence of housing classes has been established in British cities, is there a potential *housing class consciousness* too? And if there is, what form does it take? We are asking, then, whether there are forms of spatial consciousness that go beyond mental maps and lead to action, particularly local and community action. Certainly ecological segregation familiar to us since Booth (see Pfautz, 1967) has meant that those with similar socioeconomic status or social class positions have similar spatial positions in the urban structure. Much urban social geography has been devoted to the task of demonstrating just that.

From these objective differences and through the differences in interpersonal social networks, much locally based action could, has and will be based. It is very significant from the point of view of themes raised earlier in this chapter that this is frequently called '*community action*' when in fact it is *class action*. It is nearly always *locally* based, which because of the working of the housing market means *intra*-class not *cross*-class. Appeals to community spirit are usually made from the middle class when seeking wider support. Our point is that community action is based on antagonism and conflict and not on consensus, which is usually taken to be the basis of community. There is and can be no common urban consciousness.

At this stage it is not possible to more than illustrate our argument with a series of largely British case studies. We know, for instance, that fractions of housing classes have mobilized politically within a local setting: ratepayers associations to 'defend' owner-occupiers and tenants associations for council house occupiers. Two recent studies, in Liverpool and in Banbury, have gone so far as to argue that the rise of these kinds of local political action is the most significant change in politics for decades, operating as it does to a greater or lesser extent outside the already existing political structures. Hindess (1971) relates these changes closely to changes, through the housing market, in the urban structure. Changes in the urban structure are leading, he argues, to the withering away of the formal party organization in the working-class areas of cities. In Liverpool, formal working-class politics was replaced in inner urban areas by movements outside the field of political orthodoxy: squatters and tenants associations (Hindess, 1971, p. 129). Very significantly for our overall argument, he notes that 'housing has been important in grass-roots political development—not simply as a matter of bricks and mortar but as an area in which, for many people the most intimate connections between the personal and the political were established' (Hindess, 1971, p. 137). This has led to a contrast between the formally political and other kinds of political action.

In the new study of Banbury by Stacey, and co-workers (1974), it was shown that these new associations—the locally politically active pressure groups of both tenants and ratepayers (separately) associations—mobilized through social networks. Simplex social relationships between neighbours on raw housing estates became multiplex and more people got to know each other through political action. Social institutions that might be welcomed by the middle classes as indicating 'community spirit' were firmly and narrowly class-based. What spirit there was in a local tenants association was forged out of a common experience of deprivation and feelings of antagonism to the local authority— which were personified by the local councillors who were members of the existing and orthodox political parties. In Banbury, it was possible for the Labour Party to coopt some of the leaders thrown up by the tenants association, which aptly illustrates how moribund the party was until then.

Norman Dennis (1970, 1972), in a controversial pair of books about Sunderland, describes how political action does and can flow specifically from the consequences of local housing policy. In this case the action was within an existing party and against what Jon Gower Davies (1972) has called, based on his experience in nearby Newcastle, *The Evangelistic Bureaucrat*. There is no space here to develop the ongoing argument about the role of 'urban managers', yet that would be needed for a full analysis. Pahl has clearly and controversially stated why they are important; he argues 'that since territorial injustice and some form of exploitation are universal and, since the role of the State in allocating the infrastructure of collective consumption is increasing in the advanced capitalist societies, then the role of the State bureaucrats or managers must be central to an understanding of the principal processes in an urban system' (Pahl, 1974b, p. 11). Clearly, in the locality many of the confrontations in the new locally based politics are between citizens and officials. Sean Damer's (1974) vivid study of Wine Alley in Glasgow demonstrates the consequences of local authority housing policy, through its managers, in creating what he calls 'a dreadful enclosure'. Not only was there an institutionalization of inequalities in disadvantages (localities suffering as they do through the housing market from a variety of structural and institutional constraints), but as Damer points out 'they can also suffer from the very reputation of the outside world towards them' (Damer, 1974, p. 221). While Wine Alley residents resented their label and fought back (with bricks and fists), Damer argues that class consciousness 'appears impossible within (that) community' (Damer, 1974, p. 245). In our enthusiasm for the new urban politics, it should be noted that localities like Wine Alley frequently cannot organize, in part precisely because they represent the more extreme consequences of the institutional social processes described above.

Not all the new locally based urban politics must be thought of as working class. The episode of *The Cutteslowe Walls* (Collison, 1963) is a famous reminder of local middle-class action based on status panic, and Bell (1968) has written a case study of grass-roots political mobilization on a middle-class housing estate. (Many rural amenity and preservation societies represent the interests of particular housing classes: middle-class/newcomer/urbanite (Bell and Newby, 1974). These new ruralities are frequently where they are through the workings of the housing market, for since the earliest writings of the Chicago school we have known that those of the highest socioeconomic status frequently live beyond the urban periphery. Their political action has often been outside orthodox political parties. Within urban areas, there are similar middle-class actions again often based on housing class. One example that Pahl (1974b, p. 8) has noted was the collective response to a widespread threat that resulted in

> ... the co-ordination of a whole cluster of local organizations set up to oppose the concentric system of urban motorways proposed by the G.L.C. The London Motorway Action Group appeared to be more concerned with preserving 'amenity' and protecting property values and gained its support from home owners more than local authority or private tenants.

Threats from outside the locality, such as the Motorway Box, may create social relationships or communion that did not exist before (movement from B to A on our typology). This certainly was the experience of investigating the 'disruption of community' that would be a consequence of a third London Airport. The threat, especially inland, seems to have created the 'community' that would have been destroyed. The evidence (Abell, Bell and Doreian, 1970; Perman, 1972), though, shows that the airport resistance associations that personified the 'new community spirit' and represented the new politics were very middle—not to say upper-class affairs. At the working-class end, in contrast, George Clarke (1972) has described the creation first of communion and then of action within one street in London. The inhabitants of Acklam Street were dissatisfied with what they had to endure and so organized themselves in order to effect some satisfactory changes on their behalf. Clarke states strongly that in cases such as this, admittedly extreme, for not every deprived working-class street has an elevated motorway crossing, it, 'there is a chance that community power can begin to turn the scales of justice' (Clarke, 1972, p. 181). Through what we are now calling 'communion', power may come. Clarke's experience leads him to write that, increasingly, those in particular local social situations are realizing 'the power they have when they come together' (Clarke, 1972, p. 186).

CONCLUSION

What, then, are we to make of what David Donnison (1973) calls 'the micro-politics of the city'? Some, as he notes, have been part of the new official and orthodox administrative structures of the city, and yet others are 'the penumbra of independent, small-scale, unofficial political progresses which surround the accredited institutions of government' (Donnison, 1973, p. 304). Many of the micro-political innovations that are suddenly and fashionably with us are formal responses to earlier unofficial extraformal political action. It is as if lost local legitimacy cannot hope to be regained through education priority areas, urban programmes and planners action areas in neighbourhoods due for redevelopment. These all were, as Donnison (1973, p. 390) tells us, 'intended to focus resources and attention on deprived groups and areas'. We should note, along with him, that these programmes must be *redistributive* and are therefore deeply political. Micro-politics may not succeed unless they are linked to national-scale political movements. All the various community action programmes may in the final analysis be about social control, for all too frequently they are mere palliatives giving the appearance only of something being done. Yet only a nationwide or locality-wide programme can be genuinely redistributive, otherwise we will witness a succession of briefly spluttering popular local action groups that, if successful, will indeed direct resources to themselves but *away* from others who either have not or cannot mobilize—like the inhabitants of Wine Alley. For the short term and populist nature of much of the new urban politics is both the promise and the danger of communion.

This is why our overall conclusions are hesitant. We are certainly less sanguine than Daniel Bell (1974), who in a particularly enthusiastic passage celebrates maximum feasible participation. This can unfortunately all too easily mean that those who shout loudest get the goodies. For Daniel Bell, post-industrial society is increasingly a *communal* society, by which he means that public mechanisms rather than the market become the allocators of goods and that public choice rather than individual demand becomes the arbiter of services. Yet there are dangers that even as greatly an optimistic observer as himself sees in all this, for he writes (Bell, 1974, pp. 159–160):

> One of the facts of a communal society is the increased participation of individuals and groups in communal life. In fact, there is probably more participation today at the city level, than at any other time in (American) history. But the very increase in participation leads to a paradox—the greater the number of groups, each seeking diverse or competing ends, the more likelihood that these groups will veto one anothers interests, with the consequent sense of frustration and powerlessness as such stalemates occur . . . locally and nationally what we have been witnessing in the last decade, in fact, is the rise of an independent component, committed to neither of the two parties who swing vote becomes increasingly important. Thus the problem of how to achieve consensus on political questions will become more difficult. Without consensus there is only conflict, and persistant conflict simply tears a society apart, leaving the way open to repression by one sizable force or another.

Quite so, but our reaction to repression depends on who is oppressing who. In this sense we would agree with Williams (1973, p. 104) who has noted that 'community only became a reality when economic and political rights were fought for and partially gained, in the recognition of unions, in the extension of the franchise, and in the possibility of entry into new representative and democrative institutions'.

It will be in the locality, between and within classes, that this conflict will inevitably take place. This will be the new urban politics. Given that localism in the urban context has been expressed in terms of neighbourhoods, our conclusions are that it is here that we must look for the communal basis of these emerging political movements. Hilary Rose (1974) in a pioneering paper on the Claimants Union points out that they were one of just many strands of political activity focused on the home and the street. The orthodox political parties have almost totally failed to respond to them. What is more, it should be noted that so far most Marxist groups have also failed to 'locate community action as an integral and necessary part of the class struggle' (Rose, 1974, p. 199). This is a failure, too, of virtually all social scientists that we hope this chapter will go some small way in redressing.

ACKNOWLEDGEMENTS

We have had a number of perceptive comments on an earlier draft of this chapter. While we have not been able to meet all the points made to us, we are grateful to those we have discussed it with, especially David Donnison, Ronald Frankenburg, Michael Mann, Ray Pahl and Chris Pickvance, as well as the editors of this volume.

REFERENCES

Abell, Peter, Bell, Colin, and Doreian, Patrick (1970). *The Disruption of Community Life*, H.M.S.O., London.

Abu-Lughod, Janet (1961). 'Migrant adjustment to city life: the Egyptian case'. *American Journal of Sociology*, **67**, 22–32.

Bailey, F. G. (Ed.) (1970). *Gifts and Poisons: The Politics of Reputation*, Blackwell, Oxford.

Bailey, F. G. (Ed.) (1971). *Debate and Compromise: The Politics of Innovation*, Blackwell, Oxford.

Barnes, J. A. (1954). 'Class and committees in a Norwegian island parish'. *Human Relations*, **7**, 39–58.

Bell, Colin (1958). *Middle Class Families*, Routledge and Kegan Paul, London.

Bell, Colin, and Healey, Patrick (1973). 'The Family and leisure'. In S. Parker, C. Smith and M. Smith (Eds.), *Society and Leisure in Modern Britain*, Allen Lane, London.

Bell, Colin, and Newby, Howard (1971). *Community Studies*, George Allen and Unwin, London.

Bell, Colin, and Newby, Howard (1974). 'Capitalist farmers in the class structure'. *Sociologia Ruralis*, **XIV** (No. 1/2), 86–107.

Bell, Daniel (1974). *The Coming of Post-Industrial Society*, Heinemann, London.

Birch, A. M. (1959). *Small Town Politics*, Oxford University Press, Oxford.

Boissevain, Jeremy (1974). *Friends of Friends*, Blackwell, Oxford.

Bott, Elizabeth (1957). *Family and Social Network*, Tavistock, London.

Clarke, George (1972). 'The lesson of Acklam Road'. In E. Butterworth and D. Weir (Eds.), *Social Problems of Modern Britain*, Fontana, London.

Coleman, B. I. (1973). *The Idea of the City in Nineteenth Century Britain*, Routledge and Kegan Paul, London.

Collison, Peter (1963). *The Cutteslowe Walls*, Faber and Faber, London.

Damer, Sean (1974). 'Wine Alley: the sociology of a dreadful enclosure'. *Sociological Review*, **22**, 221–248.

Davidoff, L., L'Esperance, J., and Newby, H. (1975). 'The Beau ideal'. In J. Mitchell and A. Oakley (Eds.), *Women and Change*, Penguin, Harmondsworth, Middlesex.

Davies, Jon Gower (1972). *The Evangelistic Bureaucrat*, Tavistock, London.

Davies, J. G., and Taylor, J. (1970). 'Race, community and no conflict'. *New Society*, **16** (406), 67–69.

Dennis, Norman (1968). 'The popularity of the neighbourhood community idea'. In R. Pahl (Ed.), *Readings in Urban Sociology*, Pergamon, Oxford.

206

Dennis, Norman (1970). *People and Planning*, Faber and Faber, London.
Dennis, Norman (1972). *Public Participation and Planners Blight*, Faber and Faber, London.
Donnison, David (1973). 'Micro-politics of the city'. In D. Donnison and D. Eversley (Eds.), *London: Urban Patterns, Problems and Policies*, Heinemann, London.
Dumont, Louis (1972). *Homo Hierarchicus*, Paladin, St. Albans, Herts.
Fischer, C. S. (1972). 'Urbanism as a way of life: a review and an agenda'. *Sociological Methods and Research*, **1**, 187–242.
Gans, H. (1962). *The Urban Villagers*, The Free Press, Glencoe, Illinois.
Gans, H. (1968). 'Urbanism and suburbanism as ways of life'. In R. Pahl (Ed.), *Readings in Urban Sociology*, Pergamon, Oxford.
Glass, R. (1968). 'Urban sociology in Britain'. In R. Pahl (Ed.), *Readings in Urban Sociology*, Pergamon, Oxford.
Guttsman, W. L. (1963). *The British Political Elite*, MacGibbon and Kee, London.
Haddon, R. F. (1970). 'A minority in a welfare state society: the location of West Indians in the London housing market'. *New Atlantis*, **2**, 80–133.
Harrison, B. (1965–66). 'Philanthropy and the Victorians'. *Victorian Studies*, **9**, 353–374.
Hillery, G. A. (1955). 'Definition of community: areas of agreement'. *Rural Sociology*, **20**, 111–123.
Howard, E. (1965). *Garden Cities of Tomorrow*, Faber and Faber, London. Paper covered edition of 1902 revision.
Hindess, Barry (1971). *The Decline of Working Class Politics*, Paladin, St. Albans, Herts.
Kasarda, J. D., and Janowitz, M. (1974). 'Community attachment in mass society'. *American Sociological Review*, **39**, 328–339.
Keller, S. (1968). *The Urban Neighbourhood: A Sociological Perspective*, Random House, New York.
Lewis, Oscar (1951). *Life in a Mexican Village*, University of Illinois Press, Chicago.
Mann, P. M. (1965). *An Approach to Urban Sociology*, Routledge and Kegan Paul, London.
Martin, R., and Fryer, R. H. (1973). *Redundancy and Paternalist Capitalism*, George Allen and Unwin, London.
Mitchell, J. Clyde (Ed.) (1969). *Social Networks in Urban Situations*, Manchester University Press, Manchester.
Mitchell, J. Clyde, and Boissevain, Jeremy (Eds.) (1972). *Network Analysis, Studies in Human Interaction*, Mouton, Paris.
Newby, Howard (1975). 'The deferential dialectic'. *Comparative Studies in Society and History*, **17**, 139–164.
Nisbet, R. (1968). *The Sociological Tradition*, Heinemann, London.
Pahl, R. (Ed.) (1968). *Readings in Urban Sociology*, Pergamon, Oxford.
Pahl, R. (1974a). *The Sociology of Urban and Regional Development as a Problem in Political Economy*. Paper presented to the Eighth World Congress of Sociology, Toronto, 1974.
Pahl, R. (1974b). 'Urban managerialism reconsidered'. In *Whose City?* Pahl's collected papers 2nd ed. Longman, London.
Parkin, F. (1971). *Class Inequality and Political Order*, Paladin, St. Albans, Herts.
Perkin, H. (1968). *The Origins of Modern English Society, 1780–1880*, Routledge and Kegan Paul, London.
Perman, D. (1972). *Cublington: Blueprint for Resistance*, Bodley Head, London.
Perry, C. (1939). *Housing for the Machine Age*, Russell Sage Foundation, New York.
Pfautz, H. (1967). *Charles Booth on the City*, Chicago University Press, Chicago.
Redfield, R. (1947). 'The folk society'. *American Journal of Sociology*, **52**, 293–308.
Rex, John (1968). 'The sociology of the zone of transition'. In R. Pahl (Ed.), *Readings in Urban Sociology*, Pergamon, Oxford. Also in C. Bell and H. Newby (Eds.) (1974), *The Sociology of Community*, Frank Cass.

Rex, John, and Moore, Robert (1967). *Race, Community and Conflict*, Oxford University Press, Oxford.

Riemer, S. (1951). 'Villages in metropolis'. *British Journal of Sociology*, **2** (No. 1), 31–43.

Rose, Hilary (1974). 'Up against the welfare state: the Claimants Union'. *Socialist Register*, **1974**, 179–203.

Scherer, J. (1973). *Contemporary Community*, Tavistock, London.

Schmalenbach, H. (1961). 'The sociological category of communion'. In T. Parsons and co-workers (Eds.), *Theories of Society*, **I**, 331–347.

Simmel, G. (1971). 'The metropolis and mental life'. In D. N. Levine (Ed.), *Georg Simmell on Individuality and Social Forms*, Chicago University Press, Chicago.

Stacey, M. (1960). *Tradition and Change*, Oxford University Press, Oxford.

Stacey, M. (1969). 'The myth of community studies'. *British Journal of Sociology*, **20**, 134–147.

Stacey, M., Batstone, E., Bell, C., and Murcott, A. (1974). *Power, Persistance and Change*, Routledge and Kegan Paul, London.

Steadman-Jones, G. (1971). *Outcast London*, Oxford University Press, Oxford.

Tonnies, F. (1957). *Community and Society*, Harper and Row, New York.

Townsend, P. (1957). *Family Life of Old People*, Routledge and Kegan Paul, London.

Weber, M. (1964). *The Theory and Social and Economic Organisation*, The Free Press, Glancoe, Illinois.

Williams, R. (1961). *Culture and Society*, Penguin, Harmondsworth, Middlesex.

Williams, R. (1973). *The Country and the City*, Chatto and Windus, London.

Wirth, Louis (1938). 'Urbanism as a way of life'. *American Journal of Sociology*, **44**, 3–24.

Wolin, S. (1961). *Political and Vision*, George Allen and Unwin, London.

Young, M., and Willmott, P. (1957). *Family and Kinship in East London*, Routledge and Kegan Paul, London.

Chapter 7

Deprived Areas and Social Planning

Elizabeth Gittus

INTRODUCTION

Definitions of deprivation, as of poverty, are often imprecise or of limited application. As concepts, deprivation and poverty can only be seen in comparative terms and judged in relation to the particular societal contexts within which they occur. Societies inevitably contain some groups which are relatively worse off than others and within cities there are, characteristically, particular areas into which these groups have become concentrated. Deprived areas are regarded here as those parts of the city that are relatively poorly endowed with a number of basic resources, including services for housing, education, employment and health, and where poverty, in the widest sense, may be most prevalent. Deprived areas will not contain all the poor and disadvantaged in any one city, but they are likely at the aggregate scale to be the worse off and to be those areas in which the occurrence of multiple deprivation is most likely. In recent years, the theme of urban deprivation has attracted the attention of academics in several disciplines. Concern about the deterioration of the inner cities has generated a series of innovations in government policy. In Britain, increasing prominence has been given to the need for policy-oriented research. The anti-poverty programmes in the United States and, following the Plowden Report, awareness of the possible effects of an adverse environment on the development of children, have contributed to this trend (Central Advisory Council for Education, 1967).

The existence of deprived areas is a spatial manifestation of poverty. It is the purpose of this chapter to review those aspects of sociological theory and research which are relevant to this manifestation. Initially, the historical perspectives of research into urban poverty are examined and it can be shown that the 'classical' studies had great depth and range and were little constrained by interdisciplinary boundaries. The role of spatial factors within sociological analyses will be examined, and it can be shown that, besides studies in the ecological tradition, new ways of incorporating spatial variables are still being developed. Poverty as a concept will be discussed and directions in poverty research will be examined. In empirical terms, particular ethnic groups figure prominently among the most disadvantaged and are often the occupants of deprived areas. Sociological research into the problems of ethnic minorities

209

and policies concerned with the alleviation of their conditions of living will be examined. Finally, the bases for local political action within the deprived areas of the city will be discussed.

A HISTORICAL PERSPECTIVE

In attempting to set the study of urban deprivation within the wider field of analysis, it is impossible to ignore the growing divergence between those who focus primarily on the operation of market forces within the city and those whose perspective is more traditionally ecological, together with other groups of specialists in the study of local social networks and of individuals' spatial perceptions. Rather than review the literature under each of these headings, it seemed more apposite here to recall that, in the work of certain pioneers in this field, in Britain and in the United States, the separation between these various approaches is less distinct than the current academic debate might lead one to suppose.

Thus, when the onset of industralization was moulding the shape of our British towns, Engels cast his graphic description of the plight and distribution of the poorer working classes in Manchester in a form that anticipated both the Chicago model of concentric zonal development and the ecological processes of centralization, invasion and succession (see Gittus, 1960, chapter 2; and Harvey, 1973, p. 132). Unlike the Chicago school, Engels interpreted these shifting patterns in essentially structural terms, namely the superior power of the middle and upper economic classes and the working of an avaricious capitalist system.

Some forty years later, Booth's (1902–03) massive work in London pioneered the study of urban poverty in Britain. Booth began his investigations convinced that the existence of poverty, however its incidence might shock the comfortable aristocracy, would be accounted for by personal factors rather than by structural features of the economy. In short, the real issue was not 'poverty' but 'the poor'. While commentators have discerned certain shifts in Booth's ideological position during the course of his work, it is noted, too, that he began and remained firmly opposed to socialism in general and to communism in particular (Pfautz, 1967; Simey and Simey, 1960). His original plan was simply to discover the number and distribution of London's poor. But his later analysis of the causes and concomitants of their condition led him to consider such structural effects as the distribution of housing and opportunities for employment, especially the latter, and the role of trade unions, industrial organizations, welfare agencies and religious institutions (Pfautz, 1967). Methodologically, he supported the graphic description of his survey findings with the 'arts of participant observation', in order to familiarize himself with the life-styles of the poor (Simey and Simey, 1960, p. 65). Moreover, he mapped the incidence of poverty within a framework of concentric zones. He recognized the value of spatial constructs in indicating those parts of the city where poverty was concentrated. He also mapped the provision, in relation to local needs, of a range of services and institutions, including shops, places of amusement and churches (Pfautz, 1967, pp. 90–108).

In the 1920s, Burt (1925) supplemented a detailed psychological analysis of case histories for a group of London's delinquents with a tabulation, for each borough within the city, of delinquency rates and poverty rates (following Booth), alongside data on public elementary education, poor relief, overcrowding, open space, deaths, births and illegitimacy (Bert, 1925, Table 5). He used the method of rank differences to depict the spatial correlation of delinquency with most of the other inputs, notably with overcrowding, poverty and mortality rates. His study of individual cases supported the spatial analysis by identifying some of these variables among the main correlates of delinquent behaviour. Burt also drew attention to a possible bias in the crime statistics, in that misdemeanours by children from 'good' homes were less likely to be the subject of official enquiry and action—a reminder that has a contemporary ring! (see Chapman, 1968; and Hindess, 1973). Moreover, in conclusion, he argued that it was not sufficient to consider the attributes of individual offenders and that attention should also be directed to those structural features of society to which, for some, delinquency might be a form of response (Burt, 1925, 4th ed. p. 612).

Lastly, and more recently, one may recall the experience of W. F. Whyte, whose study, begun in the late 1930s, of a community of Italian immigrants to the United States, is said to have provided the material for the development of a sociology based on interpersonal relationships (Madge, 1963, p. 210; Whyte, 1943, p. 358). Whyte was an economist. He chose 'Cornerville', a slum district close to the fashionable centre of Boston, Massachusetts, largely because its features, especially the high rate of local unemployment, were those that as an economist he found most compelling. Whyte was no narrow specialist. His original list of topics was daunting. It included the set of urban resources that are typically of interest today, along with the political structure of the population and the local agents of social control, mainly the police and the racketeers. To these he felt obliged to add the more nebulous topic of social attitudes. However, in evolving the detailed plan of his research, he decided to abandon his original scheme and to make the main foci of his study the web of interpersonal relations and attitudes and the emergence of group leaders within the community. Thus, faced with the demands of the situation, he shifted his sights from structural aspects to social networks and other elements of the local 'sub-culture'.

The range and depth of the work of these early researchers are challenging. So, too, is the sensitivity with which they explored their findings. We may well ask, with Harvey (1973, p. 128), to what extent, 'with the whole theoretical and methodological apparatus that is now available, we are more able to comment meaningfully upon events as they unfold around us'.

Donnison (1974, p. 127) has called for a reappraisal of ideas about urban deprivation and the programmes that spring from them, and for serious attempts 'to bridge the gap between spatial and social thinking, between geography and town-planning on one side, and social policy and social administration on the other'. Harvey (1973, p. 37) has emphasized the need for a common framework within which geographers and sociologists may set their distinctive analytical approaches to the study of resources within the city.

SPATIAL FACTORS IN SOCIOLOGY

The incorporation of spatial factors into urban sociological analysis is not entirely new. Filkin and Weir (1972) have outlined the main features of sociologists' developing interest in 'locality' and 'location' as independent variables, with illustrations from a wide range of research projects. Green (1971) has identified a 'major trend in contemporary research towards the collective (in his application, spatial) level of analysis with which general sociological theory has always been concerned'. By combining survey methods with a Shevky–Bell designation of social areas within the city of Bath, he attempted to show how the interplay of individual and contextual factors, with regard to social attitudes and behaviour, might be discerned. For this purpose, he adapted techniques that were developed by Blau, Davis and others more than a decade ago, and to which Harvey, surprisingly, does not refer (Blau, 1960; Davis, Spaeth and Huson, 1961). Green's work is highly suggestive. But, without further information, it would be difficult to extract a setting for the study of urban deprivation from his particular typology.

Green has criticized, for being a-theoretical, attempts to construct a framework of areas, or contexts, from the multivariate analysis of census data, and has misinterpreted the original purpose of the exercise (see Gittus, 1965). But in his study of Sunderland, Robson (1969) has shown that, when coupled with the analysis of the town's historical development, these methods can produce a meaningful set of areas for the analysis of sociological data for individuals.

Robson was mainly interested in the interaction between contextual features and individual attitudes to education. Byrne (1974) has outlined a research design for the study of differences in 'social income' or in resource allocation within a northern town, where a certain degree of segregation along class lines was thought to obtain. His basic framework of areas was to be derived quite simply from a sociographic analysis of the distribution of the working class (i.e. semi-skilled and unskilled) population. Starting from the opposite end of the problem, Filkin and Weir (1972, pp. 141–144) have advocated a systematic classification of urban areas or sub-areas, by various criteria under each of the headings of 'resource-allocation', 'accessibility', 'communication' and 'symbolisation'.

Rex and Moore (1967) centred their investigation of the constraints operating within the housing market and the formation of 'housing classes', in part of Birmingham that was identifiable was the Burgess 'zone of transition'. They were particularly concerned with the position of local immigrant groups. From their study of immigrants in Newcastle-upon-Tyne, set as it was in a comparable transitional area, Davies and Taylor (1970) were able to show that immigrant groups hold differing views of their housing class position. Rex and Moore noted that, in Birmingham and its counterparts in the urban hierarchy, the twilight or transitional zone had a distinct function, in affording at least temporary shelter for those whose bargaining position in the housing market was most limited. In her study of urban migrants to a smaller Latin American town of more recent vintage, McEwen (1972) showed that it was the newcomers' lack of entry to the town's housing market that obliged them to live, for a time at least, in a shanty settlement on the urban fringe. As in Sparkbrook, it was this aspect of class position that provided the key to understanding the social divisions and the bases of conflict among the residents of the shanty settlement, the associations that were formed and the differences in individuals' prospects for mobility and integration within the wider urban society.

These methodological examples involve much more than this summary might convey. Moreover, they are directed towards various aspects of an extremely complex problem, namely that of discovering the spatial elements of the urban system and the reactions, behaviour and perceptions that are exhibited by the social elements, whether individuals or groups, at various points within that system. Some interesting contributions, which open up new lines of development in both theory and method, are to be found in the writings and research, in France, of Castells and his colleagues (see Pickvance, 1976).

Castells maintains that the sociological analysis of space is a legitimate form of activity. He suggests that urban sociology might be regarded, within the wider field of the discipline, as the sociology of space and the collective consumption, with an emphasis on the processes by which both the distribution and consumption of resources are determined, and the forces through which the whole system is open to change (Castells, 1976). Castells' further critique of urban sociology is discussed by Pickvance, who argues that much of the thinking of the French school is likely to command wide support among urban sociologists, whether or not they would adopt the same historical materialist position (Pickvance, 1974, p. 217). In any event, Castells' theoretical approach promises a coherent rationale for the articulation of spatial and social factors. Its relevance to the study of urban deprivation cannot be denied.

SOCIOLOGY AND SOCIETY

The cleavage that is currently evident between various groups of urban analysts, though not so apparent in the less academically self-conscious work of the early pioneers, is similar in some respects to a division in contemporary sociology, namely that between two distinct interpretations of the aspects of society to which sociological explanation should be addressed. One of these interpretations gives priority to the analysis of existing structures, while the other is concerned with the critique of the processes by which those structures were erected and maintained. Abrams (1975), in reviewing Bottomore's collection of essays on this critical aspect of sociology, refers to a third area of concern.

This is not just an alternative to either of the others, but is an integral part of the sociologist's task. It has to do with individual meanings (see Bottomore, 1975). Simply, in the context of the present theme, it entails the interpretation of urban deprivation as it impinges on the experiences and attitudes of the people concerned. Some aspects of urban poverty will now be considered, wherever possible, from that standpoint.

CHANGING NOTIONS OF POVERTY

Halsey (1974, p. 126), in discussing recent government policies in Britain, has emphasized the need to develop a theory of poverty and test it out in the twilight areas of our large cities. This is no mean undertaking, since poverty is a 'slippery concept', and ideas about it have changed radically in recent years.

In the immediate post-Beveridge era, poverty research in this country lost its urgency. Inspired as they were by Booth, the more sophisticated studies by Rowntree, Bowley and their successors had been built into the fabric of the welfare state (e.g. Beveridge, 1942; Bowley and Burnett-Hurst, 1915; Bowley and Hogg, 1925; Jones, 1934a, 1934b; Rowntree, 1903, 1941). The need for poverty had been reduced—or so it was believed. Its persistence, if any, was to be explained in individual rather than structural terms. By the early 1960s, however, and following translantic rumblings of concern about the number and plight of America's poor, it was realized that the effectiveness of the welfare provisions could not be taken for granted. Measures to alleviate the financial stringencies of the sick, the unemployed, the elderly, large families on low incomes, the fatherless—to name a few—needed a continual review. Moreover, some of these measures were failing to reach those for whom they were intended. The Child Poverty Action group began its campaign for a review of family allowances. Abel-Smith and Townsend (1965) analysed data from the Family Expenditure Survey to draw attention to the fact that, by official subsistence standards, the lot of a disquietingly large proportion of the population was at best precarious (see also ministry of Social Security, 1967).

A review panel, set up by the Social Science Research Council (1968), called for a renewal of interest in poverty research, and hoped that a greater variety of scholars would be committed to it. The panel identified several categories of poverty, one of which, 'down-town' poverty, extended the older phenomenon of poverty in the depressed areas to the central or inner neighbourhoods of the cities and larger urban regions. The new interest in this spatial dimension was explained by Donnison (1974, pp. 129–130):

> ... growing concern about our failure to meet the needs of the poorest people has been one of several motives for the recent revival of interest in the spatial factors which underlie social needs. This concern, which was generated earlier and is still livelier in the United States, has produced what amounts to a third explanation of social problems.

The other explanations of poverty that he cited referred to the 'social structure', i.e. a cluster of factors centred on individuals' skill, income and social status, and the vulnerabilities associated with different stages within the 'life-cycle' (see Stacey, 1969, pp. 43–50).

The argument thus became that certain groups within the 'social structure' might be at risk of becoming poor, especially at certain phases of the 'life-cycle', and that these risks might be accentuated for residents in areas where resources were limited and opportunities for betterment were few. In statistical terms, one might be tempted to hypothesize that spatial and non-spatial variables interact to heighten the incidence of poverty in certain parts of the city. But, depending on one's definition of poverty, such a statement may be a mere tautology or self-fulfilling prophecy. As will be argued, the matter of definition is problematic and the data base comparatively thin. The analysis must therefore be simple and cautious.

Using an income-based definition of poverty, Weisbrod (1965) outlined the spatial distribution of poor families in the United States in the mid-1960s. He showed that poverty, by his criterion, was all pervasive and not exclusively, nor even mainly, an urban condition. Nevertheless, the number of poor families in the central cities had increased markedly over the previous decade (Weisbrod, 1965, pp. 1–27). In Britain, the spatial distribution of poverty is still virtually uncharted. And the extent of downtown poverty, with which recent government measures have been especially concerned, remains a poorly documented theme (Halsey, 1974, p. 127). Moreover, the concept of poverty still eludes precise definition. It is relative, subjective and non-unitary. The prospects of deriving a composite measure, whose application will not do violence to the realities of the situation, remain slender (see Townsend, 1962, 1974).

Interest in the main component of poverty has broadened from 'income' *per se* to the wider notion of 'social income' or command over resources. In terms of the first definition, the early investigators set the poverty line as the lowest income that was necessary to obtain the bare essentials of food, warmth, shelter and clothing, plus certain extras that were deemed to be 'conventional necessities' (e.g. Booth, 1902–03; Bowley and Burnett Hurst, 1915; Jones, 1934a, 1934b; Rowntree, 1903, 1941; Rowntree and Lavers, 1951). In the 1960s, Abel-Smith and Townsend (1965) set a new style by relating their definition of the poverty line to the minimum income that would qualify a household for statutory assistance, given the martial status and age groupings of its members. Thus, they classed as 'in poverty' households whose income was below 140 per cent. of the statutory level. They did this for three main reasons. They argued that the statutory levels tended to lag behind changes in the real value of disposable income. Further, persons whose resources were so near the minimum were liable to be plunged into poverty through sudden misfortune. Finally, such a margin was necessary to allow for the fact that the official allowances could be supplemented by discretionary payments. In any event, their analysis suggested that the incidence of near poverty, by any realistic standard, was disquieting. And, as Coates and Silburn (1970), p. 32) argued, it was unnecessary to specify the dividing line too closely, as real poverty entailed so much more than financial stringency.

In discussing the concept of poverty, Townsend (1962, 1974) has consistently argued that the take-up of services including housing, education, health and welfare should be counted in the reckoning. The Social Science Research Council's panel recommended widening the range to included certain environmental assets that could not be purchased week by week for cash, namely open space, clean air, police protection and freedom from hazards due to traffic (Social Science Research Council, 1968, p. 25). Harvey, following Titmuss, defined income as 'all receipts which increase an individual's command over the use of a society's scarce resources' (Harvey, 1973, p. 53; Titmuss, 1962, p. 34). Harvey noted several consequences of this wider usage. It complicates the problem of measurement. The standard is open to continual extension as other services assume importance, as, for instance, those for the under-fives. Moreover, it shifts the emphasis of policies for achieving a more equitable distribution from factors related to 'social structure' and the 'life-cycle' to factors that may be termed 'situational' (Harvey, 1973, pp. 69, 85–86; and see Halsey, 1974, p. 130).

By this reasoning, Bleddyn Davies' (1968, p. 16) concept of territorial justice becomes a necessary, though not sufficient, condition for the achievement of a socially just distribution of resources among the city's residents. And initiatives by central or local government to improve conditions in the most 'deprived' areas are being directed to the reduction of poverty according to this wider notion (Donnison, 1974; Halsey, 1972; Home Office, 1968). Some policies involve measures of positive discrimination, that is apparent overprovision for those areas where 'needs' are assumed to be greatest (Donnison, 1974; Hatch and Sherrott, 1973). Such 'overkill' is necessary, according to Harvey (1973, p. 52) and Davies (1968, p. 18), in order to counter the 'hidden mechanisms' which, at the points of distribution or consumption, tend to increase inequalities rather than reduce them. Data for pre-school provision for the under-fives within Newcastle-upon-Tyne illustrate how such a policy has worked out under the Urban Programme (Gittus, 1975).

However, in accepting the wider concept of poverty and in adopting the more general notion of deprivation, the exacerbating effect of low economic resources should not be forgotten. A recent American contribution, for example, defines poverty as a set of multiple deprivations that are income-related (Baratz and Grigsby, 1972, p. 120).

In the following section, some evidence from studies within British cities will be considered, beginning with some findings that relate to this crucial monetary component.

RESEARCH FINDINGS ON ASPECTS OF POVERTY

It is not remarkable to find a high proportion of low income households in areas which, by general standards, are most unattractive. Booth, using a hierarchical classification of means that was based on an amalgam of income and and source of income, found that the poorest classes, by his criteria, were most numerous in the central areas of London, apart from the more highly valued western central sector (see Pfautz, 1967, pp. 50–57 and 90–126). In the 1930s, Caradog Jones studied the spatial distribution of income for working-class households in Liverpool. He also found that the poorer households, according to his version of the subsistence income level, were most concentrated in the central wards, in the neighbouring twilight zone and in the dockside wards to the north of the city centre. In these areas taken together, 30 per cent. of the sample households were classed as poor, compared with 20 per cent. in the remainder of the inner city and 10 per cent. or less in the outer wards (Jones, 1934b, p. 480). Jones, like Booth, attributed much of the spatial concentration of poverty to the adverse employment situation in the inner areas. Here, in Liverpool, the national crisis had exacerbated the local disadvantages of a precarious job situation and low wage rates, and had pushed up the unemployment rate beyond its normally high level (Jones, 1934b, pp. 433–434).

For the post-war years, there is a dearth of similar evidence of variations in economic need within whole cities. But studies within several central neighbourhoods have disclosed substantial minorities of households (some 30 per cent. where figures were given) whose economic resources, by the standards set by Abel-Smith and Townsend, were slender (Coates and Silburn, 1967, p. 53; Davies, 1972, p. 47; Gittus, 1962–64). In the 'Crown Street' area of Liverpool, 30 per cent. of household incomes were below 140 per cent. of the current qualifying level for assistance. This was more than double the results for the outlying 'control' areas. These outer areas were all part of one ward. They included the remnants of a former village settlement, where smaller local authority schemes had been intermingled with older privately owned or rented property, a middle-class area that was almost entirely in owner-occupation and a large peripheral public housing estate (see Brennan, 1972; Gittus, 1962–64; Vereker and co-authors, 1961).

The Liverpool study illustrated the added stringencies that might be experienced by low income households in the inner city, for here the amount of income that went to meet the basic resources of food, shelter, warmth and clothing was disproportionately high for those near or below the poverty line. In the central areas, and in advance of official attempts at control, some private landlords required high rents for inadequate accommodation from tenants who were in no position either to bargain or to go elsewhere. Fuel was purchased uneconomically in small bags. Fires were kept alight because hot water was not on tap. Clothing clubs and other credit agencies took heavy toll of those who tried to extend their purchasing power. The nature of the area's endemic unemployment has been described elsewhere, both from the official records of unemployment rates and from the residents' perceptions of their position (Gittus, 1970, pp. 324–335). The local take-up of a wider range of services, and the use of the statutory and voluntary agencies concerned with them, were characterized neither by exploitation of the services nor by widespread ignorance of them. If anything, those residents who, through ignorance or misunderstanding, failed to obtain some benefit that would have mitigated their hardship, outnumbered those who made full use of the available supports (Gittus, 1966;

and see Timms, 1961). Even among the most disadvantaged, the majority preferred to cope with their own problems. Here, as in Nottingham, the overall impression was not one of overt misery, malaise or woe (Coates and Silburn, 1970, pp. 136–137). This leads on to the deeper issues of the values, norms and aspirations of the population in the poorer areas, and how they are construed. These are topics that relate to several substantive areas of sociological theory and research. The emphasis here is on the research findings, but, in order to appreciate these fully, the reader is advised to consult the various theoretical contributions that underlie them and to which the references provide the key.

SOCIAL DIVERSITY

Strauss, (1968) in his work on urban imagery, has distinguished between two kinds of area within towns, on the basis of the social composition of their populations. He uses the term 'locale' for areas whose residents include many social groups, and 'location' for areas, such as ghettos, where the distinction social groupings are few. In this country, the evidence for the inner areas mentioned so far would suggest that it is as 'locales' rather than 'locations' that they should mostly be understood.

Even Bethnal Green, the archetype of the one-class urban community, was shown to contain several distinct elements, occupying different ecological areas with varying styles of housing and prestige (Glass and Frenkel, 1946; Townsend, 1957; Young and Willmott, 1957). Frankenberg (1966, p. 181) has suggested that the main unifying factor among these groups was their shared poverty and lack of social and geographical mobility'. Filkin and Weir, from the evidence of British cities, have questioned Parsons' association of territoriality with community (Filkin and Weir, 1972, pp. 119–120; Parsons 1969, pp. 90–94). But Pahl (1970, pp. 209–226) has conceded that territorial identity may be a cohesive force among those whose social power is limited.

In a wider sense, it would be contrary to the findings of research in the inner areas to assume that their populations subscribe to a common system of either values or behaviour. There are differences between individuals and among the local groups. Some of these differences, which have implications for policies that are community-based, will be mentioned briefly from the research findings, and then, against these findings, some aspects of the 'culture of poverty' model will be examined.

The analysis will be clearer if the nature and location of deprived areas are linked historically and currently with external or exogenous factors that have to do with the distribution of resources within the city. Against this back-cloth, the individuals resident in the study areas may be distinguished according to the routes and processes by which they came to be there, the likelihood of their moving away and their reaction to any such prospect. Housing is, of course, a major factor. The notion of deprived areas, in these terms, may be differently construed between the private and public sectors. Indices based on standards of size, quality and amenity may pinpoint areas of run-down private housing, such as those that have been classified, in an ideal-typical scheme of decaying areas, as either 'residual' or 'transitional (Gittus, 1969, pp. 27–35). In reality, some of the areas studied included both these types (e.g. Davies, 1972; Rex and Moore, 1967; Vereker and co-authors, 1961). In the public sector, several studies have been made of 'problem estates', whose low status has been acquired through the mechanisms of local authorities' procedures for allocating 'difficult' tenants (Byrne, 1975; Damer, 1974).

In seeking to understand the position of residents in the most deprived or undesirable areas in both sectors, data on individual housing histories are likely to be illuminating, and especially so for the various immigrant groups (see Research Unit on Ethnic Relations, 1975).

In research with some bearing on policy decisions, it is necessary to explore the values and preference sets to which individuals subscribe when confronted by the prospects of changes in their situation. Dennis, (1970, 1972), for instance, has provided some graphic examples from the experience of residents in Millfield, Sunderland, of the disjunction that can arise between householders' attachment to their homes and official diagnoses of their housing situation. On the other hand, studies in Swansea and Liverpool have shown that it may be wrong to assume, on the basis of extrapolations from Bethnal Green, that those who have long-standing family associations with an area will necessarily wish to remain there (Rosser and Harris, 1965; Vereker and co-authors, 1961). In the Crown Street district of Liverpool, it was found that those whose local connections, through family and kin, were most deep-rooted, most often expressed their wish to be rehoused elsewhere (Vereker and co-authors, 1961, pp. 118–119). This unexpected result appeared to reflect some respondents' willingness to subordinate their own preferences to their concern for their children's education, since, at the time, the local schools were mostly poorly equipped and the standards low (Mays, 1962). Moreover, further evidence is needed as to how far, in deprived areas, a person's local social networks are valued *per se* and how far they are mainly appreciated as temporary action sets and supports in times of crisis or emergency. (Bott, 1957; Boswell and others in Mitchell, 1969). These are just examples of the individualities that may be overlooked if it is too hastily assumed that the populations in deprived areas form a homogeneous group. More general notions of group attitudes in such areas will now be examined.

THE CULTURE OF POVERTY

The nature of the theory of downtown poverty that was fundamental to the American poverty programme a decade ago was reflected in the importance accorded to projects involving community action and social work. Central to the theory were the notions that the poor were caught in 'a vicious cycle of lack of opportunity and lack of aspiration' (Halsey, 1974, p. 129) and that 'to be impoverished was to grow up in a culture radically different from the one that dominates the society' (Harrington, 1962). Rossi and Blum included 'low need achievement and low aspirations for the self' among the value-orientations that they regarded as typical of the poorest classes (Rossi and Blum, Oscar Lewis and others in Moynihan, 1969). Thus, it was argued, that the poor tended to remain poor because, growing up in a separate culture, they were conditioned to be undemanding, unaspiring and short-run hedonistic in their outlook (Beshers, 1962, p. 31).

These 'culture of poverty' assumptions have been increasingly challenged in the United States by proponents of a more situational approach (e.g. Valentine, 1969; and see Halsey, 1974, p. 130). Valentine (1973) has stressed the need to distinguish between cultural behaviour which is the consequence of the acculturation process and that which is the response to the constraints imposed by environmental and/or structural disadvantages. Miller (1968) has illustrated this point by contrasting the experience of Whyte's Italians in Corneville with that of the inhabitants of Tally's Corner, a Negro ghetto in a blighted district of Washington, the former having much brighter prospects of going on to employment and the advantage, in the meantime, of supportive family networks (and see Schorr, 1964).

Contributors to the debate, in this country, have warned that the 'culture of poverty' thesis needs to be handled with caution. The concept of culture, though widely used, retains a certain vagueness that carries the risk of over-generalization on slender evidence (Gerth and Mills, 1954, p. xxii). The Social Science Research Council's review panel noted that the term covered many different aspects which should be studied separately and that the 'culture of poverty' approach was 'as likely to mislead as to enlighten' (Social Science Research Council, 1968, p. 10).

Clarke (1974) has examined the use of culture and sub-culture in sociology, and the relationship between cultural and structural explanations of group norms and behaviour. Like Cohen (1955), he argues that delinquent and other deviant sub-cultures, which are often associated with the poorest urban areas, may be generated primarily by structural inequalities, with local traditions and other historically specific circumstances as further determinants. Thus, deviant behaviour may be one form of response to the awareness that the desired goals of the wider society cannot be attained by legitimate means. But whether or not a cohesive sub-culture results will depend on the effectiveness of forces for legitimation or control, both locally and in the wider society (Clarke, 1974, pp. 436–440). Nevertheless, deviance is a minority form of response and, as Rainwater (1967) has argued, there are other strategies by which people adapt to awareness of deprivation or disadvantage. This viewpoint will be further considered below.

In Britain, the culture of poverty thesis, as formulated in the United States a decade ago, has gained some adherents (see the comment by Byrne, 1975). But its validity as an explanatory model of the norms, values and attitudes that may accompany the various poverties that merge in certain urban localities cannot be taken as proven.

In all the areas for which data are available, the populations included a number of sub-groups that were not clearly linked by a common cultural allegiance. In such inner areas as Newcastle's Rye-Hill, Nottingham's St. Anne's and Liverpool's Crown Street, there were groups of deviants, 'reluctant deviants' Davies called them. (Coates and Silburn, 1967, pp. 20–21; Davies, 1972, pp. 62–65; Gittus, 1969). But here, as in the problem estates studied, these deviants were far outnumbered by the 'respectables' in the local population (Byrne, 1975; Damer, 1974). Among these respectables, there were, in some areas, and notably in the twilight sector of inner Liverpool, considerable variations in economic and housing-class position and in the range of individuals' local and wider networks and affiliations (Vereker and co-authors, 1961). The populations of the areas selected for community development projects were, in most cases, similarly varied (The national Community Development Project, 1974).

In St. Anne's, where local attitudes were more systematically explored, it seemed that many residents were not unaware of the constraints inherent in their situation and that their aspirations were correspondingly modest (Coates and Silburn, 1967, pp. 69–80). Dennis (1970, p. 332) has rightly drawn attention to the narrowness of the empirical base, in British research, of assumptions that residents in such deprived or decaying areas are short-run hedonistic in their outlook, and has warned of the danger of building into official plans and policies moral judgements about such states of mind.

In the final analysis of their data, Coates and Silburn (1970, pp. 136–144) rejected the 'culture of poverty' explanation. Instead, they chose to follow Runciman's application of reference group theory (Runciman, 1966, pp. 25–28). Thus, they argued that the low aspirations of those 'respectables' who were poorest, in economic terms, reflected the fact that, while subscribing to a value system that was essentially similar to that of society at large, they had adopted a strategy of survival—a realistic adjustment to the limitations and constraints of which they were well aware (Rainwater, 1967). That is to claim that, in such circumstances, people may retain the dominant value system, 'but modify their expectations by narrowing the social range within which they are prepared to make comparisons with their own position' (Coates and Silburn, 1970, p. 143; see also Rodman, 1963).

Coates and Silburn further explored these conclusions by comparing, on certain relevant questions, the poorest respondents with the more affluent, and the committed trade unionists with the rest of the sample. Given the current interest in the notion of a 'cycle of deprivation', more needs to be known both about the forces that make for 'poverty' in the widest sense and, still more, about how individuals and groups react to such circumstances.

It must be remembered that, in residual areas like St. Anne's and especially in transitional or twilight areas such as Rye Hill and parts of Sparkbrook and 'Crown Street', residents have arrived there by a number of routes, for different reasons and with varying prospects of moving away (Gittus, 1969). Moreover, some of them belong to social categories who may be at risk of some form of hardship wherever they are housed. Holman (1970) has made a detailed analysis of such socially deprived groups in the country as a whole. He recognizes, however, that many of them are to be found in the inner-city areas and thus concludes that measures to allocate resources to them on a spatial basis constitute a viable form of social policy.

IMMIGRANTS IN THE INNER CITY

One important element in some of the inner areas is the immigrant population. It would be improper to pretend, in a limited space, fully to summarize current thinking about their situation. Moreover, it must be remembered that the relative concentration of immigrants in the inner areas is very largely a regional phenomenon and that differing degrees of concentration and dispersal characterize the distributions of the main immigrant groups. Thus, concern for the education of immigrants' children prompted the inclusion of the relative presence of persons born overseas among the indices by which the educational priority areas were defined. But the official circular to local authorities, in connection with claims for assistance under the Urban Programme, stipulated that a high percentage of immigrants would be considered only where it was ecologically aligned with other evidence of environmental or social hardship, and not independently (Department of Health and Social Security, 1968, p. 12; Halsey, 1972).

Recognizing that the whole topic is exceedingly complex, the following is a selection of ideas and research findings that seemed to be most relevant here.

The plight of the urban Negro has been one of the main concerns of the American poverty programme (Batchelder, 1965). Among northern cities, the proportion of non-whites in the population was positively correlated with grants per capita received both for the War on Poverty to 1966 and for urban renewal from the beginning of the 1950s (Alford, 1972 p. 349). Moreover, conditions in the black ghettos have drawn the attention both of campaigners for Civil Rights and of the organizers of Black Power. The rationale of each approach has been referred to the wider academic discussion of the relative utility of the concepts of class and of ethnic pluralism in understanding the position of immigrant minorities (see, for example, Lockwood and others in Zubaida, 1970; Lyon, 1972).

In Britain, sociologists' interest in race relations has progressed from descriptive studies of aspects of the integration of the newcomers, and of manifestations of prejudice and discrimination towards them, to a critical and interpretive analysis of the position of such minorities in the structure of British society, the degree of ethnic allegiance that persists among them and those explanatory factors that have to do with cultural and structural elements in the 'sending societies'. The contributions of Banton, Lockwood and Rex to Zubaida's (1970) symposium are evidence of this trend. So, too, is the initiative of the Social Science Research Council in setting up a special unit at Bristol University to pursue fundamental research in this field (Research Unit of Ethnic Relations, 1975).

Many studies to date have focused on the inner-city areas where, whether of necessity or, as Davies and Taylor (1970) have argued, of choice, many of the immigrants have settled (Desai, 1963; Glass, 1960; Holman, 1970, pp. 151–155; Lyon, 1969; Rex and Moore, 1967). The Bristol Unit is currently researching the distinctive group of Ugandan Asians, many of whom were initially housed by local authorities in their central areas, but who, in some cases, had the resources eventually to improve their housing-class position (Research Unit on Ethnic Relations, 1975). Such studies, including the analysis of housing histories, will contribute to the understanding of those constraints within the housing market that affect the prospects of immigrant groups and the circumstances in which these structural disadvantages may be transcended.

For the situation in the inner areas, the following points may briefly be made, in particular for immigrants from the West Indies, India and Pakistan, with their British-born children. Census counts from 1961 to 1971 show a consistent difference between the geographical distribution of the West Indians and that of the Indians and Pakistanis taken together. To 1971, among those born overseas, some 70 per cent. of West Indians were living in the conurbations of Greater London and the West Midlands, compared with less than 50 per cent. of those from India and Pakistan (Central Statistical Office, 1973, p. 83; Jones and Smith, 1970 pp. 166–167). Some evidence of relative concentration within these conurbations is given by a recent official analysis of 1971 data for enumeration districts in the whole of Britain (Coffield, 1975; Department of the Environment, 1975). Of the 5 per cent. of enumeration districts ranking highest on the proportion of New Commonwealth immigrants in their population, 40 per cent. were in the Inner London boroughs, 17 per cent. elsewhere in Greater London and 15 per cent. in the West Midlands conurbation, with a smaller but distinctive concentration in West Yorkshire.

Louden (1975), following Lomas (1973), has shown that, in 1971, 70 per cent. of males born in the West Indies had lived in this country for over ten years, against some 40 per cent. of the Indian-born and just under 30 per cent. of incomers from Pakistan. On the other hand, 23 per cent. of males from India and 31 per cent. from Pakistan had arrived here since 1967. The total resident populations in 1971 were estimated, from the census, as (thousands) 446 West Indians, 483 Indians and 170 Pakistanis, of whom 50, 47 and 24 per cent. respectively were born in the United Kingdom. The comparative youthfulness of the immigrant population is apparent from these analyses.

Rex (1970a, p. 114) has maintained that speculations about the future of race relations in this country may be premature, since the large-scale immigration of coloured workers from the former plantation colonies is a relatively new phenomenon. For the West Indians and Indians, however, the second generation of immigrants appears, from the above, to be now as numerous as the first. The particular tensions of this second generation will assume increasing importance (see Louden, 1975).

Many studies, in the early days of the migratory flow and more recently, have emphasized the cultural differences between the various immigrant groups (e.g. Banton, 1955; Dayha, 1974; Desai, 1963; Lyon, 1973). The most obvious and superficial contrast is that between those of West Indian and of Asian origin. But, for the latter, such a broad grouping is highly inaccurate, and even for the former it is questionable (Lyon, 1969). Dayha (1974) has maintained that, while the tendency of immigrants from the Commonwealth countries to settle in the inner-city wards has been well documented, insufficient is known of the immigrants' perceptions of their situation. For some, he argues, such a settlement pattern may be a temporary expedient, to be modified later. The Bristol researchers, mentioned earlier, will provide some evidence to fill this gap. And already, Davies and Taylor (1970), for instance, have argued that for the Asians of Rye Hill the settlement area provided a convenient ecological niche—a base for the practical expression of their entrepreneurial attitude to property and a place where, within the value system of their own culture, they could acquire esteem and prestige by providing homes for their kinsmen. The Chinese restauranteur, of course, similarly found a suitable base in the inner areas. But his more general prestige rating provides an interesting contrast, since, while members of the host society have increasingly appreciated his particular service and skills, they tend to accord to the immigrant landlord, whatever his own evaluation of his chosen function, the disesteem associated with membership of a pariah group (Rex, 1970b, pp. 44–45).

Such differences apart, it is in the inner areas, where conditions are ostensibly most unfavourable for all sections of the population, that immigrant problems tend to be defined as such, and where connections between colour and environmental squalor become rooted in the public mind (Rose and co-authors, 1969, p. 682). There are signs in the work just quoted, and elsewhere, of the unfulfillment of the West Indians' hopes that the avenues of the British stratification system would be open to them and their children, regardless of colour, —even if such hopes were qualified, for themselves, by a sanguine assessment of the resources that they had to offer. In terms of housing, employment, income, schooling, services for the very young and the scope for teenagers' leisure, there is evidence of their relative disadvantage (Collison, 1967; Halsey, 1972; Jackson, 1973; Jones and Smith, 1970; Leach, 1974; Rex and Moore, 1967). There are variations, of course, but it is in the inner areas, among those who are obliged to remain there or who choose to do so in order to escape possible rejection elsewhere, that these disadvantages may be seen to merge.

Those Asian groups who retain a measure of cultural distinctiveness and reinforcing links with the society from whence they came will differ from the West Indians, both in their reading of the structure of British society and in their expectations from it, at least among the first generation of migrants. Moreover, as has already been suggested, there are cultural differences among the Asian groups. Rose and co-authors (1969, p. 25) and more recently Ward (1972), for instance, have discussed the modified version of the plural society model that is most relevant to their case. Nevertheless, studies in the contrasting settlement areas of Sparkbrook, Rye Hill and Bristol unite in concluding that, in such areas, it is the coloured immigrants as a whole, whatever their diversity of culture and of economic resources, who tend to be both affected by the area's decline and associated with it in the minds of their indigenous neighbours (Davies, 1972; Lyon, 1969; Rex and Moore, 1967).

Deakin and Cohen (1970) have compared the rationale and relative desirability of official policies for the dispersal of immigrants from the central areas with measures for the enrichment of such settlements by allocating more resources to them. They draw the analogy with corresponding policies for the blighted areas of American cities, and the shift in the emphasis there from dispersal to enrichment.

For Greater London, they produce evidence, to 1966, of a small, and possibly class-differentiated, movement among the West Indian population from boroughs with the highest numerical concentrations to those where the number of immigrant residents is relatively few. The more general and progressive effect, on the inner areas, of selective and planned outward movements has been the subject of considerable speculation and concern. And Deakin and Cohen (1970) warn that the dispersal from the inner city, whether the result of private initiatives or of official policy, may be impeded in the future, as the persistent concentration in the inner areas reinforces the tendency of the white society to identify colour with poor housing and environmental squalor.

Advocates of the 'coloured quarter' have stressed the potential of a vigorous local community for encouraging political involvement (see Deakin and Cohen, 1970). Rose and co-authors (1969, p. 732) have suggested that the Black Power movement represents in an extreme form a progressive disillusionment, which has become so strongly felt that, for the movement, colour now transcends cultural differences. Lyon (1972) is doubtful of the ability of the 'purely racial' West Indian minority in Britain to mobilize themselves collectively in order to secure an improvement in their position. Louden (1975) has suggested that, faced with the prospect of a deterioration in their circumstances, West Indian migrants are talking increasingly of returning home.

The problems of the inner areas have been central to new government intentions, as recently announced, to tackle 'the real causes of racial deprivation' (Evans, 1975). One suggestion is 'to put a statutory obligation upon local authorities to carry out tasks to improve the lot of minority groups, over and above that shared by others in the inner city'. Also suggested are changes in the status and structural position of the Community Relations Commission, and in its relationships with the self-help groups, which some immigrant communities have set up, and with the more militant elements among them.

The possible effects of adverse labelling and the prospects of local groups' involvement in political action are topics that may be applied to all sections of the population in the inner areas. These will finally be considered in this more general context.

ADVERSE LABELLING

In discussing their scheme for a multidimensional study of poverty, Baratz and Grigsby (1972) maintain that the multi-deprived are further handicapped by the low esteem which the rest of society accords to them. Damer (1974) and Byrne (1975) have applied the concept of societal labelling, such as has hitherto been invoked in the analysis of more homogeneous deviant groups, to the study of local authority estates, which over the years had acquired ill repute among the non-residents. Their accounts are sensitive and compelling and indicate the inter-group tensions that may be generated locally by such ascriptions. And in the previous section, it has been noted that similar hostilities and resentments may arise within the inner settlement areas. Suttles (1968, pp. 323–334) has clearly shown how, in slum areas, the awareness of stigmatization can affect the local patterns of social interaction and how, in the face of this, the inhabitants seek to establish relationships based on feelings of mutual trust. More generally, one may ponder the consequences for the local residents of the application of such terms as 'social disorganization' or 'social malaise' to whole areas within the city. For here, as Morris (1957) found in his work on 'criminal areas', the labels, if accurate and meaningful, apply to relatively few within the areas' populations. While labelling theory, in such contexts, needs to be used with caution (Rotenberg, 1974), it is unlikely that the popularization of these terms will not be damaging for the residents in such areas.

POLITICAL ACTION

Finally, the poorest elements in the population are commonly supposed to be slow to exercise political power and to be ambivalent or apathetic towards participation schemes (Baratz and Grigsby, 1972; Miliband, 1974). Pickvance (1975a, 1975b) has drawn attention to certain aspects of the local social structure that may affect the prospects of residents' involvement in political action. Besides the demographic features, which have more often been cited, he underlines the relevance of the structure of social relations, the informal networks of kinship and friendship, the membership of other organizations, and the extent to which such patterns of association exist within, or cut across, the boundaries of local groupings that are based, for instance, on class or ethnicity. The existence of trust, he argues, is a further requirement if local populations are to participate in joint activity. Byrne (1975), however, instances a situation where, despite the adverse effects of stigmatization, political initiatives were successfully organized. Bell and Newby (1971, p. 220) note that, in Britain, the theme of 'community' power has been thinly researched. The issue is important, since local intervention or participation in the process of decision-making is a principle to which the present government is committed (Labour Party, 1974). Both under the E.P.A. programme and in the various schemes of the Community Development Projects, there is evidence that residents in the poorer areas can be stimulated to take part in joint action, though such interventions can scarcely be aligned with radical notions of community power (Midwinter 1972; The National Community Development Project, 1974).

Dennis (1970, p. 365), from the experience in Millfield, Sunderland, has further argued that the public's inability to obtain relevant information can be a strong impediment to their achieving political potency.

In a wider context, Harvey (1973, p. 82) argues that the ability to make use of local resources and, by implication, to share in the processes by which their allocation is decided will be constrained by the lack of knowledge and of cognitive skills. Pettigrew (1972) makes a similar point, stressing the need for the possession both of system-relevant resources, especially information, and of the skill to use them. The lack of both information and skill, in this context, is a form of deprivation that may accompany the more recognized 'poverties' in the inner city—and that has implications for many aspects of local life, whether for individuals or for groups.

CONCLUSIONS

It is not intended, here, to add to the collection of comment and prescription for the 'deprived' areas which is to be found in abundance in the literature on social policy and administration (e.g. Bryant, 1972; Donnison, 1972, 1973, 1974; Halsey, 1974; Hatch and Sherrott, 1973; Jones and Mayo, 1975; Miliband, 1974; The National Community Development Project, 1974). The purpose of this review has been to bring together, in a simple manner, certain aspects of sociological theory and research that are relevant to this particular spatial manifestation of poverty. Admittedly, the emphasis has been almost entirely on the character and circumstances of the residents in in such localities, to the exclusion of another major field of interest that may be accommodated within Castell's definition of urban sociology—namely, the study of the operations of the various public and private agencies through which resources are allocated and their distribution 'controlled' (for the importance of this field of study see, for example, Harvey, 1973; Pahl, 1970; Pickvance, 1975a, 1975b; Castells and others in Pickvance, 1976; for statistical analyses of variations in policy 'outputs' see Boaden, 1971; Boaden and Alford, 1969; Davies, 1968; Davies and co-authors, 1971, 1972; Nicholson and Topham, 1971; for relevant studies of decision-making and decision-makers see Davies, 1972; Dennis, 1970, 1972; Donnison and co-authors, 1965; Harloe, Issacharoff and Minns, 1975; Malpass, 1973; The National Community Development Project, 1974; Norman, 1975).

Four points merit underlining, in the light of the discussion in this chapter. Firstly, the statistical analysis of indicators of social deprivation is only the beginning, despite the popularity of such exercises with both central and local government and their political connotations (see, for example, Boal, Doherty and Pringle, 1974; Craig and Driver, 1972; Department of the Environment, 1975; Flynn, Flynn and Mellor, 1972; Hatch and Sherrott, 1973; Herbert, 1975; Hope, 1969; Knox, 1974; Newcastle Social Services Department, 1974; Shonfield and Shaw, 1972).

Secondly, it is clear that many of the problems of the inner areas, while locally most apparent, have roots that run back into the whole structure of

228

society. Thus, as Dennis (1958) so cogently argued over a decade ago, and as others increasingly have emphasized, the application of local measures, while obviously not to be neglected if hardship is to be relieved, can divert attention from the need for structural changes, and may leave certain crucial aspects, such as employment policy, relatively untouched (Dennis, 1958; Harvey, 1973; Miliband, 1974; The National Community Development Project, 1974). It follows, too, that certain deprivations are not wholly or even mainly to be found within such areas, and cannot fully be tackled within this framework (see for example, Gittus, 1975, chapter 9; Hatch and Sherrott, 1973; Holman, 1970).

Thirdly, uncritical resort to the notion of 'community' ignores the diversity of social groups that characterizes the populations of many inner areas.

Finally, the study of the inner city should be both intra- and inter-disciplinary, in the sense advocated by Castells (1976), namely 'the communication and inter-relating of results obtained *independently* by each discipline, or sub-discipline, in relation to the same real object', and recognizing, too, following Weber, (1949), that each approach has its own particular 'relevance for value'.

REFERENCES

Abel-Smith, B., and Townsend, P. (1965). *The Poor and the Poorest*, Occasional Papers in Social Administration No. 17, G. Bell, London.

Abrams, P. (1975). 'Review', *Times Higher Educational Supplement*, 16 May, p. 7.

Alford, R. R. (1972). 'Critical evaluation of the principle of city classification', In B. J. L. Berry (Ed.), *City Classification Handbook: Methods and Applications*, John Wiley, London. pp. 331–359.

Banton, M. (1955). *The Coloured Quarter*, Jonathan Cape, London.

Baratz, M. S., and Grigsby, W. G. (1972). 'Thoughts on poverty and its elimination'. *Journal of Social Policy*, **1** (2), 119–134.

Batchelder, A. (1965). 'Poverty: the special case of the Negro'. In B. A. Weisbrod (Ed.), *The Economics of Poverty*, Prentice-Hall, Englewood Cliffs, New Jersey. pp. 100–104.

Bell, C., and Newby, H. (1971). *Community Studies*, George Allen and Unwin, London.

Beshers, J. M. (1962). *Urban Social Structure*, The Free Press of Glencoe, New York.

Beveridge, W. H. (1942). *Social Insurance and Allied Services*, Beveridge Report, Cmd. 6404, H.M.S.O., London.

Blau, P. (1960). 'Structural effects'. *American Sociological Review*, **25**, 178–193.

Boaden, N. (1971). *Urban Policy Making*, Cambridge University Press, Cambridge.

Boaden, N., and Alford, R. (1969). 'Sources of diversity in English local government decisions'. *Public Administration*, Summer. pp. 203–223.

Boal, F. W., Doherty, P., and Pringle, D. G. (1974). *The Spatial Distribution of Some Social Problems in the Belfast Urban Areas*, Northern Ireland Community Relations Commission, Belfast.

Booth, C. (1902–03). *Life and Labour of the People in London*, 3rd. ed. (17 volumes). Macmillan, London.

Bott, E. (1957). *Family and Social Network*, Tavistock, London.

Bottomore, T. A. (1975). *Sociology and Social Criticism*, George Allen and Unwin, London.

Bowley, A. L., and Burnett-Hurst, A. R. (1915). *Livelihood and Poverty*, Bell, London.

Bowley, A. L., and Hogg, M. H. (1925). *Has Poverty Diminished?*, King, London.

Brennan, P. J. (1972). *An Exploration of Some Dimensions of Poverty*. Unpublished dissertation for the degree of M.Sc. in Pure Science, University of Newcastle-upon-Tyne, Northumberland.

Bryant, R. (1972). 'Community Action'. *British Journal of Social Work*, **2** (2), 205–215.

Burt, C. (1925). *The Young Delinquent*, 4th ed. (1944), University of London Press, London.

Byrne, D. S. (1974). *The Urban System and the Distribution of Social Income: A Suggested Perspective for the Orientation of Community Development Projects* (Unpublished).

Byrne, D. S. (1975). *Problem Families. A Housing Lumpen-Proletariat*, Working Papers in Sociology No. 5, Department of Sociology and Social Administration, University of Durham, Durham.

Castells, M. (1976). 'Theory and ideology in urban sociology'. In C. G. Pickvance (Ed.), *Urban Sociology: Critical Essays*, Methuen, London.

Central Advisory Council for Education (1967). *Children and Their Primary Schools*, Vol. 1, H.M.S.O., London.

Central Statistical Office (1973). *Social Trends*, No. 4, H.M.S.O., London.

Chapman, D. (1968). *Sociology and the Stereotype of the Criminal*, Tavistock, London.

Clarke, M. (1974). 'On the concept of sub-culture'. *British Journal of Sociology*, **25** (4), 428–441.

Coates, K., and Silburn, R. L. (1967). *St. Ann's, Poverty, Deprivation and Morale in a Nottingham Community*, Department of Adult Education, Nottingham University, Nottingham.

Coates, K., and Silburn, R. L. (1970). *Poverty—The Forgotten Englishmen*, Penguin, Harmondsworth, Middlesex.

Coffield, F. (1975). 'Deprivation in detail'. *New Society*, **32** (655), 206.

Cohen, A. K. (1955). *Delinquent Boys*, The Free Press, Glencoe, Illinois.

Collison, P. (1967). 'Immigrants and residence'. *Sociology*, **1** (3), 277–292.

Craig, J., and Driver, A. (1972). 'The identification and comparison of small areas of adverse social conditions'. *Applied Statistics*, **21** (1), 25–35.

Damer, S. (1974). 'Wine Alley: the sociology of a dreadful enclosure'. *Sociological Review*, **22** (2), 221–248.

Davies, Bleddyn (1968). *Social Needs and Resources in Local Services*, Michael Joseph, London.

Davies, B., Barton, A. J., McMillan, I. S., and Williamson, V. K. (1971). *Variations in Services for the Aged*, G. Bell, London.

Davies, B., Barton, A. J., and McMillan, I. S. (1972). *Variations in Children's Services among British Urban Authorities*, G. Bell, London.

Davies, J. G. (1972). *The Evangelistic Bureaucrat*, Tavistock, London.

Davies, J. G., and Taylor, J. (1970). 'Race, community and no conflict'. *New Society*, 9 July 1970.

Davis, J. G., Spaeth, J., and Huson, C. (1961). 'A technique for analysing the effects of group composition'. *American Sociological Review*, **26**, 215–225.

Dayha, B. (1974). 'The nature of Pakistani ethnicity in industrial cities in Britain'. In A. Cohen (Ed.), *Urban Ethnicity*, Tavistock, London.

Deakin, N., and Cohen, B. H. (1970). 'Dispersal and choice: towards a strategy for ethnic minorities in Britain'. *Environment and Planning*, **2** (2), 193–202.

Dennis, N. (1958). 'The popularity of the neighbourhood community idea'. *Sociological Review*, **6** (2), 191–203.

Dennis, N. (1970). *People and Planning*, Faber and Faber, London.

Dennis, N. (1972). *Public Participation and Planners' Blight*, Faber and Faber, London.

Department of the Environment with Home Office Deprivation Unit (1975). *Census Indicators of Urban Deprivation*, Department of the Environment, London.

Department of Health and Social Security (1968). *Annual Report*, Cmnd. 4100, H.M.S.O., London.

Desai, R. (1963). *Indian Immigrants in Britain*, Oxford University Press, London.

Donnison, D. V. (1972). 'Ideologies and policies'. *Journal of Social Policy*, **1** (2), 97–118.

230

Donnison, D. V. (Ed.) (1973). *London: Urban Patterns, Problems and Policies*, Heinemann, London.

Donnison, D. V. (1974). 'Policies for priority areas'. *Journal of Social Policy*, **3** (2), 127–135.

Donnison, D. V., Chapman, V., Meacher, M., Sears, A., and Urwin, K. (1965). *Social Policy and Social Administration*, George Allen and Unwin, London.

Evans, P. (1975). 'A change of direction in race relations policy'. *The Times*, 2 June 1975.

Filkin, C., and Weir, D. (1972). 'Locality'. In E. Gittus (Ed.), *Key Variables in Social Research*, Heinemann, London. pp. 106–157.

Flynn, M., Flynn, P., and Mellor, N. (1972). 'Social malaise research: a study in Liverpool in Central Statistical Office'. *Social Trends*, No. 3, H.M.S.O., London.

Frankenberg, R. (1966). *Communities in Britain*, Pelican, Harmondsworth, Middlesex.

Gerth, H., and Mills, C. W. (1954). *Character and Social Structure*, Oxford University Press, London. p. xxii.

Gittus, E. (1960). *Conurbations*. Unpublished M.A. Thesis, University of Liverpool, Liverpool.

Gittus, E. (1962–64). Unpublished results of sample survey of income, expenditure patterns, etc., among households in inner Liverpool. (See Brennan, 1972, and 'Income' in Stacey, 1969).

Gittus, E. (1965). 'An experiment in the definition of urban sub-areas'. *Transactions of the Bartlett Society*, No. 2, University College, London. pp. 109–135.

Gittus, E. (1966). Written evidence to the (Seebohm) Committee on Local Authority and Allied Personal Social Services.

Gittus, E. (1969). 'Sociological aspects of urban decay'. In D. F. Medhurst and J. P. Lewis (Eds.), *Urban Decay*, Macmillan, London. pp. 27–35.

Gittus, E. (1970). 'A study of the unemployed of Merseyside'. In R. Lawton and C. M. Cunningham (Eds.), *Merseyside Social and Economic Studies*, Longman, London. pp. 324–373.

Gittus, E. (1975). *Flats, Families and the Under-fives*, Routledge and Kegan Paul, London.

Glass, R. (1960). *The Newcomers*, George Allen and Unwin, London.

Glass, R., and Frenkel, M. (1946). 'How they live at Bethnal Green'. In *Britain between East and West*, Contact Books, London.

Green, B. S. R. (1971). 'Social area analysis and structural effects'. *Sociology*, **5** (1), 2–19.

Halsey, A. H. (Ed.) (1972). *Educational Priority*, vol. 1, H.M.S.O., London.

Halsey, A. H. (1974). 'Government against poverty in school and community'. In D. Wedderburn (Ed.), *Poverty, Inequality and Class Structure*, Cambridge University Press, Cambridge.

Harloe, M., Issacharoff, R., and Minns, R. (1975). *The Organisation of Housing*, Heinemann, London.

Harrington, M. (1962). *The Other America*, Macmillan, London.

Harvey, D. (1973). *Social Justice and the City*, Arnold, London.

Hatch, S., and Sherrott, R. (1973). 'Positive discrimination and the distribution of deprivations'. *Policy and Politics*, **1** (3), 223–230.

Herbert, D. T. (1975). 'Urban deprivation: definition, measurement and spatial qualities'. *Geographical Journal*, **141**, 362–372.

Hindess, B. (1973). *The Use of Official Statistics in Sociology: A Critique of Positivism and Ethnomethodology*, Macmillan, London.

Holman, R. (Ed.) (1970). *Socially Deprived Families in Britain*, Bedford Square Press, London.

Home Office (1968). *Home Office Urban Programme Circular*, No. 1, October, H.M.S.O., London.

Hope, K. (1969). 'A guide to social investment'. *Applied Social Studies*, **1**, 21–28.

Jackson, B. (1973). 'The childminders'. *New Society*, **26** (582), 522.

Jones, D. C. (1934a). *Social Survey of Merseyside*, vol. 1, Liverpool University Press, Liverpool.

Jones, D. C. (1934b). *Social Survey of Merseyside*, vol. 3, Liverpool University Press, Liverpool.

Jones, D. C., and Mayo, M. (Eds.) (1975). *Community Work: One*, Routledge and Kegan Paul, London.

Jones, K., and Smith, A. D. (1970). *The Economic Impact of Commonwealth Immigration*, National Institute of Economic and Social Research, Occasional Paper xxiv.

Knox, P. L. (1974). 'Social indicators and the concept of level of living'. *Sociological Review*, **22** (2), 249–258.

Labour Party (1974). *Labour Party Manifesto*, Transport House, London, October.

Leach, B. (1974). 'Race problems and geography'. *Transactions of Institute of British Geographers*, **63**, 41–47.

Lomas, G. (1973). *Census 1971, The Coloured Population of Great Britain* (Special Analysis for the Runnymede Trust), Runnymede Trust, London.

Louden, D. (1975). *The Adaptation and Adjustment of West Indian Migrants to Britain: A Review of Some British Studies*. Paper presented to Congress of Applied Anthropology, Leiden (see Research Unit on Ethnic Relations, 1975).

Lyon, M. H. (1969). 'The role of the settlement area in British race relations'. *Journal of Biosocial Science*, **1** Supplement 1, 163–172.

Lyon, M. H. (1972). 'Race and ethnicity in pluralistic societies'. *New Community*, **1** (4), 256–262.

Lyon, M. H. (1973). 'Ethnicity in Britain. The Gujarati tradition'. *New Community*, **2** (1), 1–11.

MacEwen, A. M. (1972). 'Stability and change in a shanty town'. *Sociology*, **6** (1), 41–58.

Madge, J. (1963). *The Origins of Scientific Sociology*, Tavistock, London.

Malpass, P. (1973). *Professionalism in Architecture and the Design of Local Authority Houses*. Unpublished thesis for the Degree of M.A. in Social Studies, University of Newcastle-upon-Tyne, Northumberland.

Mays, J. B. (1962). *Education and the Urban Child*, Liverpool University Press, Liverpool.

Midwinter, E. (1972). *Priority Education*, Penguin, Harmondsworth, London.

Miliband, R. (1974). 'Politics and poverty'. In D. Wedderburn (Ed.), *Poverty, Inequality and Class Structure*, Cambridge University Press, Cambridge. pp. 183–196.

Miller, S. M. (1968). 'Invisible men'. *Psychiatric and Social Science Review*, **2**, 14.

Ministry of Social Security (1967). *Circumstances of Families*, H.M.S.O., London.

Mitchell, J. C. (Ed.) (1969). *Social Networks in Urban Situations*, Manchester University Press, Manchester.

Morris, T. (1957). *The Criminal Area*, Routledge and Kegan Paul, London.

Moynihan, D. P. (Ed.) (1969). *On Understanding Poverty*, Basic Books, New York.

The National Community Development Project (1974). *Inter-project Report*, Information and Intelligence Unit, London.

Newcastle Social Services Department (1974). *Social Characteristics of Newcastle-upon-Tyne* (mimeo).

Nicholson, R. J., and Topham, N. (1971). 'The determinants of investment in housing by local authorities: an economic approach'. *Journal of the Royal Statistical Society*, Series A, **134** (3), 273–320.

Norman, P. (1975). *Managerialism: a review of recent work*. Paper presented to Conference on Urban Change and Conflict, convened by the Centre for Environmental Studies at the University of York, January.

Pahl, R. E. (1970). *Whose City and Other Essays on Sociology and Planning*, Longman, London.

Parsons, T. (1969). *The Social System*, Routledge and Kegan Paul, London.

Pettigrew, A. M. (1972). 'Information control as a power resource'. *Sociology*, **6** (2), 187–204.

Pfautz, H. W. (1967). *Charles Booth on the City*, University of Chicago Press, Chicago and London.

Pickvance, C. G. (1974). 'On a materialist critique of urban sociology'. *Sociological Review*, **22** (2), 203–220.

Pickvance, C. G. (1975a). 'On the study of urban social movements'. *Sociological Review*, **23** (1), 29–50.

Pickvance, C. G. (1975b). *From Social Base to Social Force: Some Analytical Issues in the Study of Urban Protest*. Paper read at the Centre for Environmental Studies, Conference on Urban Change and Conflict, University of York, January.

Pickvance, C. G. (Ed.) (1976). *Urban Sociology: Critical Essays*, Methuen, London.

Rainwater, L. (1967). 'The city poor'. *New Society*, 23 November 1967.

Research Unit on Ethnic Relations (1975). *Report on the Work of the Social Science Research Council's Research Unit on Ethnic Relations*, University of Bristol, Bristol.

Rex, J. A. (1970a). *Race Relations in Sociological Theory*, Cox and Wyman, London.

Rex, J. A. (1970b). 'The concept of race in sociological theory'. In S. Zubaida (Ed.), *Race and Racialism*, Tavistock, London. pp. 35–56.

Rex, J. A., and Moore, R. (1967). *Race, Community and Conflict: A Study of Sparkbrook*, Oxford University Press, London.

Robson, B. T. (1969). *Urban Analysis: A Study of City Structure*, Cambridge University Press, Cambridge.

Rodman, H. (1963). 'The lower class value stretch'. *Social Forces*, **42** (2), 205.

Rose, E. J. B., Deakin, N., Abrams, M., Jackson, V., Peston, M., Vanags, A. H., Cohen, B., Gaitskell, J., and Ward, P. (1969). *Colour and Citizenship*, Oxford University Press, London.

Rosser, C., and Harris, C. (1965). *The Family and Social Change*, Routledge and Kegan Paul, London.

Rotenberg, M. (1974). 'Self-labelling: a missing link in the societal reaction theory of deviance'. *Sociological Review*, **22** (3), 335–354.

Rowntree, B. S. (1903). *Poverty: A Study of Town Life*, Macmillan, London.

Rowntree, B. S. (1941). *Poverty and Progress*, Longman, London.

Rowntree, B. S., and Lavers, G. R. (1951). *Poverty and the Welfare State*, Longman, London.

Runciman, W. G. (1966). *Relative Deprivation and Social Justice*, Routledge and Kegan Paul, London.

Schorr, A. (1964). 'The non-culture of poverty'. *American Journal of Orthopsychiatry*, **34** (5).

Shonfield, A., and Shaw, S. (Eds.) (1972). *Social Indicators and Social Policy*, Heinemann, London.

Simey, T. S., and Simey, M. B. (1960). *Charles Booth, Social Scientist*, Oxford University Press, London.

Social Science Research Council (1968). *Research on Poverty*, Heinemann, London.

Stacey, M. (Ed.) (1969). *Comparability in Social Research*, Heinemann, London.

Strauss, A. L. (1968). *The American City: A Source Book of Urban Imagery*, Aldine, Chicago.

Suttles, G. D. (1968). *The Social Order of the Slum*, University of Chicago Press, Chicago.

The National Community Development Project (1974). *Inter-project Report*, Information and Intelligence Unit, London.

Timms, N. (1961). 'Knowledge, opinion and the social services'. *Sociological Review*, **9** (3), 361–365.

Titmuss, R. M. (1962). *Income Distribution and Social Change*, George Allen and Unwin, London.

Townsend, P. (1957). *The Family Life of Old People*, Routledge and Kegan Paul, London.

Townsend, P. (1962). 'The meaning of poverty'. *British Journal of Sociology*, **13** (3), 210–227.

Townsend, P. (1974). 'Poverty as relative deprivation: resources and style of living'. In D. Wedderburn (Ed.), *Poverty, Inequality and Class Structure*, Cambridge University Press, Cambridge. pp. 15–42.

Valentine, C. (1969). *Culture and Poverty*, University of Chicago Press, Chicago.
Valentine, C. A. (1972). 'Models and muddles concerning culture and inequality: A reply to critics', *Harvard Educational Review*, **42**, 97–108.
Vereker, C., Mays, J. B., Broady, M., and Gittus, E. (1961). *Urban Redevelopment and Social Change*, Liverpool University Press, Liverpool.
Ward, R. (1972). 'How plural is Britain?'. *New Community*, **1** (4), 263–270.
Weber, M. (1949). *Methodology of the Social Sciences*, The Free Press of Glencoe, New York.
Weisbrod, B. A. (Ed.) (1965). *The Economics of Poverty*, Prentice-Hall, Englewood Cliffs, New Jersey.
Whyte, W. F. (1943). *Street Corner Society*, University of Chicago Press, Chicago.
Young, M., and Wilmott, P. (1957). *Family and Kinship in East London*, Routledge and Kegan Paul, London.
Zubaida, S. (Ed.) (1970). *Race and Racialism*, Tavistock, London.

Index

235

236

238